# Out From Under
Sober Dykes And Our Friends

# Out From Under
## Sober Dykes And Our Friends

Edited by Jean Swallow

Spinsters, Ink
San Francisco

Copyright © 1983 by Jean E. Swallow

All rights reserved. This book, or parts thereof, may not be reproduced in **any** form, except for purpose of reviews, without express permission of the publisher.

Reprint Acknowledgements:
    Some of these pieces have been published previously.
    "Four Poems in Search of a Sober Reader" appeared in a slightly different form in *Sinister Wisdom* #19, Winter, 1982.
    A longer version of "What is Calistoga?" was published in *Common Lives/ Lesbian Lives* #4, Summer, 1982.
    "Killing Me Softly" is reprinted from Sydney, Australia's *Girl's Own*, March/April, 1982 issue, with permission.
    "Alcoholism: Violence Against Lesbians" was expanded from an article which first appeared in *off our backs*, August/September, 1982.
    "Confessions of A Not-So-Ex-Alcoholic" was condensed from the preface of *Jesus, Jesus!* (copyright by Red Arobateau, 1976, all rights reserved) and is used by permission.
    "Turning It Over" is copyright 1979 by Meg Christian (Thumbelina Music BMI) and is used by permission (all rights reserved).
    "In Training" first appeared in *The Words of a Woman Who Breathes Fire* (Spinsters Ink, 1983) and is used by permission.


10 9 8 7 6 5 4 3

Spinsters, Ink
803 DeHaro Street
San Francisco, CA 94107

Cover Art: Susan Sanford
Back Cover Photo: Jay Linder
Copy-editing: Annie Stuart
Design and Production: Sherry Thomas, Linda Jupiter, Jean Swallow and Linda
    Szwniszewski at Elephant Graphics, San Francisco
Typesetting: Jean Swallow and ComText Typography, San Francisco
Printed in the U.S.A.

ISBN: 0-933216-08-4
Library of Congress Catalog Card Number: 83-050762

## Acknowledgments:

This book has been a full-time job for me for over a year and I could not have possibly done it alone. It is quite clear to me that I've needed every bit of support I could get. Even though some of it came from places I least expected, many people have been quite generous.

I will be thirty when this book is published and there was a time I never thought I'd live that long. Some people literally helped keep me alive during those years and I would like to thank them. They are: Gail Owens, Cheree Briggs, Cheryl Jones, Debbie Anderson, Liz Harris, Wilma Reichard, Creighton Humphries, Marie McIntyre, and Cindy Lindsay.

It would be hard to thank them enough, but Marcy Adelman, Diane Spaugh and Cindy Lindsay started me on this road to recovery and I will be grateful they took that chance for the rest of my life.

I would also like to thank several men who helped me make this book: my boss, Demetrios Papahadjopoulos, who knew what I was doing and though grumbling for a year every Tuesday, let me work a non-standard, 4-day, 40-hour week so I could write on the other three days of the week; my word-processing co-worker, Jim Harris, who was very kind about lending me disks and extra rush time on our shared equipment, who keyed the first draft of the bibliography and helped with proofing, and who has been a great gay support to me; and Rick Wilson, who gently and graciously guided me and the manuscript through the computer typesetting process.

There were many, many women who helped me do this book by supporting me in spiritual and material ways. Specifically, I would like to thank: the women of the proofing crew: Cindy Navarro, Kathy McHenry, Jay Linder, Meg Jochild, Diane Spaugh, Jan Adams and Rebecca Gordon; Annie Stuart for great copy-editing; Meg Jochild for making me laugh by telling awful lesbian jokes, for personal, political and professional support, and for transcription of some of the interview tapes; Sally Golden for getting me a difficult-to-find transcriber so I could do the rest of the interview tapes myself; Rebecca Gordon for help with soliciting submissions, and Rebecca and Jan Adams for the loan of their two-woman light table; Cindy Cleary and Joan Pinkvoss for encouragement; Karen and Claire and the women at the West Coast Lesbian Collections for research in lesbian publications and organizations; Susan Sanford for mid-morning phone calls when I couldn't call out; and Dodici Azpadu for helping me to know when to stop.

I would also like to thank the women who are my family for their love and their belief that I could grow myself big beyond my most hopeful vision, in this book and in my life: Diane Spaugh, Catherine Risingflame Moirai, Marian Michener, Jay Linder, Sim Kallan and Sherilyn Thomas.

And finally, I would like to thank the women who wrote for this book, for the incredible sharing and wisdom and strength they have given us all, by the work they did to stay alive and the work they did that is included here.

Thank you all.

## Dedication

To Sher, and to the life and love we have created together.

# Introduction

## by Jean Swallow

This book started on a warm sunny day in July when my lover/partner Sher and I sat in the tall grass and I pulled out the grass by the stalk and swore and cried and Sher said, "Well, if you don't know of many other people and you don't know of any more books, you may have to make your own book."

I rolled my eyes around to her. "Sure," I said, "just like that," I said and snorted. But then I decided I would because I did need it. That day in July I was feeling bad; my best friend was moving away for no good reason I could see, my old girlfriend was getting serious about the woman she has since commited to and I was feeling so lonely I was about to take the plunge into a recovery group.

At that point I was a year and a half sober. I had gotten sober with the help of these women who loved me, but not with an organized group. And book fiend that I am, I had looked for reading material, but I could find very few books that discussed recovery. It was like being in a desert at noon in the middle of summer: I knew there was something alive out there, but I couldn't find it. So there sat Sher, who was beginning her own recovery process, only we didn't know that yet, and me feeling sad and furious because my best friend was moving away.

I sent out a call-for-material the next week. I sat on the floor in my little corner apartment with the door open and the sun streamed in and I made up all the envelopes and the mailing list. The next day, I walked to the Post Office and smiled at the dyke post person and mailed out 1,500 flyers to everyone and every place I could find.

Very soon, the replies began to trickle in. Some women wrote wonderful letters. Some, I heard later, were affronted, "Who did she think I was, some dried-up old drunk?" An old friend of mine didn't realize it was my book and tossed the flyer away; she thought it was from one of those crazy way-out California types. Right she was.

For the next year, this book and my own recovery filled my life. On my lunch hour, I would go down to the medical library where I worked and look up what there was to read about women and addictions. There wasn't very much. And there was even less about lesbians, and almost nothing about recovery. It was discouraging.

But I got submissions to the book. Some were wonderful and made me happy and I re-read them immediately because they were so fine. Many of the submissions were not about recovery but about days of drinking or drugging, and I sadly put them aside. Some of the submissions had wonderful parts; I wrote and asked the writers if they would consider working with me on the stories. To my delight, some did. They wrote me letters; I wrote back. I began to feel like I knew women from all over the country.

And then it became clear to me I was going to have to do more than edit to make the book happen. I had heard of lesbians who were working with addicted women: lesbians who had information we could all use, but for whatever reasons, hadn't published it and hadn't the time to write now. I decided to try to interview those women, to get their words in the anthology, to help make available to us the wisdom gleaned from those healers. Many of these women did agree to interviews. We talked about parts of recovery for which almost no information existed: what happens to our bodies and our sex lives; what happens after the first year; what are issues for third world lesbians and lesbian couples in recovery; how we can make recovery programs work for us. Like the women in the rest of the book, we talked about what was happening to us and why. Each interview was remarkable, and each woman said things that helped me in my own recovery. More than once I cried and then felt reassured as I wrote up the interviews.

I was reassured by the naming these women did. As the book came together, I saw we all had named and made less powerful some damaging part of our lives. For those of us who were addicted, we were able to say that we were alcoholic or addicted, that we persisted in a drinking or drugging behavior even after it interfered with the rest of our lives. There were co-alcoholics who spoke for this book too, those of us who didn't use the drugs addictively, but by devoting ourselves to loving someone else so much and ourselves so little, we made an addiction of our own. Para-alcoholics wrote too, those of us who have learned the abusive behavior without the use of the drug. And there were adult children of alcoholics (ACA's) willing to try to tell the struggle of sorting through all the roles we had meshed, until we dug hard enough and long enough to see what exactly was at the bottom of the searing pool of acid which circled our hearts.

There was sadness in this naming, but also damage transformed into powerful wholeness, and comfort in common chords. As the time passed, I realized that all of us had a recovery process. Each of us, whether alcoholics or addicts, co's or ACA's, went through a roughly parallel recovery. The way in which the substance or the person was an issue in our lives was different, but the process we went through to get free, to reclaim and relearn, to recover our emotions and our lives, seemed to be very similar. This similarity became more apparent when I noticed that the submissions for this anthology were not falling into categories of alcoholic or co, addict or ACA. Rather, the submissions were falling roughly into three types: pieces about the day-to-day recovery lessons, pieces about politics and theory, and pieces about how we go on. As I began to sort through and see the pattern, the book began to jell and the submissions were like a goldmine, growing brighter every day.

And then, and then it was time for the book to be done. I fretted. Another writer said let it go now and she was right. Looking back, it's easy to see the book fulfilled my wildest dreams for help for me, for a marking of where I was and where other women were. I *have* felt not so alone.

I think there will probably be people who are not lesbians who will read this book too and that's okay with me. If you are our friends, know you are welcome. If you are in recovery yourself, and if you can, take the experience we have to offer and apply it to your own situation. I assume there will be straight people who read this book. It seems to me that like all so-called "minority communities," the women in this book have unique, precious parts of our cultures that the mainstream could benefit by greatly.

If you are a lesbian reader who has not yet thought about these issues, it is unlikely that you will **not** recognize someone here... probably someone very close to you. In the lesbian community, according to a study released last summer\*, the statistics are: 38% alcoholic, 30% problem drinkers. For a lesbian, those statistics mean you either are one, or you love one.

You either are one or you love one. In the mainstream community, according to a recent Gallup poll, there is alcohol abuse in every one of three families. We all come from somewhere. Who do you remember drunk?

And what have you seen that involved destruction due to alcohol? What relationships have you seen destroyed because of co behavior or addictive behavior or even that slow death of almost any intimacy for the ACA's? What about community destruction? Within the last year, three important lesbian community institutions/businesses I know of have failed,

---

\*Please see the bibliography at the end of the book for notations on this and other helpful/interesting information mentioned in the anthology or discovered by contributors.

either publicly or privately, failed with alcohol or drug abuse or chemical behavior rampant in the institution when it went down. And when they failed, women set on each other in blame, to blame, to find every reason, any reason, besides the fact that substance abuse or chemical behavior was altering their perceptions of the world.

I hope we can start talking about these losses. I hope we can stop blaming each other and learn to take responsibility for our own growth, our own abusive behavior and our own recovery. We need to start doing our own work. We can stop altering who we are and how we are by chemical behavior. I don't think that drugs and drug behavior are the only reason this community and personal destruction is going on, but I do think that it contributes significantly. And I don't think we have looked at the effects of drugs and drug behavior on our community yet and I think we are missing a big part of the analysis if we don't.

Since I came to this feminist movement almost ten years ago, I have repeatedly heard talk, indeed have heard the gospel, that we must throw off the messages of the patriarchy if we are to be free. This is as true today as it ever was. What we must recognize is that substance abuse is part of the patriarchy; that it is not a way out, or even a resting place. It is a lie. It is every bit as much a lie as sexism, capitalism, classism, racism and homophobia.

Substance abuse and abusive behavior depend, like all the others, on denial and half-truth, on scarcity models, projection and rationalization. They are the words of the patriarchy made life. Substance abuse and abusive behavior do not help us in dealing with patriarchal oppression either. In fact, they have the same effects on us: low self-esteem, anger, depression, hopelessness and loss of purpose. There is a major difference though. Sexism, racism and the rest are done to us; we do the substance abuse to ourselves. And we can stop.

I can promise you, any revolution we make will not start in a bar. And it will not be run by women who use, or who actively engage in abusive behavior, whether or not the chemical is present.

We need to start talking about this. We need to begin now. My hope is that this book may spark some discussion, as an offshoot, as a kind of lesbian wave effect. But that is not why I did this book. I made this book for me, and Sher, and other lesbians in recovery.

This is a book about recovery. This is a book about how we live after that cold day in hell when we finally said, that's enough, that's enough, oh my god, that's enough.

It's a book about how we go on living. These aren't stories about how it was, because I think there is already enough of that: myths and stories and lies from the mainstream, birth and lesbian cultures we each inhabit throughout our lives.

No, this is not about drinking. And it's not about dying. This is a book about living and recovery. It is about how we do that and what happens when we try to do that. This book is for those times we are alone in our recovery; we can pull it out and say, for once in our lives: oh yes, yes, I *am* in the right place, this *is* what is supposed to happen.

Recovery from alcoholism and drug abuse is about recovering memory and reality and vision. It is about recovering the balance we always should have been able to have. It is about discovering emotions. And then it is about what you do with those emotions once you know what they are. In some sense, recovery isn't just getting something back so much as it is beginnings; it is about learning how to grow up. It is about learning how to love each other and ourselves. Recovery is about making community and so is this book.

This book is a kind of community that shares through print, one way among many others to alleviate the isolation and fear substance abuse has created within us. In this book are a whole group, a community, an exultation of lesbians in recovery. It is our stories, our feelings, the small truths we've found. It is our markings for a trail.

Recovery is not any one place. Sometimes it is agonizing, so bitter, so aching it is hard to believe there is life beyond it, that there will be anything beyond this moment of incredible stunning pain. And then life goes on, and there comes a sweetness too, so sweet, such tender soft sweetness that sometimes it transmutes into a moment on a soft summer day and almost a kind of joy.

Mostly though, recovery is a combination of the two, a bittersweet journey forward. Sometimes, it is a journey we have to make with only faith or trust or holding our breath, to be able to go through, to go on. And sometimes, it helps to have a vision of where we are going. I believe that which we can envision, we can make real. All the contributors to this book have written a vision of what our communities would look like if they were clean and sober. I have marked our visions with a flower, a rhododendron, and the visions are as varied as the many kinds of blooms of that flower.

But mostly this book is an effort to name our memories and our reality now, willful attempts to make real the past and the present so that we can go on, so that we can know where we are.

This book is a record of our life here when we finally decided to live. It is a record of our journeys, our fights, our joy. It is a road-map and a vision, a sharing and a song. Come with me. Come inside this book I've been reading for the better part of a year now and watch how the journey unfolds. Know that you can live. Know that you are not alone. Know that there are pieces of real joy when you take the bittersweet journey into recovery, when you do get out from under.

# The Rhododendrons

About half way down the county road that cuts in from the coast to the farm, the vegetation changes abruptly from the lushness of the redwood forest. Suddenly, the trees grow only about five feet and are not so green and the entire section looks like scrub brush from the hard mountains. The plant life able to sustain itself there at all is stunted: 200-year old cyprus are only as tall as redwood saplings, though if you were to cut them, the rings of their years would be so tight you could barely count them all.

The place looks like it has been held down by a giant hand and not allowed to grow. It looks wild and sparse and hard, gnarled. But every spring the rhododendrons bloom there in profusion. Somehow, the rhododendrons grow to their full, complex heights, and blossom with a cascade of flowers.

Back home, the mountains of North Carolina are covered with rhododendrons and their sisters, the azaleas and mountain laurels. If there is some kind of disaster on the mountains, a fire or flood or landslide or strip mines, eventually the rhododendrons come and take over the devastated mountain side, covering the earth and blossoming in the spring, their dense green leaves sheltering the earth in the hot summers, icy winters.

It takes time for them to grow, but parts of the mountains blaze with the rhododendrons: this plant that grows amidst disaster, after all was seemingly dead or lost. You can travel roads crowded with rhododendrons in bloom, so full they seem to cushion the road, so many the air is full of them and all you can see are the incredible flowers: flame orange, bright white, blush pink to magenta to lavender and deep purple, all mixed, all shimmering together under that blue, blue Carolina sky.

If my lesbian community were clean and sober, I believe that is what we would look like: alive and growing despite everything and blooming in all our ways. And I believe it is possible, even in the stunted forest of this alcohol and drug-filled world.

# Table of Contents

|  | Page |
|---|---|
| Introduction | vii |

## Part 1: The Days Of Our Recovery

| | |
|---|---|
| Breath Of A Gorilla Girl<br>*narrative by Claudia Kraehe* | 3 |
| On My Two Year Birthday<br>*poem by Suzanne Hendrich* | 8 |
| Fall Journal<br>*journal excerpts by A.* | 11 |
| The Line<br>*poem by Mary Wheelan* | 25 |
| Four<br>*narratives by Faith* | 27 |
| In Training<br>*narrative by Kitty Tsui* | 34 |
| 1973 I Decided To Stop Shooting Dope<br>*poem by Sim Kallan* | 44 |
| Reminders<br>*narrative by Sharon Stonekey* | 46 |
| Turning It Over<br>*song by Meg Christian* | 50 |
| What Is Calistoga?<br>*narrative by Jean Swallow* | 52 |

## Part 2: The Healers Among Us

| | |
|---|---|
| A Process Of The Cells Learning To Function Again<br>*interview with Karen Pruitt* | 65 |

| | |
|---|---|
| To Keep From Being Controlled | 71 |
| *interview with Misha Cohen* | |
| Recovery Is Power In The Now | 79 |
| *interview with Suzanne Balcer* | |
| In Sobriety You Get Life | 84 |
| *interview with Celinda Cantu* | |
| It's A Wonder We Have Sex At All | 93 |
| *interview with Jo-Ann Gardner Loulan* | |
| There Is A Jewel In This Process | 102 |
| *interview with Marty Johnson and Mary Bradish* | |

## Part 3: The Politics Of Our Addictions

| | |
|---|---|
| Four Poems In Search Of A Sober Reader | 117 |
| *poems by Catherine Risingflame Moirai* | |
| Creativity, Politics And Sobriety | 122 |
| *essay by Abby Willowroot* | |
| Alcoholism: Violence Against Lesbians | 129 |
| *essay by Nina Jo Smith* | |
| There Is Another Way To Fundraise | 134 |
| *essay by Alana Schilling* | |
| Killing Us Softly | 138 |
| *essay by Margot Oliver* | |

## Part 4: The Way Forward

| | |
|---|---|
| This Kettle Of Fish | 147 |
| *poem by Cathy Arnold* | |
| The Meaning Of Rapture | 148 |
| *letter from Trisha Larkin* | |
| Refrain | 151 |
| *poem by Cathy Arnold* | |
| Sobering Thoughts | 152 |
| *narrative by Alice Aldrich* | |

Confessions Of A Not-So-Ex Alcoholic 161
    *narrative by Red Arobateau*
Womanrest: Sometimes In Sobriety You Have To
    Make Changes 170
    *narrative from tapes by Karen Voltz*
First Tries Don't Always Work, Chapter 5 177
    *novel chapter by Judith McDaniel*
Recovery: The Story of An ACA 187
    *narrative by Jean Swallow*
The Day After Tomorrow Show 199
    *script by Patricia Piasecki*
Three Glasses Of Wine Have Been Removed
    From This Story 204
    *novel excerpts from Marian Michener*
The Sober Dyke 221
    *narrative by Sherry Thomas*

Bibliography 235

# PART I:
# THE DAYS OF OUR RECOVERY

# Breath of a Gorilla Girl

## (A Fairy Tale)

### by Claudia Kraehe

### The Home

**O**nce upon a time, there lived a mommy gorilla, a daddy gorilla, and their darling daughter, Gorilla Girl. They lived in a stone hut in the suburbs, forested by Safeways and Burger Kings.

### The Dinners

Were endless. Granddaddy gorilla (Walter Cronkite) was usually present, which was a good thing, since the gorilla family had a hard time talking with each other. When the daddy gorilla came home from work, he was irritable. In fact, even before he went to work, he was on edge, his veins pushing through his forehead every time he spoke. The mommy gorilla also worked. Her task was to keep the daddy gorilla calm, which she did by laboriously pushing food onto plates. For her own part, Gorilla Girl kept as quiet as possible, pretending she was the moth that was sitting on Walter Cronkite's ear.

### The Glasses

Mommy and daddy gorilla had a hobby. They collected glasses. There was the set of six with silver rims and painted sparrows; twelve glasses that were frosted and decorated with pine trees; short, wide glasses with little Scottish figures in dresses (ah, the beginnings!); twelve glasses with gold roses; glasses with owls and seals for stems; small, thumb-sized glasses; glasses with the family emblem, "G".

Gorilla Girl liked to look through the glasses for they turned the hut into a hall of mirrors. The red glasses, the blue glasses and the green glasses, made the hut an ocean bed in which she was a scuba diver, her breath bubbling upwards. But Gorilla Girl did not like what mommy and daddy gorilla put into the glasses — to her, some of it tasted like pee; other kinds had the taste of lighter fluid.

The years passed and the collection of glasses grew and grew, until the kitchen could not contain them all. There was the set of twenty-four glasses with flags from the different countries that had to go in the attic, along with the authentic beer steins from a Munich hofbrau. Soon the attic was filled. Then came the glasses with the various kinds of dogs and the others with the famous musicians that had to go in the basement. Then the basement filled.

Gorilla Girl found herself walking about the house on tiptoe, breathing very softly, so as not to disturb the adult gorillas or the glasses.

At first, the mommy gorilla drank with the daddy gorilla in order to keep him company, but then she too began to find life hard. Not only did she have a part-time job outside the hut, but keeping daddy gorilla content was a full-time job in itself. Also, washing all those glasses was making her very, very tired. She began drinking more, and at the same time, would nag the daddy gorilla not to drink so much.

Gorilla Girl watched them, and noted that after two or three drinks, mommy and daddy gorilla seemed to like each other more. Also, they seemed to like Gorilla Girl more too. Gorilla Girl told herself that surely if the reddish fluid could make the gorillas get along better, it must be wonderful stuff. And she began drinking from the glasses too.

Since there was always food and money in the hut, and since the mommy gorilla always got the glasses into the dishwasher, and since the daddy gorilla did not pass out on the floor, but nodded to "sleep" in his gorilla chair, *and* since Gorilla Girl was so quiet she went unnoticed, no social worker visited the gorilla family. Instead, someone from *Home and Gardens* heard about the marvelous glass collection and came and wrote a story for the "Elegant Dining" column.

## The Forest

Mommy and daddy gorilla arranged for Gorilla Girl to be transferred to another circus — an institutition of higher learning in Ohio. The mommy gorilla hoped that Gorilla Girl would get a B.A. in English and with a little shorthand, become an Executive Secretary at an ad agency. With any luck, she would land the Advertising Director.

Gorilla Girl studied very hard and that had its rewards. After four years, Gorilla Girl had:
1) produced a sixty page paper on macaronic verse and even wrote a few verses herself and gotten them *published;*
2) mastered the art of posing gracefully on stools in front of counters;
3) learned — thanks to Madeline Blanchard, a French foreign exchange student — that she liked gorilla girls a whole lot better than she liked gorilla boys.

## Belle of the Bar

Gorilla Girl graduated to another institution of learning — Jack's Bar (for Gorilla Ladies Only). At first she continued to breathe her small breaths, for she found that being around other gorilla girls was sometimes like being at home — that she had to watch what she said for fear the other gorilla girls would not like her politics. But she found that after four cans of 3.2 beer, the gorillas forgot about politics and she felt her breathing becoming louder and more free than ever before.

Night after night she danced, her majestic gorilla girl body prancing, spinning into the air, her fur groomed and glistening, slick in the lights.

Gorilla Girl, Gorilla Girl
You're something fine
Gorilla Girl, Gorilla Girl
Come home with me sometime.

## Grandma's House

Gorilla Girl flourished in bar life, finding herself with many admirers. Soon, however, she began going to the bar during the day and rather than being with anyone, she chose to sit on the stool and contemplate *life*. After five glasses of Rose, no one was quite so wise or profound as Gorilla Girl.

In the restroom at the bar, there was a roach motel on the floor. Gorilla Girl would peer in it and see the cockroaches devouring the glue they were stuck in, and she would burp, telling herself she was very glad to be a gorilla and *not* a cockroach.

## Mirror, Mirror

The years passed. Gorilla Girl began feeling not well. She no longer had the admirers — they were tired of hearing the same profound thoughts over and over again. Then too, the days bothered her eyes, and she often just slept. At night, she would drink until a blackness overcame her. But it wasn't the blackness which tormented her, rather it was those in-between times, when she would come to and lie there feeling pregnant, pregnant with worms.

One night, Gorilla Girl staggered into the restroom at the bar. In the dim light, she looked into the mirror and saw that her fur no longer glistened, that her face, once warm and aglow with wine, was bloated and pale. She saw herself:

1) passed out on a table;
2) collapsed on the dance floor, and the dancers ignoring her;
3) waking in a bed (who had been there with her?)
4) not as a real gorilla, but as a battery toy that had run itself into a corner and remained there, frantically whirling.

Gorilla Girl became aware of her Pabst Blue breath, stale with vomit. She saw her own fear emerging in colors — yellow for the world; red for the anger; green for herself. In all colors the fear came, and like a cobra, the fear was encircling and choking her breath.

And Gorilla Girl began to shiver.

## Out of The Forest
## (Putting Gorilla Girl Back Together Again)

## What It Took:

1) The friend who didn't just dance away from Gorilla Girl, but who gave her the phone number of other gorillas who couldn't control their drinking.
2) Going to meetings, where what mattered was not how clever you were, or whether you said "right on" things, but that you were willing to begin again.
3) The therapist who knew about gorilla girls and drug abuse, and who wanted to help Gorilla Girl.
4) And time — days and days of learning how to live without alcohol. (It was nine months before Gorilla Girl's fur began to shine; twelve months before her brain began to clear; more months before she *knew* what had happened to her.)

## A Happy Beginning!

Does she live happily ever after? Fear, anger and depression are still part of Gorilla Girl's life, but without the alcohol, hope and excitement are there too.

Here are just some of the changes:

When she walks past the park during the day, Gorilla Girl doesn't need the glasses to see that the browns are deep and rich and that the greens are thick with life.

*The Spot!* Prior to sobriety, sex had become sheer work, if not impossible. Now, after two years of abstinence from drugs and alcohol, the spot between her gorilla legs will now and then dance, causing Gorilla Girl to blush and beam.

True, sometimes she still wakes to days which seem quite weighted, but once in a while, in the early morning, Gorilla Girl will open her eyes and watch her own clean, deep breath pushing through her chest, rising like lamb's wool, and feel that this pulse, this life, is just beginning.

**CLAUDIA KRAEHE** lives and works in San Francisco. She is completing a master's degree in Creative Writing.

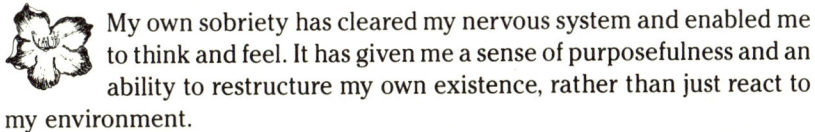

My own sobriety has cleared my nervous system and enabled me to think and feel. It has given me a sense of purposefulness and an ability to restructure my own existence, rather than just react to my environment.

I am just one person. But already I see, and learn from, in the groups that I am in, women wakening from a death, women taking the hours that drinking stole from them, and using those hours to reshape their lives.

From my heart, from my gut, I am grateful that I did not have to sober up alone, that already a sober community had begun, and that I could look to women who had developed the power to assume responsibility for their own lives, and learn from them.

# On My Two Year Birthday

## by Suzanne Hendrich

Did you see the woman who wanted to be a cake?
The cake in the window, so perfect and still.
Every bakery has one.
Icing rose petals like eggshells pale and cracked.
Visible dust on the white background,
The fragile art overwhelmed.
Relentless.
Life.
Its changes mark those who cannot change.

When I was a girl they made me change.
Out of tee shirts, out of blue jeans.
Into appropriate dress for a lady.
Into refinement, the pedestal perfect.
Out of exuberance, appetite, heroism.
Into stunned silence, reticence, fear.
I tried to change back but they just wouldn't let me.
I found something new, the love of a woman.
Equal and free we would feast and fly.
But they just wouldn't let us. They extracted a price.
The lesbian price is a bottle of gin
and how drinking it in can wash you away.
I was numb with the chill of crushed ice on glass,
no nourishing bowl to restore warmth.
I was numb to the bone with confusion.
I could not respond to an insult or to love (my broken dream).

I could not dream      but I could experiment.
If this doesn't work then try something else.
Try beer if gin fools you. Try not drinking at home.
Try giving it up and see how that likes you.

It didn't like me

But I was in love
with a woman who felt things,
who felt things that I'd never known.
And I wanted that more than anything.

I was in agony, but it was a feeling I couldn't deny.
I suffered for what I didn't have, either drinking or her.
It was the same pain.

I loved that woman beyond my bounds, for along with her came my feelings again:
1. surrender to appetite, natural world.
2. Today I can feel, I can cry, I can breathe
3. the light air of freedom until I'm full.
4. I can crash around in the underbrush of my past, unscathed, looking for treasure.
5. Today I can take precious moments to let someone help me know who I am
6. and I can be forgiven.
7. I can move on.
8. I can own my acts.
9. I can change
10. every day
11. I can know the best in me
12. and let it shine.

Let it shine.
The heroic light of foolish women
who give up everything to be free.
Let it shine.
A feast of lights.

Today I will eat the cake.
Life.
Relentless.
Whose changes mark those who could not change
but did.

**SUZANNE HENDRICH:** I am working on a Ph.D. in nutrition at UC Berkeley, studying plants which may have cancer-protective effects. I am a member of A.A. and Al-Anon. I live in Oakland with my lover and sober friend, Kim.

Clean and Sober Community? We would all have clearer eyes — from the changes inside. The feelings we drank over to avoid would be our guides. They'd guide us to know ourselves, to respect our selves and each other. We could show the world what it means to be true to one's self despite the obstacles that fear puts in our way.

# Fall Journal

**by A.**

Sept. 29
Wed. noon

**N** says there's good junk in town. He's at work today. I keep passing by him with the standard line: "i need some good drugs." I've been debating it for three days. Since i went to the narcotics addicts meeting at the state pen & said i was hurting & had been thinking about taking some drugs. After the meeting L offered me a couple of Dilaudids. I only refused because D from the program was walking right in front of me and heard the whole thing. I've been clean & sober a year & eight months. It's the most beautiful thing that ever happened to me, getting clean and sober.

At first it was my hip — i dislocated it & it's still inflamed — it hurts. But it's not that, really. It's not the lover who isn't perfect or the one who is. It's not depression over fall or quitting tobacco. It's not the donuts at break every morning — it is — it's sugar and shakiness but mostly i just want to get high. I just want that feeling — my blood feels it — relief — relax — let down the tight, the tension, let down the image, the strong concerned woman who speaks well & cares when others are hurting. Let her lie down, give her a break. It's not that i *can't* hold it up any more. Just why bother? Just what's the point? Just i want to get high just one more time. Or maybe forever and who cares anyway? One more woman gets loaded and misses a day of work or o.d.'s or doesn't feed the cats one night. So what?

And new drugs. I never tried heroin before. Or have i? Or Dilaudids. Maybe they'll work real good. I've missed out on something nice, it seems — i'll have to check it out sooner or later so why put it off? A year & a half — why not blow it now rather than wait til i've got two years, or three.

And the other voice says maybe i won't come back, maybe this is yr last chance, girl. She says if morphine didn't get you high how come you think junk is gonna make it? She says you know how full of shit you are, you know you'll either get strung out or give up before you really get good and high. It's gone, babe, the good high. It doesn't work anymore.

And the people at the meeting last night — they cared — they weren't used to me cool behind shades with an aura of poison darts, with walls a foot thick and i don't have anything to say. They were there; they made me smile even though i'd promised myself i wasn't going to. What would they feel for me if i said fuck it? "Another one bites the dust." So what. Let the dead bury the dead. Just another dyke who couldn't cut it. You know she spent a lot of time hanging out in the bars. . .

Grow up or die, girl. Maybe you can win one round of russian roulette. Maybe. But yr hooked on gambling. Once you get started, don't you think you'd keep playing? Til the end of the game or Bottom again and no way do i ever want to rerun that place. So i could get high and then kill myself real quick before it gets bad again. Grow up or die. It's not fair, of course. So what.

Wed. eve.

I am sitting in a friend's bathtub. The water is quite hot and i am starting to feel uncomfortable. It occurs to me that i have a choice: i can leave the hot water if I want to.

I have already made a date with N to score on Friday.

My tools were ripped off last night. Everything i'd worked for these last two years. Before i got clean and sober i didn't have the bucks together to buy tools. My trade has been ripped off. One of the guys at work said that's like rape, ripping off someone's means of making a living.

I'd like to get high. Everything i've worked for these last two years. . .

---

B says if you decided to get high, promise you'll call me first. I say i don't make promises.

---

N says maybe you'll change yr mind by Friday. I say maybe. We grin at each other.

---

I'm not scared — how strange. What is courage? It would certainly take more courage to stay straight. I put my shades back on, smug. I know something you don't know & yr not even gonna know you don't know it. The year of the pre-adolescent continues. When you start being unconscious at the age of 14 you never quite get over puberty, i think.

Grow up or die.

---

You know, the last few days have been so tense, so high-strung. It's a relief, really, knowing i'll wait until Friday & then i will or i won't. As soon as i arranged meeting with N, people stopped shying away, asking me if i was really o.k. Suddenly i can laugh, relate, relax. No more debates. No more hell. I will or i won't. Fine.

Sept. 30
Thurs. 6 a.m.

It's been like pulling teeth to get up in the mornings on time lately. Today my hip was well enough to run on. No problem getting out of bed. No depression. I'm up early, ready to go. Felt a little uneasy saying my morning meditation prayer — not sure exactly what to ask for, i guess. But i do want to stay clean and sober today. Maybe not tomorrow — but sober, yes — please help me stay off the booze. That's one i know for sure i've had enough of.

I fantasize about what i'll say at the addicts meeting on Tuesday. I put energy into being there. I want to get high but i want to come back. It's o.k. if i don't. I know that's a possibility. But the best would be to do it & get it over with & start living again. So why do it in the first place? Because i want to get high, of course.

---

Noticed myself irritable while i was driving A to school. She was chattering away, i was trying to listen to the tape deck. Since getting clean & sober, i've rarely been annoyed at not being able to shut children out. I've been able to be really with them & have enjoyed our time together. I don't want to lose that.

---

Everyone's telling me how good it is to have me smiling & laughing again. Still a good con after all this time.

*13*

Oct. 1
Friday eve.

Waiting for N. Another hour at least. My ride to Boulder for the rugby games isn't going tomorrow — i opted out of a ride today in favor of sticking around this eve, scoring. Rugby, love of my life, even you i ditch without hestitation in order to get high. After all this clean time too. It surprises even me. I've been myself all day, my normal lighthearted self with only a twinge of butterflies in the stomach, well concealed.

7:15. I wonder sometimes if someone or something or myself will save me in the nick of time? Will it be as good as my hopes? — as bad as my fears? — just another high?

---

No show. What a joke. Come back in an hour or two & maybe...
There's nothing else i want.

I work on an article i am writing on anarchy and trade unions. I drink chamomile tea and try not to think about: what if it doesn't come through? Will i give up or will i stretch this out another week, another Friday, another maybe?

---

Oct 2
Sat. a.m.

No show last night. Today, for sure at 10:00, 12:00, 2:00... Today for sure. Please, N, come through for me.

The violence, the anger is boiling inside, has been for a few weeks. Danger point. Express or suppress. No rugby, no whip to express it with. Come on, babe, come through for me. I can't keep making small talk forever. Only so long can i continue to have "frank" discussions with loving friends about alcoholism and drug abuse with this fireball in my gut, threatening to surface at any moment. Living a lie. Once again. It's all so natural but hard now that i know if i'd just let go, surrender, there could be some peace in my gut. Could there? I've tried. I've spent hours this week being open and honest with people who know. One secret only i've kept from them. Come through for me today, N. The suspense is killing me. There's a time bomb in my belly that wants to channel its explosion through my fist.

May i stay sober today. If i drink, for sure, my fist will not uncurl.

Come through for me, N; come through for me sweet calm heroin. My blood is bursting.

Waiting waiting waiting 10:00 12:00 2:00 3:00. If i'd wanted out, i've had plenty of opportunities.

Please.

"Why must we pray screaming?" — Patti Smith

And then there are the thoughts i would never admit even to myself, much less put down on paper —

Blistered nerve endings. I feel my eyes throw up a blank bland wall of protection thicker than shades and darker than desire or fear.

Full moon.

Parked around the corner. Waiting waiting waiting. Don't trust a junkie. Cops. Don't trust cops either. Materialize, you bastard. Now.

And if he doesn't show — if he splits with the money — do i accept it as fate? Do i find another slow suicide? Do i just wait til i earn another week's pay & try again?

Cops returning — haven't been this paranoid in years. Materialize yrself, man.

The art of patience. What a bitch this trip is when yr strung out, huh?

Was that him? Waiting waiting fucking waiting. Self-destruction never came easy for me. I've really had to work at it. It's made for excellent melodrama though, never a dull moment. Even waiting is high tension.

The glass windshield pulls at my fist. I'm wanting to tear something open **open** let it out explode spit flames split atoms release express or suppress please come cover these exposed arteries these shredded tendons. Soothe like butter on burns these blasted braincells. A little break a short respite from this endless attempt to keep the cool together. I am held together with bits of sharp wire, pulling slowly apart, ripping muscle strand by strand.

---

Oct. 3
Sun. a.m.

Couldn't get the stuff from T-town — had to score something not so good from someone who won't cop for N so he sent a friend & the bags came back short. Oh yes, i've done this before, it's all so familiar, tie off, the needle, the rush. So next Friday there's a good deal i can get on some really good stuff.

Oct. 4
Mon.

God's on vacation.

I wear yr earring, call back yr sure hand on my arm, the slow sweet push the liquid in it's clear tunnel becoming shorter & shorter slipping quietly into the tiny puncture that opens the universe to me that cracks the wall between me and danger and the calm stagnant pool of soft gentle tough of yr hand as you brush away the tiny drop of blood yr eyes low yr breath subdued.

A long long time since a man has touched me this tentatively or this sure.

I thought this might be a good piece. I could have died writing it, still could. I am not safe yet, never will be.

I smoke another cigarette. It sickens me, as have all the others.

Yesterday was not so poetic. I lay in bed wanting high wanting anger. In a moment of clarity i grasped the only out i know. I dressed, took all my money — just in case i might want to score — not believing it would be easy. I called A from the program. She came & got me, drove me to a meeting in Bomb City. A narcotics addicts meeting. We were the only ones there over 18. She was the only one there with more than a few days clean time. She drove me to an alcoholics meeting. She took me to the Club. "You'll never get high enough," she says. "I know. I've tried." I go home with her, cry & pray to the full Moon, to my Mother Earth. Where are you, where are you? My gut is empty. I wait for full but it doesn't come. I stretch out on the borderline between humility & humiliation. I want. I want high, i want clean.

I smoke cigarettes. I eat what is placed in front of me. I gag. There is no comfortableness in my body or soul. I want high, i want clean, i want anywhere but this limbo, this balance on the edge of a sword.

J has written me a poem of her pain. All i can think of is: if that bitch interferes with me getting high i'll kill her. I choose the knife i will use.

No work today. I write. I smoke cigarettes. I listen to Patti Smith, same songs, over and over. I sneak secret looks at the tiny red marks in the crook of my arm, acknowledging that there are three new ones among many old ones. I wish i could remember the other times. Were they just blood tests? Would it make any difference? Would it change what i know? What goes up must come down. The irrevocable sentence of gravity upon the human soul. You'll never get high enough. You never did, you never will. Will you die trying? Having turned my will and my life over to the care of Heroin, as i understood it, Heroin failed me. So now what? God is on vacation.

I pack lunch for tomorrow, pack clothes for rugby practice, smoke another cigarette, play the tape over one more time. So now what? I suppose i could put on my boots. I suppose i could do the dishes.

My face is awful in the mirror. I wear shades to protect myself from my own image.

There are people who care about me. They are not on vacation.

I could be like them, maybe. What are they doing right now? Perhaps they are doing the dishes. Perhaps they are caring about someone. Someone besides themselves. Grow up or die, my adolescent, self-centered girl.

I have a choice. I could get out of the hot water. It's cold out there. It hurts it hurts.

Friday is not here yet. I could put on my boots.

Mon. eve.

Just dead inside. Went to rugby practice. My hip started hurting so i stopped. And i didn't care. Didn't care anymore if i play this weekend or not. Maybe i should just stay home & get high. Got a letter from my lover. So what? The best relationship i've ever had & so what?

So i went to the bar after practice to catch a ride, thought about putting my finger in a head of beer to keep it from spilling over. Didn't. Went to a meeting.

Called K & she says write down a couple of ways yr powerless today & a couple of ways you've been taken care of:

I am certainly powerless over wanting to get high. I was powerless over my sponsor leaving in the middle of the meeting before i could talk with her.

I got a ride into town from a friend as soon as i got to the top of the hill. K was home when i called.

K says act as if you had faith. Maybe i will try praying again, on my knees like they tell me to. I'll try anything. I'm so scared. It's so close & i don't know if i'm strong enough to stand up to this ocean tide pull on my veins.

Oct. 5<br>Tues. a.m.

I am half hoping to see N at work today. If i can connect (doubtful) i will, then go to the bar. If not, i'll go to the gay alcoholics meeting & then to the narcotics addicts meeting. Is this turning it over? O.k. God, you want me clean, make it impossible for me to get high.

Tues. eve.

So i go to work today & in walks N and says "i'm going to T-town tonight." So i immediately pull out my money & give it to him. "8:00", he says. Waiting again. The death card in the tarot reading has me a little scared. Not scared enough i guess. I tell my friends i've got a meeting to go to and hit the streets. Nowhere to go. Where can i wait? I get handed life on a silver platter & say, no, thank you.

This was going to be story of how i met temptation, fought & won. No winners. Just one scared little girl who can't let go.

I don't even want this. I don't even want to get high any more. Why am i doing this? And yet i know i will.

*17*

Oct. 13
Wed.

I tell B i got high. She says you were cruising for a bruising weren't you?

Why is it so easy to write about falling down, so hard to write about getting back up?

I got high last Tues. night. Good & high. Went dancing. Felt no pain. Talked, laughed, danced with people i hardly even like sometimes. And people i do. M knew. She asked me if i was high. I said yes, it's a lot easier this way. Will anyone ever believe me again? Will i?

I prayed my ass off all the way to work on Wednesday. I prayed hard. I prayed scared. I prayed to everything, God, To Whom It May Concern. Something opened in my heart. It wasn't very big. That's o.k. When you work so hard to close up, even little punctures are major breakthroughs.

(I was at K's house, eating tortillas at 5:30 on Friday. I looked at the clock. I cried. Relieved. It was too late to meet N. I made it.)

I've spent the last week arguing myself in & out of growing up, faith and fear, God vs. the Electro-Magnetic Theory of the Universe, head and heart. Am i willing? To grow, to change? Sure i'll change my whole life to stay clean but i still want to live in the same place, hang out with the same people, go to the same bars, listen to the same music; i don't want to give up my job, my plans or my rugby team.

Willing to change they tell me. Willing to let go of everything. Grow up or die.

I surrender.

I take it back.

I surrender again. I give fucking up! I can't do this anymore. Take it God or whoever you are you better exist.

Do you love me?

Does the Electro-Magnetic Theory of the Universe love me?

Are you there?

I want to believe in you. I want to believe you are capable of love. I want to believe you know. What is it you want me to do?

Stagnation is not working. I want to change. (This hurts.) I want to grow. (I am terrified.) I want to believe there is something good & intentional in the universe. (Do you love me?) I want to bring peace & love to the world. There is enough hurt, enough confusion. Just a little, just a little good, can't you use me for something good, there must be something i can contribute. I will try to love. (This is going to be a bitch.)

Someone is trying to love me. (I'm scared.)

There is a kind of joy that doesn't jump up and down. It sits quietly, unpretentious, undramatic. I had no work today so i went to LN's house. She is a recovering addict/alcoholic too. She had written about her life. She shared it with me. Thank you.

Oct. 14
Thurs.

Can't tell my pain in words, or my blessedness either. Life goes on, you know. Nobody will pack my lunch for me or wipe my ass or apologize for me just cuz "i'm having a hard time with drugs, you know." That's good. The apology makes me feel better, the lunch will be more nourishing & i can wipe my own ass, thank you. You must be growing up, girl — you can wipe your own ass. Small accomplishments. LN & i were talking about what great prestigious & good things we did when we were getting loaded, how nowadays just paying the rent seems to be a big deal. When i grow up i want to be. . . maybe myself. Grow up. You're good World, yr good Electro-Magnetic Theory of the Universe. Yr o.k.

Life goes on. Thanks.

Oct. 17
Sun.

Yes, sometimes I want to use again. Sometimes i crave it. Sometimes life is a bitch.

Today, though, the sun was shining, i got some wood in, spent the day with clean and sober people, the children were beautiful, music was beautiful, the badlands and the golden trees were exquisite. All my needs were met perfectly today. Joy happened & i opened up & some changes were thrown at my wide-open gut. Yes, i cringed, i shook inside, but the conversation went on, life went on. I laughed. I laughed from my gut. I smiled & joy smiled back all around me. Is there any way to say happy & grateful & not sound trite? Don't know. And who gives a fuck what it sounds like. I'm happy, joyous and free. I'm o.k. I made it today, that's what counts. Clean and sober. Takes work. Time to get down to it, write down my resentments, my rationalizations. Clear it up with the Universe so maybe next time — tomorrow maybe — when the shit hits the fan i'll see it coming. O Freedom. O, my sweet high, you don't run my life today. Neither do i. Blessed Spirit, whatever you have for me to do today, help me to do it well. Walk with me, guide me, i run with the wind & the running is easy. Teach me to feel the wind change direction. Teach me to run with you & i will not be afraid anymore. I believe it is somewhere beautiful. I am enjoying my body in motion. It is like flying to run, riding the wind.

Oct. 19
Tues.

So i fantasize about getting high, changing the fantasy to how i say no, break the needles, throw away the dope. I can choose to think whatever i want to. I can choose to think clean.

I am tired of trying to be cool.

Oct. 20
Wed.

I can't do this. Nobody else can do it for me. There must be some Magick at work because i am clean and sober today. Magick can & will work miracles for me every day of my life if i let it. There must be a Spirit, a God, & that Spirit must be capable of infinite unconditional love. I am a fool, living at this moment in a state of grace, loved by Magick more fully than i have ever loved myself or been loved by anyone else. I am a child of the Universe. I claim my full inheritance of joy and pain. I claim my right to love and be loved, yes i want and will learn to receive love. Wide open to each word, scream, breeze, car horn or smile that touches my gut, i stand free and unafraid. I will know fear again, i will experience confusion and doubt. So what. I am only one child among millions. Right now, at this precious point in time, i sit on a couch in a cold room with golden trees outside my window. I write in a red notebook. The tightness in my belly rises to my chest and begins to escape in small tentative tears. Right now there is joy and gratitude. I want to live. I want to feel.

Oct. 21
Thurs.

I wake each morning immobilized by fantasies, cold, and depression until the last possible minute. Then, having blown it already, i debate whether the day is worth living, force a prayer, get up & make myself a good breakfast anyway just in case i should decide to live today. Belatedly i begin to move, to attempt to repair the damage already done to my psyche and my day by getting up late. But the fantasies are less often about using, more often about staying violently clean. Is this an improvement?

Progress, not perfection, they tell me. O.k. God, where are you, let's get on with it.

Oct. 22
Fri.

I'm having a lot of trouble with the *concept* of loving a Higher Power. I can feel it in my heart sometimes but my mind tells me i can feel anything i want to so i'm probably making it up. Only trouble is: if there's no loving God what's the point & if there's no point i'm gonna go get high & i'm pretty sure if i do that again i'm not gonna make it back. So in order to stay alive i keep believing.

How can something love but not be jealous or angry or stupid sometimes? Unconditional love i guess. Maybe Magick loves people like i love flowers. The beautiful ones, yes, i love them. But if you were to put an orchid and a dandelion with half it's petals missing side by side — no, i don't love the dandelion less — or more. I love flowers. I am glad they exist. Maybe Magick loves recovering addict ex-hippie construction-worker dykes with dishonest tendencies like i love the dandelion. I'm no St. Francis or Emma Goldman or orchid or anything but what's wrong with dandelions? I like them. They're like sunshine on the ground. I want to be like sunshine on the ground. When i grow up. Or tomorrow morning. Or tonight right now as i curl up with my cats and blow out the light and say thank you goodnight. O.k., Loving, you win. Even my devious brain can't deny you now. I love flowers, you love us.

Oct. 23
Sun.

I have wanted so much. I set goals for myself: have my own crew; get published — to be known for my erotica & political theory; that deep-down wish that S would still want me. Yesterday i had the job, got my writing accepted for a book & after a year & a half, spoke to S on the phone. She still wants me. I already have the lover i've always wanted. I find this morning that all those things that came to me suddenly yesterday — i don't care about them so much anymore. I'd let go of them. I'd decided clean & sober was really all i want. I even got the leather jacket i'd been fantasizing into existence for eight years yesterday. I didn't realize i'd even stopped needing these things til suddenly they're all here & what i'm most interested in is a friend to talk to.

Oct. 24
Mon.

So now i'm asking myself what the fuck am i gonna do now. Work's come to a dead standstill. I forget to ask what can i do to be useful? Is there someone i could be helping out right now? Is this time off cuz i'm needed for something else? Sure was glad K was unemployed those desperate days.

I'm so strong you tell me. You don't see the hours i lie on my bed like a piece of dead meat, bare & beat on like cube steak raw & gristly & i can't get up can't move just can't the air's too heavy. It's not pretty, me lying here sunk into my bed like lead weight until i scrounge up the courage to put on my jacket & shades & go out & smile at the world & talk about the spiritual awakening. I don't mention the hours i lie on my bed doing nothing, paralyzed by the weight of my own head bleeding internally & not bothering to try & stop it.

Oct. 26
Tues.

H.P. seems to have everything under control. Yesterday i find out — no work indefinitely, so i figure what the hell i have time to hang out at V's & we have a great morning & she turns me on to: organic gardening — if you put chemicals into the soil or vitamins it doesn't matter. The plant will grow & be healthy. But the soil will be depleted by the chemicals or nurtured by the vitamins. The soul, the artist, the human, will grow, and often grow beautifully, in a body that is fed by chemicals. But sooner or later the body will be depleted and will die. So yes maybe i can still write pretty when i'm high. So what?

So anyway, after i got that one into my brain & after i got my laundry done & got to a meeting today & got to where there's no pressing essentials to do, i find out i have work tomorrow. And stuff like that. It's starting to be a regular thing how everything falls into place right on schedule, only i never know the schedule beforehand.

I stuff myself with pie & rice & eggs & ice cream & broccoli & tea & coffee & smoke lots of cigarettes & i do not put a needle in my arm.

I go to meetings & i sweep my floor & i get up late every morning & i leave the lovely wine glass on the table.

I pray & i fantasize about violence & i talk to people who seem to be interested in growing & i apologize to J & then the next day i'm all distant again.

My face looks better except for the darkness that has never been under my eyes before.

I have stopped running in the morning cuz it's too dark at 5:30. I feed my cats i read i write i brush my teeth i don't walk by N's house, do not pass go, do not collect $200 worth.

Everything goes exactly as planned. I am not on the planning committee.

Oct. 27
Wed. a.m.

Today it is enough to sit in my own space, fire going, a good breakfast and jazz on the radio, my cats warm and well-fed, dishwater warming on the stove. Time to run, in-between the raindrops. Time to read. Don't know if i will work at all today because of the weather. Do know i want broccoli for dinner and my own bed tonight. Do know i want to go to sleep clean.

Wed. eve

I wish i could go to a planet where there are no drugs. It's the same thing, same place, i'm just a street bum again, walking around carrying all my shit in backpacks with broken straps walking around endless cuz one more time i hitch to town to not have any work for the tools i'm lugging around, no rugby practice for the sneakers & sweats & missing all the events i'm dressed up for & it's just the same old scene, not even enough money to go in some restaurant so i keep walking around. Flashback. So many autumns & out of work. Walking around town. It was nearly tolerable high. Tolerable newly sober & on a pink cloud the world new & wonderful. But no pink clouds this time & my gut cries for oblivion. One more backpack strap breaks, walking dark cold streets. I give up. Surrender. For a moment there's almost a smile. I'm salvageable. A few blocks later it leaves. I arrive at a friend's. Want to get on the phone & cry help but i make what conversation i'm capable of. Another evening passes clear across town from my connection. Staying in town tonight — work tomorrow if the weather holds. If.

So i'll go to sleep clean. So thanks.

Oct. 28
Thurs.

So everything fell into place today. Again. Have faith. Two weeks of work. Maybe more. At the house of someone in the program. My boss & she & i all went to the noon meeting. The sky was clear. Hitching home was easy. Supper's cooking. My belly hurts from drinking coffee. I have letters to write. I have friends to write letters to. (The dishes are clean.) I am so grateful for my life. I have to get up early tomorrow to get Z's car to the shop, go to work, hitch home, cook dinner, pray, get blessed, smoke cigarettes, not drink coffee, feed my cats. These are the facts as they appear to me right now. That's all i have to say. I've been writing this for a month now. I feel good now. I'm clean & sober now. Thanks. Thanks to A & K & D & L & K & Everything. Thanks for the lessons, heroin, i hope i don't meet up with you again soon. Or ever. Dinner's ready.

**A:** I began taking drugs at the age of 14 & used & drank daily for 13 years before i began seriously attempting to get straight. I do not give my full name because i cannot take all the credit for this piece. It is full of the words and ideas of many others who have shared their recovery with me.

Already, today, it is rare to see a beer can on the road down into the valley. The music box and the food table are the centers of the parties. In the bars there are sometimes whole tables where every glass is "safe." OJ and water, and Coke for the truly decadent. People have stopped asking me where to buy dope & how do I stand all those men at the meetings.

If only i could be sure, when its not just my friends, who know & support — if only i could go into a ritual circle of women & children from all over the state or the world and be sure that no one would bring sacred weed from women's land, or magic mushrooms in an abalone shell, or strong wine in a silver chalice, and offer them as gifts to the circle, to us, to the Goddess, and hit me right where its easiest to rationalize: this is sacred. Just one sip, one toke, it's a prayer, it's sharing, it's o.k. & come to think of it i have a lot of praying to do right now — three or four tokes' worth at least, & the cup is more than half-way round the circle & less than half empty — i can drink a little more.

Personally, i don't think the Goddess would be offended by water. Or orange juice for that matter.

# The Line

### by Mary Wheelan

I laugh.
I smile.
I joke around.
                goddess forbid I might reinforce
                someone's idiotic notions
                and pre-conceived ideas
                of what I must be like now.
                now that I've walked both sides of the line.
I laugh.
I smile.
I joke around.
                I hear the hesitancy
                and the caution in their
                now patronizing voices.
                why waste energy on them?
                educating them's not worth my time.
I laugh.
I smile.
I joke around.
                how could I possibly explain
                the growth and strength that comes
                with pain to ignorant,
                insensitive people who
                could use walking both sides of the line?
I laugh.
I smile.
I joke around.

> when no one's looking sometimes I cry,
> slam a door or break a glass.
> I have a right to feel
> pressures as anyone would
> without having to prove my sanity

I cry. I holler. I scream aloud.


**MARY WHEELAN:** About two years ago, I experienced a psychotic break while withdrawing from Valium. This was the first poem I've written since. My sun sign is Sagittarius. My rising is Aquarius. My moon is in Taurus. Recently someone who hardly knows me said, based on this astrological information, that I must be a constant battleground between the creative side of my being and the practical side. It is a constant battle. I hope someday the creative side wins the battle once and for all.


If my lesbian community were clean and sober everyone would always know the answer to the question: "What is it I really need?".

"What do I really need? I may feel like getting drunk but I know that's not what I *really* need. Do I need a hug? Maybe I need to cry. Do I need to throw a tantrum? Have I ever thrown a tantrum? Maybe I should call a friend. Could be I just need some rest or maybe I need to be bitchy. Yeah, being a bitch might be exactly what I need.

"Perhaps buying something really impractical would help me feel better. That three-piece, pin-stripe suit I looked at a few days ago would sure look terrific on me. It's expensive but hell, I'm worth it. I know something else that would help me feel better, that healing ritual I used to do daily. I haven't done it for awhile but it sure did help me to relax. A long, hot bubble bath would be real nice too. Maybe my lover and I could go out for ice cream sundaes. In fact, we could really blow our phantom diets and order banana splits.

"What is it I really need? Getting drunk is certainly not the answer."

What is it we all really need? A clean and sober lesbian community would have the answers.

# Four

## by Faith

### Revolution

Slowly I raised my scratched, quivering hand to pull my long hair over my bruised eye. Muscles aching, I lowered my hand, watching to make sure no one at the Alcoholic Anonymous meeting saw my secret. They had, of course, but they were much too kind to tell me then. Months later, someone mentioned the way I had looked at my first meeting and the anger and fear that was almost a tangible shield between me and them and I remembered. I went there because I had nowhere else to go. I had ruined my life with my drinking and my drugs; I deserved to die, but I couldn't quite figure out how to arrange that, and I had two children who hadn't asked for any of the hell they were living with. So there I was: shaking and sweating, icy-cold and nauseous and very, very frightened.

I thought of A.A. as my last chance, but I was certain that it was hopeless. I really came to verify that fact so I could stop feeling as though I should be doing something. I knew there was nothing that could be done; it was far too late for me. I will never cease to be grateful for the things that were said that night. Not to me, of course. I would have left immediately if I had thought they were talking to me. No, the people there were just talking about the way their lives had been when they drank, and how they were without alcohol. They were so real, so sincere, that I, the cynic, believed every word they said. That night when I went home, I took something with me that I had not had in so long I couldn't even put a name to it. I had *hope*.

I walked back into my house, a house I hated, with the air resounding in the arguments, fights, punches, screams and solitary tears which made up the obscene tragedy that only the marriage of two alcoholics can produce. For seven years he said I would never be able to escape him: I was too helpless. I had no skills, no education, no money, no work history, couldn't drive: I was his as long as he wanted me. I heard it and knew it to be true until the night of the A.A. meeting. I heard the stories those people told that night.

In a mere handful of days I did the impossible. I took my children and I moved away. Every night I went to a meeting and gathered strength from what I was discovering inside myself, and every day I used that strength to fight. I had to fight a lot. I fought with the Welfare people (and won), with the medical aid people (and won), with my psychiatrist (and won), with my husband (and won), but most of all I fought with myself to stay sober and keep trying. Thank God I won that too. Every day was a landmark for me and every night I went to a meeting to share my triumphs, exhilarating conquests for a person destined to die a failure a few short months before.

My life changed in many ways and all of them were good. I felt a strength and cleanness that only self-respect can bring and I was doing it for myself.

## Absolution

After several months of the new awakening a friend asked me if I intended to stay single forever. My answer was yes. Never again would I settle for second best. She was appalled and asked me who I thought would be the perfect man. Without any hestitation I told her. I described the man who had lived in my mind since I knew I was supposed to get married and live happily ever after.

Four hours later at a Valentine dance, I met him. He looked precisely as I had said he should and his personality was exactly the same as I had requested. He had been out of town for almost a year and had just gotten back that day. It was eerie, like I had placed an order and someone had filled it.

He was just as interested in me and we began a relationship soon after. It was as though the whole world responded to us as a couple. For the first time in my life, I, the outcast, was in the center of a social whirl. People planned their parties around us; we were asked to speak at meetings; nothing started until we arrived; we chose the places where everyone ate and the things we all did and we were thanked for our trouble. It was amazing. At 27, I was a prom queen at last.

He was the man of fairy tales: tall, dark, so handsome, intelligent, kind, romantic and attentive, strong and gentle at the same time and he saw me as his perfect counterpart.

Each day was glittering with promise and I was happier than I had ever hoped.

The portly matron with the sad eyes who had come to A.A. so recently, had now lost thirty pounds, wore tight jeans, skinny tops and feathers in her braids. And each time I passed a mirror, I had to stop and remind myself that SHE was ME.

Six months into the relationship came a new discovery. Everything was still wonderful; he hadn't changed a bit and I was more marvelous by the minute. I was pleased that I held up my end of the "ideal" relationship as well as I did, that I could indeed be all of the things I admired in others, honest, real and faithful. But I was bored to tears most of the time. Oh, not with everything. I was still captivated by the new dimensions I was encountering in myself and he was still all the things he was in the beginning, but as a couple, we were stultifying. Shortly after this realization hit me, the affair died a quick, quiet death. And I went out to face the world alone again.

I will be eternally grateful for this brief interlude in my life. It gave me all the things I missed in my adolescence. When I was really seventeen, I had already descended into the pit of alcoholic drinking, so I only imagined what a normal popular girl went through. This short romance allowed me to experience it all first-hand and I loved it. Now that I know that, I can make my new choices, not out of the bitterness of deprivation, but out of the fullness of knowledge.

And somewhere deep inside me, I also feel that I was handed back a part of my life that I thought I could never have. It's almost like a special blessing on my new way of life, for if I hadn't lived through this period, I would have always missed it and wondered whether my decisions were really decisions at all, or merely the empty acts of a bitter woman cheated of her youth.

## Persecution

With the "Perfect Man" out of my life, I had time to think about my future and remember my past. I began to recall some of the lies I told about myself. All through my drinking I had pretended to be someone I was not. I noticed that the only lie I told regularly was that I was a college graduate. In A.A., I learned that we make our own dreams come true, and that maybe it wasn't so much a lie as it was a dream. . . I moved to a small town nearby and began college. I also did volunteer work in my chosen field. I lived alone with my children and was having a wonderful time learning and growing. I was extremely active in the A.A. community and felt right at home.

It came as quite a surprise to me when I was called into the office at work and told that someone there had a crush on me and I should be certain never to be alone in a room with that person, or at least I should keep the office door open at all times so I could be seen by other people, as this person was *gay* and I didn't want my reputation ruined, or certainly that of the facility besmirched.

I listened very carefully and was terribly quiet. I wanted time to fully digest this information. I walked out of the office and sat down to sort out my thoughts. In the hour I sat drinking coffee and mulling over this news, I had two phone calls from a co-worker to remind me to be watchful of the woman. The audacity of those people made me furious.

Before my marriage I had often dated women casually. I'm sad to say that often it was merely for sex, but being European by birth, it never occured to me to make a production out of it. After all, I had no guilt or fears because of it. I always took it for granted that I was luckier than most people because I had the whole world from which to choose my lovers. So for that man to assume I would be repelled by the fact a lesbian was interested in me was ridiculous, but for everyone to be so concerned was insulting. Certainly no one ever said a word when a man was in my office with the door closed. How was that different unless they expected the poor woman to be so depraved that she would attack me at the first opportunity, or else that she would be so fascinating that I couldn't resist her?

Now that was certainly an interesting thought. Immediately I invited her to join the group of people coming to my home to listen to music and talk that night. I felt touched that she was so grateful; it showed me that she was used to being left out and alone. I was angry that she had to fight the isolation of her alcoholism coupled with this unfair rejection because of her sexual identity.

In the weeks that followed, the inevitable happened and I quit my job, telling them they had so intrigued me by their warnings that I simply had to date the woman and see if she was all that awful. (All the while I enjoyed their discomfort wrapped in the warmth of my growing love for this fragile girl-woman who frightened them with all her honesty.)

My life became a series of warm soft evenings, full of laughter and music. I was given the finest gift of my life when she brought me a Meg Christian album. For the first time, I heard someone sing of my feelings, and she did it with joy and a profound sense of pride that strikes me fresh whenever I hear her sing. Those evenings with those albums became magic to ward off the evil of the days. I had become branded.

People I had grown to love didn't quite hear me when I spoke; when I entered a room, I was deafened by the silence. People who had always talked to me of their lives, families, and marriages, no longer shared those things with me, as though now I could not understand. The very worst part of all this was that it was a very small town, and everyone tried to be oh-so-polite. No one ever mentioned it. After I learned to live with my ostracism on that level, I was still given a job working with teen-agers, but it was made quite clear that it was because of my excellent qualifications and my discretion that I was working there. They cited examples of other people who wanted the job, but were unsuited. All three examples were of lesbians who were not so discreet. None of them ever talked about their private lives but they were apparently more physically obvious. My children had to eat, and I needed a job, so I did the work I loved with my mouth shut tight and my heart like a flower that longs to open, but can't because there is no sunlight.

I kept hoping that if I were persistent, we would all get beyond the awkwardness, and with some beautiful people, that happened. But most people were rigid in their disapproval. Every day as I left my house filled with love, I prepared for battle on the silent level that is so terrible. I had my uses, it seemed. I became the person who was given all the cases of people with sexual identity problems, and I never compromised there. I told them all to follow their hearts: to pretend that no one in the world would know what they were doing, to close their eyes and envision their lives the way they would be perfect. If they did that, and came up with a same sex partner, I made sure that all our work would never contradict that in any way. At least I could maintain my integrity on their behalf.

Inside I was dying from the rejection. I had come to depend on A.A. meetings for my peace of mind and I could no longer do that. The people I worked with were there. If I were honest about myself, I was through, even though most every one knew already. Actually telling someone I was in love with the woman I had been living with for two years could cause our adolescent program to shut down. If I mentioned it at meetings, newcomers would be frightened away by our perversity. The list of reasons I was given to maintain my silence is long and wearisome, even now. Sadly enough, the reasons worked. I was quiet and dying from it.

## Evolution

I knew I had to do something to merge my home life with my spiritual life, so every couple of months we drove 200 miles to an A.A. meeting for gay people. I was so thrilled to find it existed that I would just go, sit and smile. I didn't take part because I was always too torn by my betrayal of myself. I wanted to hear how other people coped. It saved my sanity, but just barely.

The change came in 1980 when I went to the 45th A.A. Anniversary Conference in New Orleans. I went to a couple of meetings in the Super Dome and then I heard that they had two gay Hospitality Suites, one with continual A.A. meetings. I went to the "International Hospitality Suite" first and there were only a handful of gay men there and the meeting was over. Almost unable to choke down my disappointment, I thought of going back to the hotel to sleep for a while. I was persuaded to drop by the "Houston Hospitality Suite" before I went back to the hotel, but I had no hope of it being any different. Out of 25,000 alcoholics, I had seen a total of five gay men up to that point. I was certainly ready to believe none of us were allowed to speak up.

I pushed open the door to the "Houston Hospitality Suite" and was immediately hugged and pulled into a laughing crowd of about 100 people. I was enveloped in that style of love that knows no limits. I sat and talked to people for hours that evening and thought I had never been so full in all my life. At midnight there was a huge crowd of people for the gay A.A. meeting and my world turned upside down. The meeting just continued. Everyone was told they should feel free to leave when they were tired and come back rested and catch the tail end of the meeting. I thought surely this was an exaggeration until it got to be 4:30 a.m. and there were still many of us in that meeting.

All of a sudden it seemed we went from about 25 members to eight women and one man. The things that were said that night were the most heart-breaking, miraculous and incredible things I've ever heard. Women opened their very souls. Many cried silently in pain when one would talk of her tragedy. Moments later, the same women would convulse quietly with mirth when another woman shared her stumbles along the path of growth. Every one of us that were there talked until we were empty, drained of all the things that hunched us over in sorrow. All of the things that we had carried alone for so many years were shared by seven other women and made that much lighter. I feel as though I saw all the miseries of the world in that room, and I was privileged to be a part of the almost unearthly beauty of women taking each other to the pit of hell and loving each other well, bringing each other the sheerest joy I have ever known.

I was healed in places I didn't even know were hurt, simply by the magic of lesbians giving to one another, giving the one thing the world can't take away: the ability to be so in tune with others of our own kind that we pass the strength among us to weave the spell of overwhelming unconditional love.

When I left New Orleans, I knew that never again could I be an outcast. My wonderful women were everywhere, waiting to turn my tears into affirmations of joy. I will always know that whatever I suffer, if I can be with these strong sober women, the cost is not too high.


**FAITH:** More than six years ago, a wild-eyed, shaking, desperate failure walked into a room full of strangers and began a metamorphosis that is still in its initial stages. The wild-eyes became wide eyes — open to the magic of discovery. The shaking became throbbing — to the beat of life. The desperation turned into expectation — of the joy and growth hidden behind every pain. And the failure; she simply left — to make room for the new woman — 33 years old, with a college degree, a job she loves and 2 children she adores. Best of all, in the not-so-genteel poverty of a Southern California city, there is a woman surviving, with dignity, pride and the knowledge that each chemical-free day gives her the opportunity to have a better tomorrow. She is me — and I am a miracle.

The feelings in the small square would be of warmth and gentle comfort. The laughter would tinkle, bubble and boom all around as the women met to share their day. The creativity unleashed would show in their hair, their clothing, their homes and their gardens behind them. The flashing bold eyes, quick smiles and easy caresses tell of a world devoid of dishonesty, mistrust and isolation that comes when we hide from each other in the cold grip of a chemical prison.

I hope to see you all there — in our town — clean, green and serene — for I love the *reality* of you even more than I feared the you I saw through my pain-blurred stupor as I prayed to be numb. Your drug-free, love-filled lives validate my dream and allow me to strive to share in yours.

# In Training

## By Kitty Tsui

### For Marilyn King

**R**abbit turds. The floor was covered with them. The tops of primo California-grown sinsemilla laid out in neat piles according to size. The smallest buds, called especial, were the only grade that had the green outer leaves left on them. The other buds were cut free from their protective covering until the inner core was exposed, a cone of delicate hairs shining with resin.

Rabbit turds. She laughed out loud. In between all her odd jobs she had been on food stamps, Medi-Cal, student financial aid and unemployment. But only in California, she thought, could she make money planting trees in the mountains up north in the spring and manicuring the state's second most valuable cash crop in the fall.

Rabbit turds covered every inch of floor space in the room. She surveyed the scene with pride. Each turd had passed through her hands to be trimmed and shaped. And though the work had required concentrated and often painstaking labor, the job of manicuring some forty large, healthy plants was well-paid and one that afforded a fringe benefit. Smoke.

She exhaled slowly, savoring the fragrance of the smoke. She could smell the resin that had accumulated on her fingertips and could taste the sweetness in the back of her throat. She stretched in the chair and yawned. She was exhausted and her back was hurting again. She dialed p-o-p-c-o-r-n and got a busy signal. She tried again. A dry voice announced: the-time-is-six-ten-exactly. Thank you, she mimicked as the voice continued, the-time-is-six-ten-and-ten-seconds.

She couldn't believe it was only six. It felt like bedtime. But what did it matter? This was why she had always chosen to live alone; even if it meant cutting back on other necessities. She could eat and sleep whenever she wanted to. Play music loud. Walk around in the nude. She didn't have to answer to anyone behind the doors of her own home.

Too early to crash, she reproached herself. She looked listlessly through a box of tapes. She was tired of the same old tunes. She turned on the radio but had a hard time choosing between jazz, classical, rock or the KPFA evening news. She turned the radio off.

Almost immediately a munchie attach struck. She knew better than to waste any time fighting the urge. For popcorn for french fries for a Coke or a meal. It didn't matter that she had just eaten. Smoke made her want to eat again. And again and again. With a seemingly insatiable appetite.

She went downstairs to the refrigerator. There was a very old jar of kimchee, a bag of yellow onions, two green apples, a carton of eggs and some left-over rice. She cut up half an onion and fried it with two eggs. Then she tossed in the rice, added some drops of soy and ate from a wooden bowl.

Seven o'clock. That meant she could watch M*A*S*H, Sanford and Son or the network news. None of the programs struck her fancy. She yawned. Another smoke would help pass the time. Then perhaps she could go to bed without feeling guilty. After all, it was getting dark outside and the moon was already rising above the crest of the Berkeley Hills.

In a dream she is looking into a mirror. Her eyes are bloodshot and her lips are cracked and dry. She bends over the washbasin and splashes cold water on her face. Squeezes a line of toothpaste onto her toothbrush. When she opens her mouth to gargle, flames shoot out from between her lips. A towel catches fire. The room fills with smoke so dense she cannot see. The phone rings. She gropes around for it. Her fingers connect with the receiver and she picks it up. She tries to force sound from deep in her gut. Sweat is pouring from her face and from under her arms. Her tongue is locked behind clenched teeth. And the only sound she can hear is the sound of the dial tone.

She woke up coughing. The sheets were cold and damp around her body. The world was black outside her window and she wondered if it was early morning or still night. Her head was heavy. Her chest felt as if there were many layers of sheets wound tightly around her.

Ahhhh! A loud exclamation burst from her lips. She was suddenly wide awake, staring into the darkness. Fragments of a dream disturbed her. She tried to coax images from the recesses of her mind. Being chained. Immobile. Silence. Smoke. A mouth. Her teeth.

She knew that her teeth dreams were anxiety dreams. She'd had them for as long as she could remember. Teeth stained and black. Teeth missing. Teeth loose in her mouth. Teeth falling out. No teeth at all.

She curled into a fetal position and tried to shake the dream from her mind. Sleep would not take her. She lay awake listening to the sound of the clock beside her. It was ten past three. She shivered and drew the quilt up over her face. She was not going to be intimidated by a dream. Especially one she couldn't even remember.

When she woke up her head was hurting and her eyes felt swollen and sore. The room was still in semi-darkness. Outside, fierce winds shook the limbs of trees with wild abandon. Must be the early winter storm that had been predicted, she thought. The meteorologist at Channel Seven had been right about the storm's timing. Even as the thought went through her mind she heard the sound of rain pelting against the window pane.

The room was cold. She got out of bed reluctantly and threw on her clothes. A thick cotton T-shirt, long sleeve thermal underwear, flannel shirt, jeans and two pairs of socks.

She went downstairs, put water on to boil and stepped outside to get the morning paper off the front porch. She sat down to two pieces of toast thick with butter and a cup of strong black tea which she drank with milk and honey. She skimmed the front page, lingering only on an item about a woman who had bitten the tongue off a Berkeley man who had tried to rape her. She laughed and thought, only in Berkeley. Then she added, good for you, woman.

Her horoscope read: relax and wallow in the attention you get. This is your moment in time, or soon will be. No point in holding on to old ways that have become restrictive and burdensome.

Reading the horoscope itself was an old habit from her hippie days. She would smoke a joint and consult the daily paper to see what the stars forecast before venturing out into the world. Of course if the signs were not auspicious she might have chosen to stay in the house all day listening to music, smoking dope or working on an intricate jigsaw puzzle that was always half-finished, spread out on the floor of the living room.

No point in holding on to old ways that have become restrictive and burdensome. She wondered what that meant. She'd given up coffee and alcohol and rarely ate beef or pork. She tried to avoid sugar but allowed herself to indulge in an occasional vanilla bean ice cream from Vivoli's or a can of Coke. She'd been raised on sugar. In Hong Kong where she'd grown up, one didn't drink water during the hot, humid summer months. There was an unlimited variety of soft drinks to choose from. Coke, Pepsi, Vitasoy, Green Spot and Schweppes cream soda, ginger ale or sarsaparilla. And she'd made it through many sweltering summers on ice cream — mango and coconut were her favorites — and iced drinks made from red beans, syrup and condensed milk.

Nowadays she ate brown rice and whole wheat bread, took vitamins and drank spring water. There was nothing wrong with her diet.

Or her relationships either, she mused. Her dealings with people were fine. She had grown up a loner but had established some deep friendships. And though she was involved in some long-term feuds with friends and ex-lovers, for the most part, she valued her relationships. And she loved her grandmother dearly.

Old ways that have become restrictive and burdensome. She wondered what that meant. She'd given up drinking and drugs. Pills, psychedelics and cocaine, that is. Marijuana was a harmless high. It didn't fall into the same category as the other drugs at all. Grass wasn't a hard drug. She didn't consider it to be a drug at all. Just a pleasant relaxant after a day's stress.

Giving up booze hadn't been easy. She'd been drinking since high school. Growing up a shy, introverted girl, drinking had given her a great sense of confidence. Drinking made her feel loose enough to drop her guard and she could play and joke and laugh out loud. The protective armor would crumble from her body and crash to the floor. And she wouldn't care. Drink made her feel at ease. Secure. Accepted. Loved.

She drank when she felt lonely. There'd been times in her life when alcohol had been her best friend. Booze didn't argue, disagree or talk back. Booze was always there. Was easier than a phone call, quicker than the mail and more comforting than a hot bath. She drank when she was depressed. About money, a job, a lover. She drank to celebrate a birthday, a holiday, the next-to-the-last-day-of-school. It didn't have to be a big occasion. She could turn any day into an excuse to drink. Somedays she drank just to pass the time.

Giving up booze hadn't been easy. And there had been many tries since the first try. But she had been determined to ditch the monkey that had been riding on her back for almost ten years. Not only because of the hangover. And the blackouts.

She was determined to ditch the monkey because drinking made her lose time. Hours, days, weeks passed by her faster than the landscape from a moving train. Her friends were going to New York, Europe, Asia. With books in print, shows at established galleries, performances on stage. Friends were sporadically appearing on TV talk shows and even cropping up between the pages of *People* and *Time*. Zake's play had opened in New York for a very successful stint off Broadway. Just last week right on Market Street she had seen her face plastered on a huge billboard that advertised the play's San Francisco run.

Everyone was going somewhere but her. She was still hanging out in her apartment listening to War singing,

mu-sic is what I like to pla-a-ay
oh yeah. . .
let's have a picnic
go to the park,
rolling in the grass
'till long after dark. . .

She was determined to ditch the monkey because drinking had made her hate herself. And she had only just recently begun to realize it.

Giving up booze hadn't been easy. She'd tried so many times before. And all her attempts were heavily peppered with threats and ultimatums.

So many promises. So many days that were all Day One. Tomorrow I'll quit, she promised herself. Next week. Thanksgiving. Christmas. New Year's Day, a new start. Her birthday. Her grandmother's birthday. The anniversary of her grandmother's death. By that time it was Thanksgiving again and she'd not been sober a month.

All her front teeth are loose. She can feel a cavity in the back of her mouth. She tries to call the dentist but cannot get a dial tone.

First she stopped drinking hard liquor. That had been easy. The mornings after were hell. Besides, it cost a dollar seventy-five for a Courvoisier-up-soda-back-with-lime in a bar. And she could easily put away five or six. That could get very expensive, especially if she was buying drinks for someone else too.

Abstaining from hard liquor had been easy. She still had beer and wine to keep her happy. Then she resolved to give up wine. That had been a little harder. She loved to drink white wine. With romantic sounding names like pouilly fuisse and flume blanc. Even the commonplace chablis and chardonnay had names that rang poetic to her ears. She loved drinking white wine. Driving across the bridge to sit in the afternoon sun at an outdoor cafe in the Haight. Dinner for two at the Neon Chicken. When she could afford it she bought French wine to cover up the fact that she was drinking alone. In her own company.

Wine was easy to give up because she was still permitted her favorite drink: cold beer. Dos Equis when she could afford it and Schlitz malt liquor when she was broke. Even when she was broke she made sure she could still buy beer.

She is in Hong Kong walking along the narrow streets. There are crowds of people pushing past her. All of a sudden she tastes blood inside her mouth. She can feel her back teeth with her tongue. They are loose and about to fall out. Alarmed she puts her hand to her mouth and runs to hail a taxi. People jostle against her and block her path. She sees an empty cab and tries frantically to flag it down. But her arms are like lead and she has no power over them. She starts to shout but the roar of the traffic drowns out the sound of her cries.

Smoke. On the day she gave up beer she still had her smoke.

She gave up drinking. Instead she smoked. Regularly, depending on availability. She was listless, lethargic. She was numbed and relaxed. Could escape from whatever routine or responsibility was calling. She was safe for a time.

From sleep she is awake but she cannot open her eyes. She tries to move her head, her hand, any part of her body. Can't. Strains. Tries to move her tongue. Tries to force sound from deep in her throat. Her nose is plugged up. She tries to blow. White, sticky mucus comes out.

She woke up coughing. Knowing she'd probably been coughing in her sleep all night long. Knowing that smoking regularly fanned the flames of the fire.

She was depressed a lot. About something or another. She didn't want to see anyone and stopped calling her friends. She found it hard to get around or do anything she didn't absolutely have to do. She did do a lot of binge eating. Might be a salad with lots of sprouts one minute and a chicken burger with french fries smothered in ketchup the next. Might be anything on the table or in the refrigerator that looked appetizing at the moment. A tangerine. A banana. An old bear claw.

She is on stage about to address a large audience. She says to herself, better not smoke yet or you'll fall asleep. A voice whispers, or get paranoid. Another voice pipes in, or crazy. A voice shouts, or spaced out. Or stoned.

She woke up in a daze. Everything around her was foggy, unfamiliar. She wondered if she was really awake or had merely entered another dream. Her head ached. She closed her eyes but knew it was already too light in the room for her to go back to sleep. She stretched, took a deep breath and reacted in pain. Her chest was tight and constricted.

She was in the grip of another monkey.

She crumpled a small bud between her fingers and rolled a thin joint. She lit up, inhaled. It was the weekend. She could smoke day and night.

Her horoscope read: a tendency to indulge should be checked. Get rid of clutter. Make a promise you will keep.

She studied herself in the mirror. Her face was lined and weary, the brows drawn. A combination of inactivity and overeating had made her stomach and ass sag. Her thighs were pale and puffy. She had little energy and no enthusiasm at all. Her sex life was zero. She had trouble remembering her dreams.

A tendency to indulge should be checked. Get rid of clutter. Make a promise you will keep.

Tips for cold turkey, she read. Drink plenty of water. Teas and juices. Listen to music. Take hot baths. Practice deep breathing. Meditate. Masturbate. Plan a trip. Make new friends. Do some outdoor activity. Exercise.

The sun was in her eyes. Her left ankle hurt like hell. She tried to avoid running on concrete whenever possible but living in the city had its drawbacks. She glanced at her watch. She couldn't believe she'd only been at it for ten minutes. To distract herself from the pain she zigzagged between trees planted at intervals in the sidewalk, careful to stay clear of dog shit that dotted her path. She looked at her watch again. She couldn't stop yet. She had planned to run for twenty minutes a day. Rain or shine. Today she was sweating under the midday sun. Yesterday it had been so cold she could see her breath dancing in front of her like a kite in the wind.

Late night. The house was cold. She tried to save money by not using the gas heater. She wore layers of clothing — shirts, sweaters and even coats in the house. She sat in bed trying to read. Her mind kept wandering. After awhile she realized she couldn't even remember what she had been reading.

She got up and started to pace, rubbing her cold hands together vigorously. Her nose was cold and so were her feet. Three pairs of socks and her feet were still cold! She looked over at the bookcase where she had hidden her stash. She was doing really good. It had been five days since her last smoke.

She paced the floor. She took a deep breath and imagined she was inhaling a lung full of sweet smoke. She walked past the bookcase. Surely a few tokes wouldn't hurt, she told herself. It could be considered relaxation therapy. Besides, no one knew except for her.

She rolled and smoked. She inhaled deep and held it until she felt a rough tickle in her throat and had to let go, coughing violently as smoke poured from between her lips. It didn't take her long to get high but she thought she might as well finish smoking what she'd rolled.

Shit, she thought. Back to Day One. The monkey was still riding high. Laughing. And getting fat.

Shit. She could have fought the urge. She should have fought. With tears, with threats. Anything. The only way she could continue was to fight.

She lasted a week and a day on her jogging regimen. Her legs hurt and her back was bothering her again. She finally admitted to herself that jogging just wasn't her thing. Besides, as young as she was, she didn't want to be seen running up and down the street gasping for breath.

In a dream she sees a jade plant with brilliant red flowers. She remembers the trunk vividly. It is dark brown, knotty and thick as a strong dyke's forearm.

Gym. When she was fourteen she hated gym class with a passion. Not because she didn't like sports. She did. There was hockey in the winter, track and field in the spring and netball in the summer. Not because she didn't like sports but because she hated to change in front of the other girls. She was fourteen, thin as a rail and had no tits to speak of. According to her biology book she was a "late-bloomer". All the other girls had bras and she was still wearing little cotton undershirts. She was very self-conscious. Even little Kimberly Fung had tits. And Karen Smith's one nipple looked bigger than what she saw on her own chest. She hated gym with a passion.

She started smoking again. The cycle she was trying to break sucked her right back in. She was depressed for no apparent reason and stayed in that rut for days. She had a hard time remembering things and she procrastinated more than ever. She knew she had to stop but she didn't know how to. It was easier to roll than to fight.

She didn't know what to do. Water she drank plenty of. Ditto for teas and juices. She loved music and was always soaking in hot baths. To keep warm and to soothe the nagging pain in her back. She practiced deep breathing whenever she could remember to but had no desire to meditate or to masturbate. At least not on a regular basis. She had no money to take a trip and felt too vunerable to make new friends. She hated jogging and didn't know what other activity to pursue.

In a dream she is sitting on someone's lap. A pair of strong, comforting arms surrounds her. She turns and discovers it is herself.

She was getting desperate. Smoke was running her life. She knew she had to stop but she didn't know how to. Self-discipline had never been a strong point. Perhaps if she had to pay a fee or join a club it would give her the incentive to stick with some kind of activity, she thought. What the hell, it was worth a try.

She was working temp in an office building downtown when she decided to join a gym. At least to go check one out. She looked through the Yellow Pages. Talked with one owner on the phone.

A faded sign read: Olympic Health Studio. Bare boards. Racks of weights. Mirrored walls. Weight machines each occupied their own place on the floor. It was mostly men who were working out. Men of all ages with broad backs and shoulders, thin hips and big thighs. Men with muscles bursting from their bodies.

There was an air of seriousness about the place. There was no dolled-up receptionist or complimentary visits here. One year membership. Take it or leave it. She paid her dues and was initiated into the world of weight training, sweat and hard work.

She was introduced to the different weight machines and given a program of exercises. At first the sight of men with bulging muscles intimidated her. There were not many women and the ones she did see on a regular basis used 5 pound weights and did bent knee push-ups in fancy leotards.

She knew she was strong; she'd just never been tested. She remembered with a spark of pride how her grandmother used to tell all the old ladies in her building about her granddaughter who could carry a fifty pound sack of rice all the way down Grant Avenue and up three flights of stairs without stopping for breath.

It was exhilarating for her to move a dead weight. 10 pounds. 15, then 20, 30. To grasp a cold dumbbell in the palm of her hands and move it for eight reps. Ten. Then twelve. To feel the cold metal grow warm in her hands. To strengthen her body. To build muscle and realize the power of her mind. Whenever the going got hard she urged herself on, her inner voice shouting: yes, yes, you can do it.

She sweated and strained. She did one set. Then two, three and four. She set goals and pursued them. She learned to pyramid: warming up with light weights, then increasing the poundage with each set and going till she could go no further. Arnold Schwarzenegger's prescription for getting strong and massive. Not that she wanted to look like Arnold. She just wanted to push herself to the max.

She skimmed muscle magazines for tips and information. Read about the importance of a sound nutrition program. Studied articles on women's weight training and bodybuilding routines. It was too bad she couldn't remember much from the year she studied human anatomy in college. Still, she was reading, studying and sweating.

She worked out three times a week. Her routine started with a twenty minute stretching session. Then she would exercise all the large muscle groups: chest, thighs, back, shoulders. Early on she found that the exercises she dreaded the most were ones for the abdominal muscles so she interspersed these throughout her workout.

Drugs and alcohol used to run her days. Where to cop from, how to pay. Rolling and smoking. Drinking and hanging out. Now she went to the gym and pumped iron.

She loved this new-found activity. It was exciting and full of challenge. She met and started to work out with other women who were also training with weights. Soon the sound of explosive breathing and the smell of sweat was as familiar and pleasing to her as a Sunday afternoon in bed with a woman she loved.

To supplement her weight training she went to a local pool and swam laps twice a week. She studied food combination charts. Changed her diet. Cut out sugar, salt and fried food. Began calling her friends and stopped watching junk TV.

In a dream she is standing on a beach looking out to sea. She raises her arms to salute the rising sun. Fire envelopes her body. From out of the flames many women emerge. An Amazon with wild hair, broad shoulders and muscular limbs. A thin woman dressed in silk and brocade holding a fan. A barefoot woman in baggy peasant clothing. A Buddist nun with a shaved head in billowing grey robes. A beautiful woman with deep dimples, her grandmother in the prime of her life. The flames subside. She stands naked and whole before the rising sun, her woman ancestors in a line beside her, hand in hand.

This was a dream she carried with her often. It gave her great strength to know she was a vital link in the chain of life.

She had not been smoking or drinking for some time. She could hardly believe it herself. The monkey tried to tempt her from time to time. But she knew she'd only be back at Day One with a headache and a sore throat. And no respect for herself. Again.

The refrain she trained to was: yes, I can.

She was experiencing definite changes. Her stomach muscles firmed up. Her shoulders broadened. She began to see muscle definition in her biceps and her calves. The pain in her back was gone. She stood tall. Her eyes were clear and bright. She felt great and she knew she looked good.

And for the first time in many months, she was loving herself. Pumping iron was paying off.

Drinking and drugs had shielded her from life. From feelings. From people. From herself. She knew she could continue to train with weights. But she also knew the monkey would always be watching. Waiting for a moment of weakness to jump on her back. She knew the only way she could continue to live was to fight.

Yes, I can, she said.

Dare to fight. Dare to sweat. Dare to live. Dare to dream.

Her horoscope read: this is your moment in time.


**KITTY TSUI:** is the author of *The Words of a Woman Who Breathes Fire* (Spinsters, Ink: San Francisco, 1983), an artist, an actor and a recovering alcoholic. She bodybuilds for her health, strength, discipline and sanity.

community of women
clean and sober
healthy and whole.
working, sharing, caring
learning and loving.

community of women
struggling and singing
swimming against the currrent
surviving the storm.

# 1973 I Decided To Give Up Shooting Dope

## by Sim Kallan

**1973** I decided to give up shooting dope
     the same way I began     for someone else
I began for my first lesbian lover
I stopped for my best friend

all of which took 3 years

I got the drugs out of my body and found a new addiction.
     her name was Karen.
later, I changed back to drugs.
she changed her name.

we stayed together as long as we possibly could.

It was like jumping off the high diving board and holding
your breath under water.
it's fine at first.
when it starts to get hard, well, it's not all that bad.
then you get determined and stubborn.
by the time you let yourself surface you're hurting.
I was shooting cocaine.

all of which took 6 years.

Since then I've been working hard to find my self
the toughest part is asking for help
but I'm doing it.
I'm starting out again.
it's the most fun I've ever had.
I get to take risks, but there's no real danger.

I'm alive.


**SIM KALLAN:** is a grateful clean and sober Jewish dyke. I was born in Brooklyn in 1949. My journey has so far brought me to San Francisco. I live with my sweet lover and my old friend Lillian, the cat. I'm the luckiest womon I know.


If our community were clean and sober then we could look at the world as we experience it and ask ourselves — What am I choosing for myself today?

If our community were clean and sober and we asked ourselves that question — we'd have the ability to answer clearly.

If our community were clean and sober and we acted on our own behalf — we'd experience success.

# Reminders

### by Sharon Stonekey

I walked to the village through the dark night. Although I had just moved there and was not familiar with the sidewalk's ups and downs, I thoughtlessly trusted each step as if it were my childhood town. The two places reminded me of each other; both were old and historic with aging trees and children's voices in the air.

My lover and I had just moved from a small working class neighborhood, where we had been harassed because we were lesbians. It had first started with the kids at the bus stop as we passed, and had escalated to rocks on our lawn, shaving cream on our windows and a boy in our yard one morning idly walking with a rifle. Then the older boys, the 20- and 22-year-olds in cars and on motorcycles had begun yelling "lezzy" at us as we left the house. I was getting increasingly afraid that if we stayed, one of us would be raped, probably me since I haven't learned how to punch. We had tried all the right things: turning around and talking to them, explaining about discrimination, talking to their parents, getting a male friend to rough-collar two of them and later simply yelling back at them. None of it had worked.

So we moved to this new town about twenty miles from the city where we worked. We loved the house, our first two-story place with green shutters and original woodwork inside. We were nervous though, knowing homophobia is a classless commodity. In these early days, we held our breath lest the harassment start so soon again.

I kicked the leaves as I walked, wondering what I would find when I got to town. I was a recovering alcoholic and my A.A. meeting book listed a meeting every Friday night in a church in the village. I would be a newcomer and being a bit shy, I feared being made the center of attention and I feared that the men would be overtly sexist. I hoped I could get through the evening relatively unnoticed and unannoyed.

I had drunk or been drunk every day for 12 years, which had been my entire adult life. Stomach pains and nausea, memory losses, outbursts of anger and violence had become common-place in my daily life. I was aware I was alcoholic almost from the beginning and now finally all these years later, my overwhelming inability to stop, despite my fears of an early death by car accident or by deterioration of my organs, had spurred me to seek help.

On the advice of my therapist I went to a rehab for alcoholics. There I struggled through the loneliness and abuse of being the only lesbian and the only feminist among a random assortment of alcoholic Americans. I tolerated the loneliness and discomfort because I simply didn't know what else to do. For me, being a lesbian feminist meant being strong, and I couldn't be strong if I were helplessly drinking. So I listened carefully at the rehab and took what I could use and discarded what I couldn't.

Now I was in my second year of recovery. The second year was easier than the first, but there were still temptations and I still needed to be on guard. Having the hang of abstinence meant never being secure that I had the hang of it.

At first, like everyone else, I groaned at the idea of going to A.A. It was a program designed in the 30's for white, middle class men. It seemed to have little to do with, and was offensive to me, a lesbian feminist in 1980. But I tolerated it, too. I had been brought to my knees by alcohol and I was scared. Despite my dislike of A.A., it remained the only support group in town. Gradually, I found ways to redesign and interpret it so that it was compatible with me and my feminist values.

When I got to the church, I found a meeting which looked like many other meetings I had been to. The coffee urn was going on the side of the room accompanied by sugar, Cremora and spoons. Chairs and tables were set up. A.A. literature was on one table and cigarette smoke hung in the air. About 40 women and men were there laughing and talking before the meeting.

I poured myself some coffee and when I turned around to look for an empty seat, a man approached me. "My name's Paul," he said.

I extended my hand. "Susan," I replied.

"Are you new to A.A.?" he asked.

"No, I just moved here. I've been in A.A. for a while."

"Oh," he said in a friendly way. "Well, welcome to our meeting."

"Thank you," I said. "Thanks a lot."

"There are lots of nice people here if you need phone numbers."

Getting phone numbers and calling other A.A. members was a means of support the group used between meetings. I sat down in the back by some women. One of them had two small children with her. They both had coloring books and stuffed animals, and made toddler noises as they played.

I looked around the room for somebody like me, a lesbian, a gay man. There were some possibilities. Statistics had it that there were four of us there, but no one I could immediately identify.

The meeting began. A woman was chairing. I was glad about that. She read the explanation of A.A. which was read at every meeting and then she told us some of her drinking history. Both her original family and married family had been broken up because of booze and like everyone else she was glad to have this reprieve from a poor and disordered life. She called for a topic and someone suggested comparing a day in our drinking lives with the day we had just had.

We went around the room and everyone spoke or passed, in turn. It was a nice group of people who knew each other by name and laughed easily at each others' jokes. I was reminded of my own drinking by their stories: of my hurting body, of mornings finding evidence of cooking an entire meal which I didn't remember, of calling friends and apologizing for saying things I hadn't meant. I received the nourishment and reminders I needed from this group, from this assortment of small town housewives, shopkeepers, gas station attendants, farmers, orchard pickers.

A man named Gary spoke. I had felt a rapport with him when I surveyed the room. He looked like me, an aging hippie. "Well, I must be in a minority here," he said, "because I've had a terrible day. I blew my stack at my job, threw my hat on the ground and gave Jesus Christ a middle name." Everybody laughed. "And on my way home I swore I wasn't going to bring my foul mood with me, but within a minute of walking in the door my son gave me news which set me right off again and I yelled at him, yelled at my wife and then felt guilty about it. And then," he continued, "I was on my way here and I ran into an old girl friend who's a full-time teacher, a part-time ski instructor and a full-time lesbian." The room exploded in laughter. He then explained that it was probably his fault (he used the word fault) that she was a lesbian. I became very quiet, noticed the women I was sitting near weren't laughing either and wondered what I should do. I felt my anger implode within me and I thought, "I won't say anything. When it's my turn I'll pass and I'll never come back."

I wondered where the other three homosexuals were in the room and how they were handling this laughter at what we were. The three women to my right all passed. I decided I *must* say something. I remembered the old neighborhood and knew I couldn't come out here. I might be revealing myself to a neighbor or the chief of police. I pulled my strength together and ever so seriously said that at least now there's a chance for a good day. All the problems didn't go away when I stopped drinking, but at least now there's a chance to begin to change. (I meant change the world).

I walked home kicking the leaves through the night, feeling vulnerable, knowing there were enemies in each car that passed. I rehearsed what I wanted to say: "I came to this group for support and I haven't been supported; I've been laughed at because I'm a lesbian. Is this group open or isn't it? You wouldn't like being laughed at just because you're an alcoholic."

My lover was home when I got there, enjoying our beautiful old house. I told her what had happened. She became angry, cursed the group and stormed around.

Later we talked quietly. "I would have liked it," I said. "I would have liked walking there on Friday nights and being part of that group." She held me closely and we became quiet, knowing there were no easy answers for us.

**SHARON STONEKEY:** (b. 1949) grew up in suburban New Jersey. She attended NYU School of Performing Arts and graduated from SUNY-Albany. She is both a writer and performer. Her play *Jail Cries* appeared in *Chomo-Uri* and she performed it Off-Off Broadway as well as at many universities and women's prisons. To subsidize her writing, she coordinates the legislative office of NOW-NYS. She has spent the last three years recovering from alcoholism. She enjoys herb gardening, running and watching disasters on television. Currently she is writing short stories and lives with Donna Reynolds in Kinderhook, NY.

Recognizing one's own feelings and wisely acting upon them is a major element in achieving psychological wholeness. Alcoholism and drug abuse are two of many possible impediments to this process. If chemical abuse were suddenly absent from lesbian communities, there would still be a long way to go in achieving harmonious relationships and communities in which each individual approaches her full potential. I believe each woman must look to herself and explore who she is and who she can become while we collectively struggle toward Amazonian utopias.

# Turning It Over

## by Meg Christian

1. Summer is fading, the wind's a little cold, I, — I feel the seasons as they're turning in my soul. And I'm feeling kind of lonely, but I'm mainly o.— k.— I'm just all I can handle at the moment, Feeling my changes, feeling my pain, Turning it over, (Such a relief to let go of the reins!) I'm turning it over — a— gain.—

1. To next verse
2. To Bridge

And o these re- vo- lu- tions slow-ly spin me out— and draw me in. ——— Oh,

(To next verse)

2. Trying to save you, trying to please,
   I nearly tore up your house looking for my own keys.
   Now I'll clean up all my mess, and I'll go on my way,
   And I'm all I can take at the moment —
   Turning the corner, turning the key, turning it over,
   (To the One who can run it without any help from me!)
I'm turning it over again.

BRIDGE: And oh these (our) revolutions slowly spin me out and draw me in. . .

3. Oh, one thing's for certain, one thing's for sure
   I just cannot fight with anybody, any more.
   All that old righteous anger just ate me to the core.
   And all I have left are these moments
   of turning for comfort, turning to friends, turning it over,
   (Keep taking it back, then I have to do it all again.)

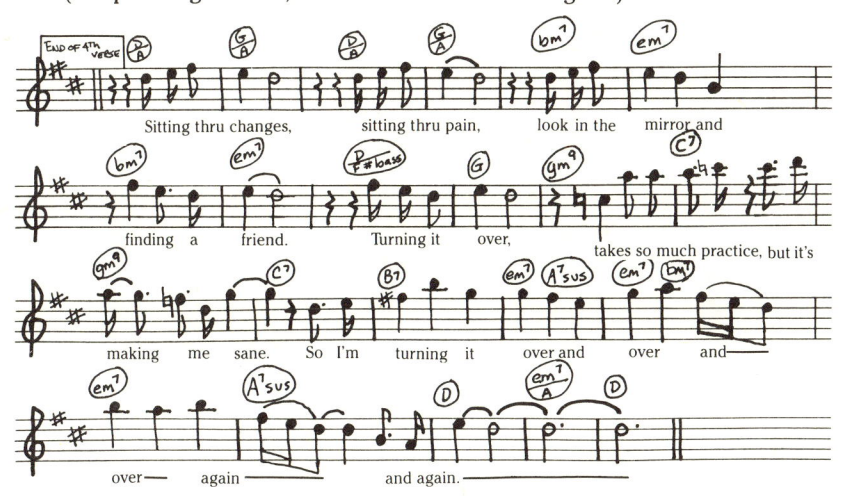

*Sitting thru changes, sitting thru pain, look in the mirror and finding a friend. Turning it over, takes so much practice, but it's making me sane. So I'm turning it over and over and over— again and again.*

**MEG CHRISTIAN:** Singer, songwriter, multi-talented musician, Meg Christian co-founded Olivia Records, the largest women's recording label. Olivia's first release was Meg's *I Know You Know* (1975). Since then, Olivia has released two more albums by Meg: *Face the Music* (1975) and *Turning It Over* (1981). All three albums are available from Olivia Records, 4400 Market Street, Oakland, CA 94608.

Meg was on tour when this book was being assembled and was unable to contribute her vision for a clean and sober community.

# What Is Calistoga?

## by Jean Swallow

### Part I: The Way Back

    This year I rediscovered my grandmother's tea by the smell of it alone—by accident, while it was brewing in someone else's cup.
    "What's that?" I said, hesitant, sniffing the air, trying to pull back to the smell, pull myself back, though to just where was not certain. Smell some more. It smells like, smells like: her kitchen in Pawtucket. A long kitchen with a pantry and a giant gas stove set right in the middle of the room and along the side, a porcelain sink. I can see my grandmother limping from the stove to the dining room, carrying serving dishes full of food, but never spilling. A doctor had cut a nerve in her leg while delivering her last child, leaving her with one leg permanently shorter than the other. Her husband treated her as an invalid until he died. But I didn't know all that then. I thought she moved so deliberately because she was majestic. I didn't know small women who walked with a limp weren't supposed to be majestic. She was the only matriarch I knew as a child. I knew that much by instinct; I wish I had known then she was a prisoner too. And I certainly wish I had remembered the tea, though the milky sweet taste of cambric tea made from it still floats somewhere in my mouth.
    So when I tasted and smelled the lapsang souchong tea again this year, I thought about my grandmother and her kitchen. I suspect she bought the tea in bulk, this was New England, I can see the tea boxes now. But I am not really sure; I have so little memory of her after my childhood. She fell and broke her hip and her mind shortly thereafter and they sent her away. She died then, no matter how much longer they say she lived. She left me some of her books and her china — I sold the china in a fever for almost nothing

and the books are the furniture in Cindy's front room in Atlanta; I despair ever getting them out here and miss them, even now.

But then, there are surprises out here in California. The smell of that tea and the smoky bold taste of it fill my own kitchen now. I offer the women who come to visit a cup of my grandmother's tea, or Calistoga; there is no alcohol in this house.

Unlike the tea, Calistoga is new to me. It jumped into my life, nudged itself a place and saved me more than once. Talking to East Coast friends over the reclaimed tea about my reclaimed self, or in letters to women who knew me when I drank bourbon like water, the question keeps coming back. What is Calistoga?

Well, Calistoga is only bottled water and though they say it's "naturally carbonated," I've since found out it is filtered through asbestos—so I'm not really gaining anything over the water that comes out of the pipes in the city of San Francisco—I just think I am. But health is only part of the reason I drink Calistoga. The other part is that it steadies me. I know it's only water. Of course the tea is only tea too. But this is California. And though there is no more magic here than anywhere else, life and love have converged at stranger places than this to make magic with something no less ordinary than plain bottled water.

## Part II: Courting

Last month, I bought myself the first pair of blue jeans I've had since college. They fit tight; I bought them tight and with buttons instead of a zipper, not only because "501's" are fashionable in this town, but because I like to wear them without any underwear after I've made love, and the buttons are safer than a zipper, I found out.

I've been thinking quite a bit about all kinds of clothes recently. I think most women who've just fallen crazy in love think about how they look. I could be wrong, but for myself, I can say that I am very interested in provoking a certain kind of response. That response might be translated into English as wild abandon or passionate aggressiveness. Maybe not. I've never had anything in my life like this and I can't imagine that there is an English word for it.

But I *am* finding clothes for it. Clothes that cover my breasts without hiding them, like I want to do when I am at work. Clothes that show my ass, that show her I want her to want me. The first time we made love, she gasped and said "you don't look anything like you do with your clothes on." Well, clothes have been my armor. I have the kind of body men think they are supposed to like and I have hated it ever since my father helped me figure that out.

So I am trying to reconsider my own body. I am trying to find all the passion I have hidden from myself during these last few years. As a "radical lesbian feminist," I haven't gotten much power. What I've gotten is to be morally superior, a self-righteous cannibal. Finally, I noticed I was giving away hunks of my own flesh to avoid being eaten. One of the pieces I gave away was my passion. "Real" feminists don't have vaginal or, dare I say it, anal orgasms. And of course, we don't talk (in detail) about things like *that*. It's "too male." Oh, we write about it some. Romantic descriptions of kissing and "the pearl" and then coming and that's that. I mean, we have to mention it at least once in a while. We are perfect, right?

Wrong. If I have to trade my perfection for my passion, I'll consider it a good deal. I want my passion, I want my own power back. But I've needed help. The clothes are helping. I like it. I also like giving her clothes. Last week I gave her a New England cotton sweater, the kind with a high collar and two or three buttons to the yoke. The collar sweeps up towards her neck and she leaves all the buttons undone and when I cup my hands around her chin and then draw them down under the collar, spreading the wings as though the sweater were the lips of her vulva, it is all I can do to hold on, catch my breath, regain my balance and then slowly start again, bend over and kiss her neck, lick her strong shoulder bones, the soft skin just above her breasts, and then spread the sweater wider to take her breast into my mouth, teasing her nipple with my teeth.

And right about this time, before, I would have stopped, picked up a glass of wine and teased her some more with that, drawn her into my mouth with it, swirled it on my tongue. Images of love-making without alcohol are not part of my memory. How romantic can it be with bottled water, anyway? I'm learning. This is the first time I have started a lover relationship sober. It's very different. It's very wonderful. All the tastes are different.

Still, it's a tug-of-war. The memories I have of before, before I was sober, come in two packages. It is hard to open up the package of the bad memories because I can barely stand to look at them. I could barely stand to look when it was happening. There are good memories, on the other hand, memories of drinking and dancing until three, my sweat-gleaming self dancing for the woman I loved, teasing her with my body, wrapping her around me in the public/private places queer discotheques are, teasing until we couldn't stand any longer and went home and made love until the sunset rose. I don't remember so well, don't want to remember, the nights I smashed the car coming home, or puked my insides out in front of everyone, or even just the nights I sat in the booth and cried because of some drunken pain. Is this ugly to you?

It was ugly to me, too. And to my lover who finally got so angry she stopped making love with me. She wasn't angry about the scenes or the car. She was angry because it felt like I wasn't there, angry because it felt like I had taken another lover, a lover who comforted and soothed me better than she could, a lover she couldn't compete with. She never told me then.

She said she couldn't, was afraid I would leave and I did leave, later, after the alcohol had kicked out my brain so much I couldn't figure out how to get dressed. I thought if I left and could start over, I wouldn't drink so much.

Well, I did start over. Many nights I stayed home, cooked a special dinner, waiting for my new lover to come home from work and we ate and talked and slipped gentle into bed and tenderly made love. There were long days of staying in bed and reading and drinking and loving each other in that gentle way. Like this one better? Okay, let's have the whole story: how about the nights I was already drinking before she got there and passed out after dinner. Or the days we fought in bed because of the alcohol. Or the nights when we said nothing because the pain was so great and the alcohol so soothing.

Or how about the times I don't remember at all. The days we spent floating, Bloody Marys for breakfast, or champagne if we were celebrating, and then vodka tonics for her, bourbon for me until supper, with wine, the list just goes on, but what happened to the days? Listen, these are not war stories. I thought we were having a good time. This is about being strong dykes who drink. This is about seeing where the matriarchy begins and where the victims stand side-by-side.

Finally, I did stand side-by-side with Diane, both of us shaking, and said, no more, this is enough for me. I'm not going to leave you too because of this. Now other women, women who didn't know me then, find it hard to believe my memories or my friends who remember much more than I. One woman said, "But why didn't you stop sooner, you're smart, how come you didn't figure it out before?" I *had* figured it out before. It *was* ugly to me. And partly that was the point. Partly none of that mattered.

It does matter now though; it has been more than a year since I stopped drinking. I can stand steady now. I can finally try to find out what happened, now that I don't spend every day just trying to make it without the stuff. So I have to go back, back into the memories and find out what is left, what happened, where my life went. I have to. You see, I intend to stay sober.

But even now the alcohol pulls on me, the alcohol memories. I try to remember to have *all* the memories as well as my more recent discoveries. One of these discoveries is a wonderful thing about being sober. You remember things. You don't have to worry about what you said, because you know what you said, because you were sober. You remember each detail, each touch, each taste.

She comes up to me in the kitchen from behind, slips her hands to my waist where she rests for a moment, just fitting, and then slides them down, over the front of my very tight jeans and cups both hands over the buttons, pulling me back towards her, pulling my ass into her. I lean my head back on her shoulder, searching for her mouth, her tongue. One of these nights,

I'm going to unbuckle her belt, slip her pants over her thighs, lay her down on the kitchen floor and slide my fingers into her right there. We don't have to worry so much about eating food because we aren't drinking. It can wait. Maybe we can't. And I can tease her with a glass of Calistoga, as well as I could with a glass of bourbon. I can take a lime and rim a glass of Calistoga just as well as anything else. Calistoga floats through my love-drenched mouth leaving it clear for other tastes and god, she tastes good. Listen, it's just bottled water, remember? It's me, this time. It's me doing this. Me and her and nothing else.

## Part III: The Holidays

It's rainy here, this holiday season in San Francisco. Doesn't get much below 50°. It is hard to get used to; even in the South it seemed like holidays when it got cold and the ice came to glisten on the wires. There are no seasons here in the city. Across the bridge, only the short distance to Berkeley, the trees are finally turning. But in the city, it mostly rains.

It is the holiday season. I am alone, most of my people are out-of-town and I am trying to find a new rhythm here, trying to figure out how to have this month sober.

"Do you have a plan?" Marian asks. "Yeh," I say. "I'm going to stay sober." "How?" she asks. Marian always wants to know how. This is a little more difficult. I have stayed sober by gritting my teeth. It's worked but I think there is a lot of unfinished business hanging around, getting ready to snatch me back at the most unlikely places and, like Marian, I don't want me to be unprepared.

Like Thursday night when I went to a school Christmas pageant because a friend's child had a part in the program and I was sitting there feeling very smug and haughty like I do when I'm around middle class, straight, white Christians and then all of a sudden they started singing my mother's favorite Christmas carol and someone started to sing the high part just like she does and I shivered and thought "You jerk, just where do you think you come from anyway?"

Because even my blood remembers how my mother likes "Angels We Have Heard On High." And I can not help but remember how lovely her face looks when she sings it, her throat arched for the glorias, her long slender fingers holding down the pages of the Congregational hymnal. I remember it the way I remember how her face flushed when every year, at exactly the same time, she and my father would argue, quietly, the way middle class people do, about the correct way to hang the lights on the Christmas tree. She would be standing away from the tree to get a perspective on it, holding a glass of brandied eggnog in one hand, the other hand on her hip, her head thrown back and her face flushed from the alcohol and the argument. He would be standing on a stepladder, his hands full of lights, his drink already drained on the coffee table. All of us children would have to be there; trimming the tree was a mandatory family gathering. I would be hiding in the big chair, trying to get out of the way, trying to look invisible, thinking if we didn't have the tree, I wouldn't have to be there.

When I left their house I stopped doing trees. But this year, trying to retrieve myself, I went with Sher to the country to find the perfect tree, cut it down and bring it back to the city. And I thought everything was going to be okay when the sun set over the bay and cast the city in gold just as we were driving back. The car was filled with the smell of pine and the pitch rubbed into my hands the way it did when I was very little. When we got back to her house I was feeling so good I could handle the presence of eggnog and the carols but when it came time for the lights to go on the tree, I froze and backed away, wishing myself invisible before I could catch myself.

I've been backing away all these years. But I can't back away from the parts that are already in me. The first drink I ever had was at their table. When did it start? When did it start for them? I called to find out.

It turns out that my grandmother did not drink; oh, she might take a little sherry now and then but my father says he remembers her at parties, looking for a potted plant to pour her drink in. He thought it was very funny. "It wasn't fashionable to drink until after Prohibition," he said. "She didn't like it much," he said.

"When did *you* start drinking," I asked. There was a long pause on the phone. "When I started traveling, your mother and I started to have drinks to celebrate when I got home on Friday nights." Another long pause. "And then it just got more and more and more," my mother said. She said it without bitterness, almost hopelessly.

I think about this. How much don't they remember? How much has their memory gone like mine, lost evenings and years to the drinking? But they didn't learn it at home. So what did my grandmother drink then, on those long New England nights when the snow muffles all sounds by the weight of packed softness? She must have drunk lapsang souchong. It does not go back forever. It will not go on forever.

I don't know how long my struggle will go on. I know this month is going to be day by day, night by night. And the nights, oh god, sleeping has got to be one of the worst parts of it. I don't think I'm the only alcoholic who drank to go to sleep. Holiday memories and being alone. From as far back as I can remember, I have had favored demons who only step out after 2 or 3 a.m. And it doesn't matter if I'm sleeping or not. They will visit in my nightmares or they will step out on their own, in the wavering bedside light, if I can't sleep. I smell them first, feel their breath next. Often they approach from an angle behind me, and out of my peripheral vision I can just see the edge of them, can feel them waiting, breathing but not touching, waiting for me to turn around to their ragged fingernails scraping across my face.

They like it best when I'm alone. Then they can whisper to me, taunting: "How come you're alone, how come no one wants to be with you, not worth much are you, can't take it can you, what a baby, everyone else sleeps alone, you got something wrong with you, something wrong, wrong with you?" And there is no one there to talk back to them. Except me. And no sounds ever come out of my mouth when they are there. Thursday night they stayed with me until 4 a.m. when I outlasted them, finally. I counted sit-ups. I imagined myself doing flawless, easy sit-ups and I counted.

Not unlike counting sheep, you understand, and certainly not what Marian calls a "novel thought." But it worked for me. When I was a child I hadn't been able to do that, wasn't "coddled" or consoled or even listened to at bedtime. This was New England, remember. But try as I might, the terror remained with me through my childhood, into the rest of my life. At fifteen, I thought alcohol was an adult solution, so I didn't need to learn any other solutions. Now I do. Step by step, inch by inch.

So that's my plan. Step by step, inch by inch, hour by hour if I have to, like Thursday night. I have to go back and go through the old pain, find new solutions for it besides drinking. I know it doesn't sound great but it's been worse. I've had worse holiday seasons when I was drinking something other than tea and Calistoga.

## Part IV: Friends

Marian and I hang out together. We are writers together. We work in the same building, doing the same kind of job. We have lunch together almost every day. She has been my best pal here, once we had cleared up the confusion about how best to love someone you are not going to sleep with. We do the things best friends do: we have helped each other through beginnings and endings, have fallen in love at the same time; we both love bridge and writing and women.

But we never drank together, which always seemed strange to me. I stopped drinking about a month before I met her and she stopped about six months after that. Now when we go out together, it's always Calistoga or tea. Sometimes when things are wonderful between us and the sun is shining and we have an hour for lunch before we have to go back and face the secretarial world, sometimes I think to myself, Jesus it would be nice to share a beer with this woman, right here, on someone else's front steps, in the middle of the day, in the middle of the queerest city on earth, right here with my best friend.

And sometimes I say that and she says, "Do you really?" and I always say no, except it's hard for me to remember that I want to say no. But she has a funny way of saying "do you really," like when we were trying not to eat white sugar and I would be craving a cookie and she would look at me, scrinch up her nose and say "Dogshit. Those cookies are dogshit. Just look at them, don't they look like dogshit to you?" And I would have to agree, of course they looked like dogshit. Who would want a cookie after that?

Sometimes now when I say I want a cookie or a drink all she has to do is scrinch her nose up and say dogshit. Sometimes it's enough. We haven't talked about not drinking too much, I'm not sure why, considering the range of conversations. And I had been really sure I'd missed something by not being drunk with her at least once until I finally talked to Cindy again.

Cindy is my best friend since ninth grade. She knows parts of me that no one else will ever know, because either I don't want to remember or I can't remember because alcohol hides things. For the last two years, we barely spoke to each other. When we finally broke the angry silence this past fall, we talked about something we had never talked about before: how she felt about the years when I was drinking. It is a familiar story to me now but she had never told me how angry she had been, even though she was the first one to tell me I was an alcoholic, on my birthday, over eight years ago.

This time, we were walking up the Castro Street hill almost out of breath, when she told me she felt like I had always left her when I was drinking, that the times I remember as good, had ended badly but I wasn't around for the ending; I had passed out. That she wondered if I had always been drinking before I got to her house, that the really good times had been when there hadn't been any alcohol at all.

Well, it was a good thing the hill was so steep. I didn't have to look at this woman who I have loved fiercely for more than fifteen years, who remembered times when I didn't drink, who loved me through all of it but finally couldn't stand it any more. She didn't want to punish me by telling me now, she said. She was proud of me. But the old hurt crept into her voice and I was ashamed that I had never noticed it before.

I didn't know what to say; finally, wisely, I kept my mouth shut. I had already apologized earlier in the day for being so self-righteous with her, for thinking she had become a part of the beast because she is straight and works as the highest-ranking woman in a large corporation. She wore make-up to go to the zoo, I had reminded myself when my love for her threatened to surge over my politics. But this was my best friend, a woman who had more than once dragged me off the streets of Washington D.C. because I was too drunk to walk. And *I* had been too good for *her*. When I finally came to my senses, I wanted her to know I was sorry.

She had accepted that apology gracefully, said of course I was wrong, but didn't rub it in when she could have. And then on the hill I didn't know how to apologize for the years of drinking; I'm not sure she even wanted that apology any more than she wanted the first one. So I just kept the moment for my memory, holding it for a weapon. Now, when I think of it, I think about the green buds coming out on the trees on that Castro Street hill and reaching up, pulling a bud off and rolling it my hands because I had nothing to say.

I think of it whenever I think I'm missing out on something with Marian. One day last week, when the weather cleared, Marian and I went out to lunch, walking and picking something up to eat at the corner store, walking and eating and talking and soaking up the sunshine, like we always do. The way lunch works is that we both get different things, no matter where or what we are eating and then we both eat from each other's sack or each other's plates. This was something that just naturally occurred about the third time we ate together and the custom has stayed with us. So that day I was eating cheese, and giving her bites and she was eating chips and feeding me them. Then she peeled an orange while I drank the Calistoga. We were talking about sex and lesbian literature.

"It's because it's magic and it's always hard to find words for magic," she said. She was getting orange all over everywhere. This is another characteristic of our friendship. She never has a napkin, I usually do. But not that day. I looked at her and laughed at her dripping, orange-filled hands.

"You want some orange?" she asked, hopeful. I laughed.

"No," I said, "You want some Calistoga?"

"Yeh," she said and then waved her hands around. I laughed again and said, "Say when," as I started to pour the drink into her open mouth. She nodded, laughing.

"The fountain of knowledge," she said, gasping. "Now we'll be able to figure it out."

"It's no fountain of knowledge, you fool," I said, both of us laughing. "It's only Calistoga."

## Part V: The Way Forward

I have a new apartment now, done in shades of the palest gray paint made. It is a wonderful apartment, with a garden outside and just enough room for me inside. Cindy is coming to visit soon. I think she will like the place. Marian helped me paint it one afternoon when I struggled not to cry.

The new courtship is rockier than when I first bought the jeans; the old relationship fights through old battles, tries to find itself around new pain. I am alone a lot. There are many nights when I still can't sleep.

But I am no longer interested in earning my place in the patriarchy by making a public spectacle of my self-destruction. There are other things I can do, other places I can be. And I am not so interested in victimizing myself before they can get to me, whether *they* means the patriarchy or the cannibals. A friend recently said, only partly joking, "don't you find my self-reliance attractive?" Well, I do but self-reliance is one thing; not admitting to needs is another. That is self-destruction and I do not find that attractive any more. I need my grandmother and my mother and my past. I need my friends and my lovers and my present. Most of all, I need myself, my passion and my power.

So the refrigerator is full of Calistoga, there is water in the kettle for tea. I am still healing, tearing out parts of myself like I was a garden with weeds, tearing out patches of cannibalism and drinking and replanting with new patience and the smell of old memories. I guess I'll be forever going back to get the good things I left behind and going forward day by day, step by step in this strange part of the world where the hills turn green in the winter and where there is more than magic in life and love and bottled water.

**JEAN SWALLOW,** 30, is a lesbian feminist writer and editor who works as an administrative assistant in the liberal heart of the beast. She lives now in San Francisco with her partner Sher and the cat Alixander/Salamander, but she was raised in North Carolina and New England. She is a recovering alcoholic. She is on the collective which publishes *Common Lives/Lesbian Lives* and co-ordinates poetry for the magazine. She spent many years working for mainstream newspapers and since then has published mainly in the lesbian or feminist press, including America's *Common Lives/Lesbian Lives, Lesbian Inciter, Feminary, Women A Journal for Liberation, Womanspirit, Lesbian Contradictions,* and New Zealand's *Bitches, Witches and Dykes.* She has been writing stories and poems for years, but does not think it is an accident that her work has only begun to feel right since 1) she started writing for other lesbians, and 2) she stopped drinking.

# PART II:
# THE HEALERS AMONG US

# A Process Of The Cells Learning To Function Together Again

## An interview with Karen Pruitt

Karen Pruitt, 50, is a registered nurse at one of a half-dozen all-women's residential rehabilitation programs in the country. She has been a nurse since 1955 and has dealt with alcoholics on and off since that time. For the last three years, she has been working specifically with alcoholics in an in-patient setting. She tells me that in general, there are ten times fewer treatment facilities for women than for men.

We talked in the kitchen of her sunny apartment in San Francisco's Western Addition. Her white hair was rumpled; she had tried to get a little sleep in between our early morning interview and her late night shift, but her sky-blue eyes were steady. She grew up in a small town in California and calls her family "real WASP," with tee-totaling, moralistic grandparents and a father she describes as a "blue-collar worker who drank mainly as a class thing and not very much at all." She considers herself a "concerned other" around the issue of alcohol.

She talked gently and softly and extended her opinions carefully. She said she felt alcohol was a problem in the lesbian community and that maybe she and her friends have ignored it as a problem. But it seemed more to me that in her careful way, she was considering and measuring her life, her friends' lives and how to move from that place. I felt no judgment from her at all during the interview and felt at ease when we spoke.

---

**JS:** So tell me what you do.
**KP:** Well, I don't do all that much in the way of traditional nursing except during detox and then there is more physical observation and more

medication. There are different things to do in a residential rehabilitation program than in traditional nursing, more than just helping the person physically. Detox is only the initial portion of our program and usually lasts three to five days. The rehabilitation portion lasts three to four weeks and involves group therapy, educational lectures and some individual counseling. So my job is much less demanding physically than general nursing, but more demanding emotionally. It resembles intensive care nursing in the emotional involvement with the patients and their families. I spend a lot of time talking and listening. The nurse's function, as set out by company philosophy, is to be loving and caring and that's what I try to be.

There is not much information about the physical stresses caused by recovery from alcoholism, except in the early stages of detox. Physically, detoxing from alcohol is dangerous. The biggest danger is convulsive seizures, *grand mal* seizures, just like an epileptic seizure. The other major danger is cardiovascular collapse.

Alcohol is a central nervous system depressant; it depresses everything through the central nervous system and it also has an effect on each cell, a toxic effect. And that toxic effect is also a depressant. So when people are drinking, their body functions have been pressed way down and are depressed. Then you take the alcohol away and it's like giving somebody a stimulant, like giving somebody speed. The cellular metabolism increases in every cell; the nervous system is racing; everything is racing. And that's what causes most of the symptoms of withdrawal; it's the speeding up of the system.

With seizures, what happens is that the person loses consciousness, but there is some kind of aura before the seizure that sometimes the person can feel. The aura is often, but not always, present. The person loses consciousness and all of their muscles receive a barrage of stimuli from the brain and all of the muscles go into tonic and clonic seizures. The tonic is rigid and clenched and the clonic is loose and relaxed. The vocal cords go into spasm right at the beginning. The patient will continue to have these spasms and go in all directions. The seizures most often last from 30 seconds to 2 minutes, but they can sometimes last longer. If seizures occur one after another or without cessation, it becomes a condition known as *status epilepticus,* which is a medical emergency. In general, the seizures are exhausting and that's one of the dangers in withdrawal: sheer total physical exhaustion. The movements slow down gradually and the person is usually confused for a certain time period up to hours after. It's a direct effect of alcohol withdrawal.

It's as though the brain short-circuits itself. The nervous system normally can respond to a stimulus. There is a certain period after that when it can't respond. When there is a series of rapid stimuli, everything gets confused.

I think the hormonal system is really involved in women's recovery too. I think the endocrine system is suppressed and it takes a while to get back to normal, usually about a year. This is the system that usually controls stress.

The rehab program, particularly for people who are not feeling well physically, is emotionally exhausting and we don't have any magic secrets to keep people from drinking. What we try to work on is teaching them to recognize their emotions, to deal with their emotions, to channel their emotions constructively. And most alcoholics need assertiveness training, particularly women. We try to teach them ways to deal with emotional stresses so that if they can keep the rest of their life in control, they can keep their alcoholism in control.

But getting back to the physical, there have been studies that show that alcohol is more damaging, faster, to women than men. It has to do with the distribution of body fat. Alcohol is stored in the fat and so it stays in a woman's body longer than a man's. And for some reason, though they don't know why, women seem to get cirrhosis faster than men, on a drink-per-drink scale.

Cirrhosis is a scarring of the liver tissue. The cells are damaged and they scar and the cells that are damaged do not regenerate; scar tissue forms and the liver does not function normally. It is much less efficient. Gradually, progressively, the liver dysfunctions.

Any toxic substance is detoxified in the liver. So if your liver is not functioning right, the toxins taken into your system are not detoxified as rapidly or as efficiently. This often makes the skin jaundiced and causes a backpressure of fluid which can cause a distention of the abdomen, can cause it to balloon out taut, like a pregnant woman's stomach. It can cause a lot of pressure on the veins in the legs and sometimes a shortness of breath. There are changes in posture, compensating for the pressure on the legs and abdomen.

Because of the toxins in the blood, alcoholics tend to be somewhat confused. And before they reach the confused state, they reach a point where they are not thinking as quickly and as effectively and simple things become hard.

Also, detoxification is a step-by-step process and sometimes the intermediate product is toxic in itself. Alcohol is an example of that. Alcohol is broken down into acetaldehyde, which is toxic. So people die from the toxins that build up from the cirrhosis. I had a patient, 26 years old, who died from cirrhosis.

The treatment for cirrhosis is all symptomatic. There is nothing you can do to reverse cirrhosis. You can control the symptoms and once you stop drinking or using you can stop the degeneration. This applies to both drugs and alcohol, but mostly it's alcohol that causes cirrhosis.

So there isn't much we can do about cirrhosis, but when people come to the center for detox, we can do something about the seizures. When people detox, we treat them with Valium or Librium or Vistaril, primarily to prevent seizures, but also to decrease the cardiovascular stress that happens in withdrawal, to slow the heart rate so people don't develop congestive failure. In our program, we usually use Vistaril during detox because it has fewer adverse side effects than Valium or Librium; however, Vistaril does lower the threshold for convulsive seizures. If the person has a history of previous seizures, a long drinking history (e.g., many years), has been drinking unusually large amounts of alcohol, and/or has an unusually high blood alcohol level on admission, we use Valium or Librium during detox. If a person convulses, the immediate treatment is Valium intravenously; that is followed by Dilantin orally for varying periods of time.

For people who are quitting without the benefit of medical assistance, it is crucial to have someone with you. If you have seizures, or cardiac arrest or vomit and aspirate, you'll need help. And you'll need the support of somebody else being there. Most people, when they detox, just want another drink, because the body knows if it takes another drink, it won't be going through so much pain. So if you have another person there, you have that much more support to not take another drink. If you get shaky when you stop, this person could help you with your food, and other things you might need your hands for. A lot of people get really shaky. Detox varies for people, but in itself, it is an extremely difficult time and even if you don't need the physical support, just having a friend there will be a tremendous help. This support is primarily emotional support, but that is probably *the* most important element in recovery.

The physical part of detox takes between two to five days, but three days is the most common. Then there is a mental detox period. There is a mental fogginess, people are usually confused and sometimes completely disoriented. As you get further into recovery, you return to mental alertness. It seems that there is a longer period to return to completely normal mental functioning and short-term memory seems to be affected.

Nervous tissue, if it does regenerate, usually takes longer to heal itself than, for instance, the cells on the skin. Patients who have recovered tell me that this foggy period is their principal symptom of recovery. There seems to be a short-term memory loss, around 3 days to six weeks that you can't remember, associated with the first year or two of recovery.

Physiologically, the tremendous nervous stimulation that happens with detox also contributes to this mental disorganization. Recovery is a process of the cells learning to function together again normally. Just for a ratio example, let's say during the first week, you don't have 100% of the cerebral function. And then by the second week, let's say, you have 50% back in an effective way. Then, over time, you get the rest back. Of course these figures are just made up, but the ratio seems right in my experience. For some reason, the last 5% or 10% seems to take the longest time to get back. But maybe that's because you are more aware of what you don't have back.

This isn't like amnesia; it's more like forgetting or mixing up details intermittently. For instance, you might not be able to remember whether or not you paid the phone bill last month, or you might be thinking you paid it when you didn't.

Also, on a mental level, one of the things that happens very commonly with alcoholics when they are drinking is that they stuff their anger: the angrier they get, the more they drink. And that's one of the things that therapists work on with almost everybody in the unit, is how to recognize their anger and how to do something about it besides drink. Anger seems to be real common with alcoholics.

The physical changes in later recovery are mainly a return of the body to normal functioning. There is usually a change in sexual appetite, too, decreasing for the first year or so. And there are the memory problems and common sleep disorders and the craving for sugar. I think this is related to hormonal levels and because the body is trying to return to normal.

Most alcoholics seem to be hypoglycemic, meaning they have low blood sugar. This seems again to be related to a rebound thing. Alcohol affects the pancreas. The pancreas produces insulin and has to do with sugar metabolism. Insulin drives down the level of blood sugar. Alcohol gives people a lot of fast calories, but little else and it consumes a lot of vitamins and minerals, particularly B vitamins. So there is a disturbance in the insulin level. So again, it's the timing in the system that is out of balance.

So if you are in recovery, you should eat right and take B vitamins in particular. For the sleeping disorders, try L-tryptophan, an essential amino acid, which is found in many natural proteins (e.g., liver, milk and bananas). Tryptophan is a precursor of niacinamide and serotonin. Serotonin is a neurotransmitter in the brain and this probably is the reason that tryptophan is helpful in stress, depression and sleep disorders. What happens with the sleep disorders is that alcohol represses REM sleep and so there is a REM rebound in recovery. What happens is that you have a lot more dreams, and restless sleep and frequent periods of waking in the night. And often the dreams seem to be nightmares, but again this is REM sleep in rebound. Some people have told me that the sleep disorders last for two to three years. The tryptophan will ease some of that, correcting an imbalance in the amino acids.

There are many things that happen when your body gets back in balance. It's hard to pinpoint just what might happen as things swing back together. Basically, in long-term recovery, there are the memory losses, sleep disorders and sugar cravings. And most alcoholics have very high standards for themselves and high expectations and when they aren't meeting them, there seems to be a lot of anxiety. Maybe, too, their standards are set too high.

It seems to me that the biggest thing in recovery is to start a support system. And one of the major problems with alcoholics is the isolation they have.

As an older gay woman who has experienced the effects of ageism, I think that isolation is particularly hard for gay women my age and I think there are probably many older lesbian alcoholics. For an older lesbian alcoholic who is not in a long-term relationship, it seems clear to me that the isolation compounds the alcoholism. I do think friends can help without enabling so that older women are not totally isolated. There *is* ageism, dirty-old-women jokes and younger women who are prejudiced or have preconceptions about old lesbians that really hurt. And the stigma is there, the older woman, the lesbian issue, the older lesbian issue. . . it's all there. And I myself have some preconceptions about older women that aren't true either.

The older lesbian alcoholics, particularly those who have been lesbians for many years, seem to have accepted the stigma more than younger lesbians and it has to do with being lesbians in a very oppressive situation. This compounds the problem so much that ptreatment, even with obviously gay staff members, is very difficult. And possibly, they are even rightly so anticipating difficulty in recovery treatment. But they need to know they are not alone in their recovery.

I do think that the lesbian community can become clean and sober. It would look alive. There would be less fighting, less screaming and yelling in relationships. There would still be problems, but there would be less fighting. Our relationships with each other would be better, both individually and in the community. We wouldn't waste so much time. We would be less tense and more relaxed, more active yet more relaxed. Maybe we would accomplish more. Maybe we would be able to deal with aging better. And maybe we would be more honest.

# To Keep From Being Controlled

## An Interview with Misha Cohen

Misha Cohen speaks slowly and clearly and there is a softness in her voice that is not weakness. She has been an acupuncturist and a Shiatsu therapist for the last seven years, and an herbal healer for the last 14 years. She is 31, and grew up in Miami, Florida in a middle class family. She learned acupuncture in New York City at Lincoln Detox, then one of only two methadone detox (as opposed to maintenance) programs in the entire five boroughs of New York. Politically, she is now and has been very active in anti-imperialist work, particularly in support of the black liberation movement. She is Jewish. She currently lives in San Francisco.

The following is an interview I conducted with her in March of 1983 at her healing room in the San Francisco neighborhood called the Mission. Present and part of the interview was her lover, Cindy Icke, also an acupuncturist and naturopathic healer.

---

**JS:** Tell me what happens physiologically to a woman in detox. And how does this relate to her emotions?
**MC:** In terms of Chinese medicine, you can't separate what happens in the body from what happens in the mind. It's all the same thing. With addiction, the liver is overstimulated. It has to work too hard, both when using drugs and in detoxification. In the first stages of detox, because of all the toxins that are stored in the liver, it has to work really hard to get rid of the toxins.

But it's true too that when someone is addicted, the liver is having to work too hard. And so that's why so much anger is generated in alcoholics. It works both ways. One: people who have (in Chinese medicine) excess liver conditions to begin with, for whatever reasons, often having to do with repressed anger, internalized emotions, or depression. . . all those things are related to the liver, and so people start to drink. And then they come full circle, because when you are drinking and the alcohol is going into the body, it's making the liver work really hard and become stagnant, creating a lot of fire, a lot of heat. In Chinese medicine, this often comes out as anger. And so there are a lot of alcoholics who basically relate to the world in a very angry and fearful way. . . a real strong fear, and there is a lot of bouncing back and forth between the two.

But getting back to detox, the liver starts working overtime. Also the kidneys start working overtime. Also the lungs. So you've got a lot of detoxing going on. Those are the three major organs affected. The spleen and the heart are secondarily affected. There are a lot of other organs, but they aren't considered as important in Chinese medicine.

You tend to have things happen like getting diarrhea immediately, getting muscular aches and pains. Depending on the drug, like with alcohol, you can get binges of feeling drunk, just because of the toxins still being released into the system. The liver is releasing the toxins and they are getting sent to the brain, so you tend to get absent-minded; you are very irritable, often don't want to eat. There are a number of things that happen physiologically.

**JS:** One of the things that happened to me is that I lost the first three or four months when I got sober. I mean, I remember, but just barely and sort of through a fog.

**MC:** Yes, that would relate to the kidneys. The kidneys, when working overtime, have a tendency to get weak. They are unlike the liver, which just works even harder. The kidneys tend to be related to memory, as are the spleen and the heart. If the kidneys are weak, you won't remember. As they get stronger, you'll remember more. Also, there are a lot of toxins in the body, and when there are a lot of toxins in the body, you tend to get really spacey and not remember things quite as well.

**JS:** I'm in my third year of recovery now, and I feel like my body is falling apart on me. How long is this going to go on?

**MC:** Every person is different. Every person responds differently to their environment and to internal things. In natural medicine, people say it takes a certain number of years for various organs to regenerate themselves. Some people say seven years, but I don't think there is a set number of years. Some people say the liver can hold toxins for 10 years. So it's hard to say how long it will take for someone to not experience the recurrent kinds of things that happen during recovery. But I would think there are things that you can do to help yourself through the process.

I think acupuncture as a way of rebalancing can help, and massage, particularly some kind of acupressure that rebalances the body. The rebalancing has to do with the energy flow in the body; all the different organs have their own energy flows and the whole body has an energy flow and if there are blocks in the energy flow, then the body can't be balanced. There will be some places with too much energy and some places with not enough energy.

The blocks come from internal things, like emotions, or miscellaneous factors, like not eating correctly, or the toxins being released into the body. So it's by releasing those blocks that the energy flow becomes more balanced. This is something I've seen a lot when treating alcoholics and addicts: someone will come in very agitated and within five or ten minutes of the balancing treatment, they will be able to go to sleep. So you can see exactly what that blocking is doing and by using just a few needles to rebalance them, you can see what it will do.

Massage is something that everyone can take responsibility on themselves to do, massaging themselves every day.

Herbs and vitamin therapy help too. Comfrey, for example, is very soothing. What is good in the first few days is often valerian, for calming the nervous system and as a muscle relaxant; it's really good for helping people sleep. And camomile and catnip as relaxants, to drink in teas. And blood cleansers such as burdock and red clover (but not a lot). And vitamins. Vitamin C is real important. You can detox someone from heroin very quickly with vitamin C. It stimulates the liver to detox very quickly.

One of the things about alcoholism, or any drug addiction, is that people don't eat right. Alcohol itself (and the heroin too) affects the whole digestive tract. Food then becomes hard to digest. And so sugar, which is easily digestible, is something that people eat. Heroin addicts really eat a lot of sugar. And that's all they eat. And so there is a lot of hypoglycemia.

Hypoglycemia is low blood sugar. Alcoholics almost invariably are hypoglycemic. That can affect the body in lots of different ways, but it especially causes exhaustion, inability to think and dizziness. Some people should eat six small meals that are high in protein a day to help with this. I tend to give people diets that are not real high in protein, but high in complex carbohydrates, like brown rice, millet, that kind of thing, but no sugar, not even fruit, because fruit has a lot of sugar in it.

Many alcoholics become sugar junkies after getting off alcohol. The alcohol actually creates sugar in your system. . . and so you try to replace the alcohol in your body by eating sugar. . . and the sugar tends to make you drunk. You are still getting the same effect from the sugar: you are getting high.

Part of the problem with eating a lot of sugar and refined foods is that the (vitamin) B complex is eliminated. Alcohol needs to have those vitamins to be digested by the body, as do refined foods. So especially with alcoholism, the body is depleted in B-12, B-6 and B-1. Almost all alcoholics need to have really high doses of those, especially in the early stages of detox. A lot of memory loss comes from loss of B vitamins.

I think one of the main things that happens during detox is that people tend to get a lot of infections, often due to deficiency of their immune system. Their bodies start to get rid of everything and are not able to fight infections as well. The organs already have to work so hard in detox that it's hard for the body to fight infection. So a lot of vitamin C is good to build up immunity, even up to 10 grams a day. Vitamins A and E are also important. In recovery, I think it's good that people continue to take a lot of vitamins and minerals and that they begin to change their diet so they can start to nourish and rebalance their bodies.

In the short-term recovery, it is important to take a lot of vitamins, but also in the first few days or few weeks it is also important to do some kind of healing every day. I used to treat people twice a day, people who were detoxing from heroin.

For the long-term body healing, it is very important to change your diet, do things to build up the body. Try to not eat sugar; stay away from caffeine; stay away from refined foods, foods with white flour. Try to eat positively, not a lot of meat, not a lot of fat, but eat whole grains. And to start to look at the whole self, not just the physical aspects or the emotional aspects.

This is important because alcohol and drug addictions make you not feel things. So it's real important to take food slowly and feel it and feel what it is doing in your body. And that is part of feeling, not just an emotional response, but a feeling as it happens.

**JS:** A lot of pain has been coming up for me. First I didn't know what a feeling was, now I know what they are, I'd like to know what I am supposed to do with them. It feels to me like a lot of emotional pain is getting translated into physical pain.

**MC:** I think that is a real healthy thing. I think that what it means is that the person who is feeling these things has been numb for a long time and is feeling again. There were probably a lot of physical things happening for you that you never felt before. That is one of the reasons drugs are so dangerous: serious things are happening in a person's body that aren't being noticed because of the sedative effect. So I think it's okay to be feeling a certain amount of pain.

One of the things that is really important to let yourself go through is massage, because it is a very physical kind of thing so it makes you feel something. Let it hurt or let it feel good. Also meditation is real important because it allows your feelings to come to the front so you can look at them and not block them out or have to act on them, which is real different from drugs. Also anything that rebalances, acupuncture, chiropractic, helps.

**CI:** In Chinese medicine, you are able to work with the air of the body, called the *chi*. Some of the breathing work in meditation helps replenish the kidney, helps calm you and helps slow you down. It's something you can do for yourselves and helps you take some control in your life instead of feeling so out of control.

**JS:** I feel pretty out of control myself sometimes. And my body feels out of control. Can you tell me about the emotional response to, say for example, my liver detoxifying itself?

**MC:** Well, in Chinese medicine, each of the organs is represented by an emotion. For example, the emotions that go along with the liver are fear, anger and depression. They say tears are the sweat of the liver. There are different kinds of fear, but there is a kind of fear that is combined with anger, and that is generally in the liver. I'd say that when those feelings come up, it's a healthy sign, because the liver is beginning to function better and the release of those emotions is real important. Any time there are liver excess problems, those kinds of people tend to hold things in a lot and depression and internalized anger start to come out when you try to heal the liver.

I think it affects the kidneys a lot. In Chinese medicine, the kidneys are the seat of the will. And with addictions, people can't stop. There is a dependence there. So I think there is a real strong problem with will.

And also fear is connected with the kidneys. In this society, there is a kind of fear that everybody has: everybody is very fearful. People who become addicted to something are people who have fear and are people who are using something to become less fearful. So recovery is learning how to deal with fear and anger in some other kind of way.

On a political level, I think people are forced to become addicted, really. What I liked about learning detox the way I did was that it was political work. People were politicized as to why the alcohol and heroin and methadone existed. They really exist to keep people under control. And therefore our responsibility is to keep ourselves from being controlled.

The individual responsibility of people is to look at that and to understand that they can change things and that the fear and anger need to be directed at something other than themselves or their friends or their families.

**CI:** When you are addicted to something, it takes away your power. And I think that for any people who are strong and together, the object of the government is to make you powerless. And I don't think it's a surprise that many lesbians have their lifestyles centered around the bar scene and alcohol. It keeps us powerless. It takes our focus away and really keeps us from being effective in the world. It's a way to control people by taking away their power, especially if the people are doing it to themselves; it makes it easier.

**MC:** In the 60's at the time of the Civil Rights and the Black Power movements, a lot of heroin started being pumped into the Black communities in this country and at that time, many many people started being addicted to heroin. It was available real cheap. The C.I.A. is one of the major suppliers of heroin in this country. There is a book on it, called *The Opium Trail: Heroin and Imperialism* which documents the story. The government does, in fact, stop heroin at certain times, like when people start to get very upset about housing and get organized, the government dries up the sources and then people have to start worrying about being sick.

A good example of the government's attempt at control is their use of methadone. Methadone is more addictive than heroin. It was developed by scientists in Nazi Germany, so-called scientists, who were experimenting in the death camps. They called it dolophine, in honor of Adolf Hitler. It was stolen by the C.I.A. and produced by major drug companies and brought to this country as a drug to keep people under control. Black communities and Puerto Rican communities who have a consciousness of this, have fought against methadone maintenance programs as a way of keeping people under control.

And that's how I got into it. Lincoln Detox started about ten or eleven years ago and they had a methadone maintenance program, which was getting people addicted to methadone. And then people in the community, led mainly by the Black Panthers and the Young Lords, got together and said we don't want this in our community, so what we are going to do, is to close this down and substitute it with something else that is actually going to heal people. They had to do it forcibly; they sat in and said this is our program from now on. And eventually they got the program. What they substituted for methadone was acupuncture, vitamins, diet, massage and especially political education.

I went to Lincoln Detox because I was studying acupuncture and also because politically I was doing solidarity work with Black and Puerto Rican struggles. I was one of the few white people there. It's interesting, too, that of the white people there, all were lesbians, except one or two. I think there was something about understanding oppression and being able to see what this society was doing to women that made me really want to be doing healing work with women.

Finally, after about seven years, (New York City) Mayor Koch said that the people at Lincoln Detox misused funds and he was able to surround the place with police and eventually kicked them out. The National Black Acupuncturists Association of North America was formed and they moved to Harlem and they are treating people there now. There is still a Lincoln Detox, but it isn't the same community-based program anymore.

Something that is very interesting about all of this is that in China and Vietnam, acupuncture has been the major method of detoxifying. In pre-revolutionary China, 80% of the men and about 60% of the women were addicted to opium. The addiction started through British colonialism and was furthered through the Opium Wars. Britian made a lot of money off processing the opium and selling it to the Chinese peasants. Opium was banned in Britain at the time.

So what happened after the revolution was that the revolutionaries taught the people why they were addicted, why the opium was available and the fact was the opium addicts were not able to contribute to their society. Basically, through re-education and getting rid of pushers, two or three years after the revolution there was no problem with addiction in Chinese society.

And the way that they did it was to identify the people who were pushing drugs and say, okay, you have a year to stop doing this and then the punishments got heavier and heavier.

**JS:** What do you think about people who push drugs or alcohol in the lesbian community?

**MC:** I think they should be stopped. I think that is one of the real big problems. But we don't have a society in which people get what they need: we don't get what we need in terms of adequate pay for the work that we do, respect, living without fear, unalienated conditions of work and where we live.

As long as we have social conditions where people are estranged from each other, social relationships are really skewed and people are in competition with each other. I think as long as that exists it will be very difficult to stop people from pushing drugs and alcohol. I think that two things are really important: one is the responsibility of the people who are addicted to really understand what is going on with themselves; and two, that it is the responsibility of all of us to change the society in such a way that addiction is not necessary.

Many people who are alcoholics or addicts are that way because of pain and anger, and that is a way of dealing with it. And by not seeing any other way of dealing with it, that's what people continue to do.

And I think that's why having a philosophy, and understanding there is something beyond that and we can change the world, really changes that. That's why political education is so important for people who are addicts or alcoholics. While A.A. is not a political group, it does try to show that everything we do is connected, and affects someone else and affects everything around us. . . that we are not just by ourselves, that we can do anything and it won't affect someone else, which is what a lot of people in this society believe and it's not true.

**JS:** So what would your community look like if it were clean and sober?

**MC:** I can see a lot of different things. I see a world in which there is much less violence, where people are not so violent. I think a lot about violence when I think about drugs, so I see a world that is much calmer, where people are able to participate much more in a very real way, in day-to-day kinds of things. Everyone would be able to take care of herself and each other without having to have anyone be the victim. I think one of the things that makes it difficult for us to take care of each other is that we don't take responsibility for ourselves. What healing really should be is a give and take between people. And in a clean and sober community, people would be able to do that because they would be conscious. I would see people eating things that are healthy, and caring about it, and caring about each other.

Yet I believe we must make a fundamental revolutionary change in our society, in order to bring this about. In the meantime, we can educate and change ourselves and each other so we can actually participate in this transformation.

# Recovery Is Power In The Now

## An Interview with Suzanne Balcer

**S**uzanne Balcer is the Coordinator of Women's Services at the only totally gay and lesbian alcoholism center in this country, 18th Street Services in San Francisco, CA. She is a 44-year-old white woman from Detroit, MI. She is a mother, a lesbian, a recovering alcoholic. She has worked in the alcoholism field for 12 years, nine of which were spent designing recovery programs for women. She has a lean face, graying hair, and she uses her hands to talk, to smooth the air, to ask questions. Often, she will pause for long moments before responding: considering, looking, staring into the air, or straight into you. Except when she laughs. When she laughs, she throws her head back and her eyes crinkle behind her glasses and the sound is immediate and full and you know she is not laughing for you. She is laughing for herself, but without excluding anyone present. It is a revelation to be around a woman who claims her own power.

The following is an interview I conducted with her in November of 1982 at the 18th Street offices.

---

**JS:** Tell me what you do.
**SB:** I coordinate the women's services here. We currently have eight groups going and over 60 women using the services. We have three counselors and three volunteer/facilitators. Since I came in June of '81, we have worked to expand the recovery options for women. We have tried to find ways to enhance recovery.

18th Street can be used by women to augment their existing recovery programs as well as women who have had difficulty in finding a recovery program that works for them. The women's staff here is committed to working with class, culture, race and spiritual issues in addition to the basic issues of recovery from addictions to substances. We have found that many women report difficulty finding peer support for those issues in early sobriety. Our goal is to address and work with those issues in a supportive environment so that recovery can be as meaningful as possible. We often find women are more willing to seek outside peer support groups when they have a place to work on their own issues, as in one of our smaller groups at 18th Street.

When I arrived at 18th Street, there were two groups being offered... Phase I and Phase II (substance-free longer than one month, but less than six) and we were serving women who were in late-stage alcoholism. This was due to lack of womanpower to run the program. There was only one position funded to serve the lesbian population of San Francisco... a third of whom are probably being abused by substances. The program is expanded now so that we have a wide continuum of services being offered: from pre-recovery to one to five years or more of recovery.

We also have an education/information program, where participants only have to be sober for that one day. We have retained the Phase I and Phase II programs, but now we also have a Phase III program that covers from six months sobriety to a year. Six months is not enough in terms of recovery. Six months to a year is getting there. The cloud lifts, the depression begins to clear and awareness starts, feelings begin to come up. And that is a crucial time.

We also have groups now for lesbian Adult Children of Alcoholics. We have groups for third world and multi-ethnic lesbians and a group for older lesbians. We have a wonderfully diverse staff and several consultants who facilitate groups here now. The women who work here are recovering themselves. We are just getting started with a counselor training program for clean and sober graduates of 18th Street. We are beginning to pull together alumni as another component of our network.

In general, I think a good recovery program needs a variety of things. It needs to be flexible to allow for the individual differences of clients. Along this same line it needs to be sensitive to the issues that are relevant to the populations being served. I don't believe that a program that operates on the precept that alcoholism is alcoholism can provide an environment for clients to thrive in the recovery process. We have to be sensitive to all kinds of oppressions and we need to identify them.

Often in alcoholism and addiction rehabilitation programs, all symptoms are attributed to the substance... low self-esteem, depression, anger, isolation, alienation, paranoia, distrust, self-hatred. For the lesbian, these are also symptoms of social, cultural, class and racial oppression. From the point where a lesbian is drug/alcohol dependent she is at least triply oppressed... as an addict/alcoholic, a lesbian and a woman. Oppression escalates as she differs from the "establishment"... for example, if she's older, or working-class, or third world, or a mother. A good program needs staff who are sensitive to these issues and more than that, the program needs to provide role models who are recovering and able to join women in their struggles because they have been there and are there themselves.

Programs need to provide basic and useful information about alcohol and other drugs. We need to teach basic self-care so that women can learn to nurture themselves. We need to teach nutrition, provide relaxation to reduce the stress of recovering and living in the world, provide whole-body exercise and teach ways for women to read themselves. The need for this last skill is shown by the fact that most women in recovery do not know when they are tired — only when they are exhausted. The same for hunger.

Programs need to provide networks to the clean and sober community groups. This networking begins in small facilitated recovery groups where women can break out of their isolation, to be with and have support from other women in their recovery. A goal for all should be the development and enhancement of self-esteem. Often recovering women need to be loved, cared for, and respected by others before they can love, care for and respect themselves. This is how women can empower one another.

Programs need to help women examine their survival skills. Some skills should be kept by all means, but others may need to be replaced with new skills that will enhance the quality of their lives. I believe that women who struggle to overcome their addictions are some of the toughest and strongest women around. They are miracles. I respect them deeply. They are *survivors*. I think programs can undermine this toughness and strength when coping skills are referred to as inadequate, sick or unhealthy. Given the herstories of survival of abuse by drugs and alcohol, I believe women have coped remarkably well. They have coped, many of them, with physical violence, sexual abuse and many forms of neglect from early childhood to present day.

If the woman grew up in an alcoholic home, the old skills may be really old. By the time a child in an alcoholic home is seven, she is already shut down in order to protect herself from rejection and abandonment. Many of the recovering women who are served at 18th Street grew up in alcoholic families. Their relationship to alcohol may go back to the first days of their lives. Joining their families in the use/abuse of alcohol may have been one of the few options available to provide a sense of connectedness to their families. It may have been a way to cope with the feelings of abandonment, rejection and alienation that children in alcoholic families experience.

In a way, these women were targeted for alcoholism and drug addiction before they ever used a substance. Their models (their parents) used substances to cope with life. It seems absurd to fault people for coping behaviors they had modeled by the most significant people in their lives for the longest amount of time.

I see alcoholism as an outgrowth of the ways society gives us to cope with the crazy world out there. I believe women turn to alcohol to help them cope. Some women turn to mental illness, some to physical illness. Whatever works for them, they do, and so I look at this as ways women have used to survive.

I don't think it's an accident either. Women have been specifically targeted by the liquor industry for the last five years. And it's not just women. . . it's any group that the powers that be want to single out. Look where the liquor ads are. Look what communities they are in. No, I don't think it's an accident.

**JS:** So you see your work as partly political?

**SB:** Yes. And I do this work because I really love it. It's a way that I can be political. And I do it because I see women oppressed by alcohol. It is an oppressor. I enjoy watching women grow out of their oppression and take charge of their lives, to begin to feel and experience their lives more fully and themselves more fully.

**JS:** You are a recovering alcoholic. You are also the mother of a boy-child. How has it been for him?

**SB:** It's been better for him because I know, without a doubt, that if I hadn't stopped drinking, I wouldn't be alive. And I think I've done better parenting due to my recovery skills.

But before I was aware that I was a person to get sober for, I got sober because I was afraid I wouldn't be around for him. He was the beginning step in my recovery.

**JS:** Suzanne, give me a definition for recovery.

**SB:** Okay. . . this is a hard one. Recovery is making a bridge back to a time of feeling and awareness and vitality and health. Recovery is a process where power is in the now. It is a time when we are able to venture back and pick up the pieces of ourselves that have either been relinquished, lost or covered over. Recovery is taking back all that we are, including who we are now and where we've been, what we've experienced, with all the strength and dignity that are ours.

**JS:** I know you believe recovery is a three to five year process. What do you see as the hardest places in that process?

**SB:** The first, and the most difficult is after the drugs and alcohol have been out of the body for a considerable period, say one to two years. Awareness is no longer dulled and we have to take a look around our lives and begin to make changes in order to go on growing. We need to look at who we are spending time with, and how to begin to refurnish our lives with that which will help us grow — no, that's not even enough — that which will help us thrive. And it is a time of saying no, saying good-bye and getting in touch with loss. This could mean loss of family, of friends, of relationships, and loss of many of the old defenses for protecting ourselves. One loss will provoke memories of old losses. And there is a lot of mourning to be done in the first few years of recovery.

The other really hard part of recovery is the unrealistic expectation that women have that if you are doing everything right, you should be happy, pain-free, that life should be great. And if it's not, then *you* are doing something wrong.

My belief is that life is, can be, painful and that we have to work our way through the pain. My concern is that women feel like it's their fault when things don't go right.

**JS:** What with all the studies about the large percentage of alcoholism in the lesbian community, do you think there's hope for us, as a community?

**SB:** Oh, there is always hope. There is hopefulness coming right now from the women's community. We have been fighting oppression without identifying the tools of oppression. I see alcohol and drugs, as well as prescription medicines, as tools of oppression. We have to stop using tools "they" have given us and come up with our own healthy, powerful tools.

**JS:** Do you see any changes in our community since you started working at 18th Street?

**SB:** Yes. There is more awareness of alcohol. There is less reluctance to go in and check out drinking in the early and middle stages. There is more support. There is a general awareness that alcohol is a serious problem and that it's okay to go and get help. And there are more and more role models for recovery within our community.

I am still concerned about the women who are being misdiagnosed. There are thousands of women being abused by drugs and alcohol, and the symptoms of this abuse are being attributed to psychiatric illness, sexual, racial and class oppression, the aging process or youth. Unfortunately, there are many lesbian sub-cultures who remain virtually untouched by the drug and alcohol awareness to be found in other segments of the women's community in San Francisco.

**JS:** So if your community was sober and clean, what would it look like?

**SB:** Oh, it would be just wonderful. It would be abounding with life, vitality, creativity, power, love: all of the good things. There would be healthy women and healthy children. There would be no jails, no mental institutions, no hospitals. Everything would be green and blooming.

# In Sobriety, You Get Life

## An Interview with Celinda Cantu

Celinda Cantu, 31, works for Alameda County (CA) as a drug program consultant, helping set funding priorities to ensure that treatment in the county is accessible. She has worked in almost all aspects of the alcoholism/substance abuse field during the last seven years. She is a recovered alcoholic, was the second woman graduate of the Whitman-Radclyffe Foundation, the nation's first gay/lesbian-identified recovery service.

She is a Chicana, raised in California's San Joaquin valley. She says she grew up with the American dream but in a very distinct shade of brown. She talks slowly, not slowly as though she were considering each word or as if concerned about stuttering, but slowly as she moves in her own rhythm, from her own sense of time. She laughs frequently, laughs at the ironies and contradictions of recovery. Her brown eyes close slightly when she laughs and her broad face is filled with her smile but moments later, when she is making her point, though the smile is still there, her eyes are wide and clear and deep brown and she looks as though nothing will stop her, for long.

---

**JS:** So tell me what you do.
**CC:** What I'm doing in Alameda County is working to determine how the money is going to be spent for drug abuse services. There are contracts between the county and the programs for services. So we look at the whole continuum of services: residential, non-residential, community-based organizations, detox, methadone maintenance. We try to set priorities for

funding to ensure that the people of the county, as best as possible, are served, and that treatment is accessible.

In terms of my own priorities, I always feel there is a need for services for women: directly, specifically for women. Then there is just a whole gamut of needs, in terms of culturally-specific services, residential services for youth, prevention services, family crisis counseling, looking at what happens to families in terms of recovery, all of these are priorities.

I also sit on the Citywide Alcoholism Advisory Board here in San Francisco. Right now I chair the Family Task Force. We've set our priority to focus attention on what services are being provided, or not provided which seems to be more of the case, for family members.

I view alcoholism as a community addiction. Individuals may manifest it, but the community supports it. Alcoholism is such a debilitating addiction. Once you become a certain level of drunk and you can't maintain your own addiction, you have to have support for it. You need to have co's. And there are plenty of co's out there. A co-alcoholic (co) by definition is someone who is dependent upon the alcoholic as the alcoholic is dependent on alcohol. Co's get a fix by taking care of and being needed by the drunk. Alcoholism and co-alcoholism are not mutually exclusive, so it's not unlikely to know a couple who share an addiction and vacillate between co-ing and drinking.

In the lesbian community, the bars are just a fantasic network of co-ing. If you don't have money, you can still go in there, and somebody will support you, in terms of getting drunk and maintaining the addiction. They may loan you money, find you jobs and do all kinds of networking. Again, it's the whole premise of "doing it over drinks".

Historically we haven't had many places outside of the barroom setting where we could gather, socialize and be who we are. I don't think most women go to the bar scene intending to drink. I think they go there mostly to socialize. At least in the beginning, that's the gathering place, that's the place to go. Essentially, that's how it's set up right now; that's where we go.

But the whole set-up pushes the drug called alcohol. So to take alcoholism out of it's community base, we as a community have to build alternative structures to the bars to fulfill what the bar provides, which is socializing and networking.

We also need to have an alternative within the bar system so that it is okay to be in a bar, if you want to be there, drinking orange juice or Perrier and having alternative drinks beside mixers. But the reality, I found once I had sobered up, was that the bars were (and still are) very boring. I don't have a problem with going there; it doesn't feel threatening in terms of my sobriety or recovery or any of that. Bars are just boring. The energy is down and generally I don't want to be in that space. I do go occasionally to play pool; since I sobered up, my game's improved 1000-fold, the table doesn't move anymore, and it's great. And I can dance without falling down and that's great, but the bar is depressing.

The bar scene has been given traditionally as the reason for the higher rate of alcoholism within the lesbian community. But I don't know that there's *more* alcoholism in the lesbian community than say what's out there in any other segment. We are a group that's isolated and tend to be identifiable, in that we have our specific gathering places, our identifiable community networking (which I tend to see as a plus. I mean you can be part of the lesbian community, you can experience that). I don't think that heterosexuals have that network as readily available to them, so I think we can view the lesbian community a little more definitively. The boundaries are there. I think there is probably as much alcoholism among straight women, it's just not as easy to measure. And it's not quite as visible.

I think that the information in some studies, like Fifield's, is valid. Fifield (1978) wrote her master's thesis among the lesbian/gay community in Los Angeles and found that two out of three people in the gay community were or may be problem drinkers and that three out of three needed information about alcohol. I think alcoholism/drug abuse is a serious problem in the lesbian and gay communities. It's the ten percent in the general population that I really question, I really question that. I think the percentage for the general population is greater.

If we were to look at inter-generational addiction we would see something else. I consider myself the adult child of an alcoholic. And I learned the addiction from day one. This whole area of information about growing up in a substance abuse environment is now coming to the forefront of recovery communities. The information being gathered has not been thoroughly analyzed or disseminated. From what I've read, a whole new fascinating aspect of how one acquires addiction is emerging. In viewing alcoholism, we have to take into consideration the fact that alcoholism has only been viewed as a health issue since 1971 on a national level. The A.M.A. is still fighting over whether alcoholism is physiological or psychological. Who cares? The fucking drunks die.

That would be nice information if we could understand it. At this point, I think understanding addiction is almost a booby-prize. In unlearning addiction, I had to really come to terms with it, confront it and create something different. In that process, if I understand it, that's great; if not, so what? I'm still not drinking, I'm alive.

What we need to look at is the accessibility of drugs. I mean if you look at it, alcoholism/drug addiction is one of the most powerful, political, oppressive tools that exists. Oftentimes, like during Depression, during the Recession, you'll find that there is much more heroin, pure-grade heroin and street drugs available. It keeps the masses down. An addict is not going to get up and mobilize a community around a particular issue.

The whole liquor industry has a lot invested in its product. And they have been able to keep the fact that alcohol has anything to do with alcoholism away from any kind of media and the masses. Basically, the industry has been putting out that alcoholism is an individual disease and yes, there are going to be those people who abuse our product, but they as individuals abuse it. At this point you don't see warning labels on alcohol that say this is a water-soluble, mind-altering depressant toxin. The liquor tax is the second largest source of income for the federal government, second only to the income tax. So it seems pretty obvious to me who has the power over money and information about alcohol/drugs.

So many of us become addicted. And what happens now with a woman who comes into treatment? If she is a lesbian, her options are very limited. If she can afford to go to Los Angeles, she can be open about her lesbianism and have residential services at A.C.W. (Alcohol Center for Women). If she's lesbian and has food, clothing and shelter taken care of, she has a variety of out-patient programs. Within the city (San Francisco), she has A.A. or whatever networking she can connect with. So there are things out there but they are very limited.

If she is a Chicana lesbian, she needs to look at the issues for her. I was politically correct and dying on my bar stool. As a Chicana lesbian, working class, with a Masters in social work, I had to get my shit together. There were no services out there that even identified me as existing. And when I thought about going for services, there wasn't too much. The Whitman-Radclyffe Foundation was the only gay-identified service. I just said fuck it, I need it. Every one on staff was blond hair, blue-eyed. Their values for success were basically the prosperous white American male dream: that you had a job, you had a lover, you had your apartment set-up: all very middle class in orientation. Their vision for my recovery was that I would get myself together around some of this stuff.

Now the fact is that as a Chicana, my identity is really different. I have a cultural intactness that I first identify myself as a member of this larger group, known as Chicanas, La Raza, which is connected to other Latinos, then I am my father's and mother's daughter and then I am Celinda Cantu. This is my identity, this is how it comes down.

The American dream is that you are you, as an individual and despite your roots, you can go for whatever you want, all it takes is work. For me, that doesn't mean shit. I know that as a Chicana, I get treated differently. I also know that I celebrate differently and that I have a basic identity that nobody gets to touch or gets to try to take away. In essence, I have a celebration, I have a cultural heritage. A lot of it has been ripped off; there has been so much acculturation and blending of values, but in essence, I have my way of celebrating. So when Christmas comes around, I celebrate my way.

The attempted rip-off I saw coming down was in terms of the very white and diffused values that the recovery programs offered. The essence of the message I was getting felt very alien. I felt sadness because they had no history of how people celebrated or why they were celebrating. The holidays were questionable for them. For me, there are historical roots, in terms of Catholism, cultural music and foods. It was almost like they read Emily Post to find out what the proper Christmas dinner was. I think that's pretty sad. To not have any grounding in the celebration made me ask how they could call it a celebration.

For me, it has always been clear that I had family. I used to laugh at how white people got punished as kids. . . their form of punishment was that they got grounded, they had to stay with the family. For me punishment was I had to leave and spend some time with other people. And so it was that basic.

In terms of my own recovery, and for other third world women, I believe that there is a lot of cross-cultural stuff that happens and part of that is just coming from that core identity. As a culturally intact person, I have systems that are unique, that are my own. And the sadness is that those systems are constantly being ripped away and assaulted and violated. The family, self-identity, cultural celebration, how we dance, what we eat, some very basic human kinds of things are all things that in recovery can be stepped upon or dismissed or listed as taboo, like you shouldn't have those kinds of connections because everybody is drinking in your culture or whatever. That's bullshit.

So how I dealt with it was that I basically began to question the need for alcohol, as opposed to what's wrong with my culture. For me, it was taking the information and assessing it and taking it for what it was worth. I dismissed a lot of things. Part of it was I had to realistically deal with the fact that alcohol was going to be out there; I mean I am assaulted by it all the time. For me now, I don't think about drinking like I don't think about eating thumb tacks for breakfast. It's that ridiculous; it's that stupid. I view alcohol as such an unnecessary function in one's life. For me, there is an element out there that can kill me; it's like playing Russian Roulette with five loaded chambers and pretending that I'm going to win. I just don't need it. It's not necessary to me.

So, in this way, I can be all of who Celinda Cantu is and also make it clear to people that I don't drink, and if they can't deal with it, that's their problem. It's real clear to my family that I don't drink and I've been able to set the norm there, people apologize for drinking around me and that's great.

In terms of recovery, I think there has been a lot of misinformation put out there about alcohol and alcoholism. A.A. is a wonderful support system, but in essence it is Christian; it is male; it is white and it comes from the real middle class orientation. And certainly the principle of recovery has been well-documented and well laid-out through A.A. But the thing is: the main cause of alcoholism is alcohol. The thing that is going to kill you is racism, sexism, classism in terms of alcoholism treatment. These issues (and others) will stop you from getting the information that you need to deal with the addiction. There are populations out there who are dying at a quicker rate; women are dying at a quicker rate. So we need to say "Look women, we can't hide behind our tits anymore!" and talk about what's really going on and set up structures in order to do that. The problem is that most of the information we get is filtered through men or is male-identified.

In terms of recovery for third world women, we know what isolation and internalized oppression and self-hatred is about. But alcohol is not going to be the key to deadening the pain; all it will do is kill us. It's a basic and simple formula. Alcohol equals death: a death brought on earlier, much more violently and unnecessarily. As women of color we know who we are, we have a sense of our culture, we have a sense of our celebration. We are not going to get it through alcohol. And alcohol is the most effective political way to die, as the system is now set up.

The information I have to share with women of color is that you are not alone, that alcohol is not necessarily part of our culture, that in fact it kills us quicker and takes away our culture much more than any racist act can do and that we are not supposed to survive. And I say survive. If they are going to get us, let them get us sober, we will leave a much more visible trail.

I am not going to do it for them; I was doing it for them for a long time. If they want me to die, they are going to have to do it for themselves, because I am choosing life not death.

For the woman in recovery, what I have to say is that recovery in itself is a miracle. In recovery you get to choose between life and life. But there are no guarantees. We know that, but we tend to forget it. The whole media hype is that life is just and fair but we know that is bullshit. Life is not going to change until we are alive and are able to scream and be angry and change the system. If we die behind it, i.e., being drunk, it's not going to change and we are just going to prove the stereotype.

In recovery, you have to take into consideration that you learned the addiction well — that you learned to perceive the world through an altered state, through a depressant drug which essentially puts you in touch with jealousy, pain, fear, anger, hurt, low self-esteem — not a whole lot of glorious attitudes to have for human existance. And the drug induces those feelings. You have to take into consideration that the drug stays in your system and it takes anywhere from nine to eighteen months to get it out of your system. The seventy-two-hour detox just gets you to stop shaking. You have learned to perceive and operate while in the chemical state. So for the first year and a half, you are basically still operating with this drug running in your system.

You have to allow your body to heal itself, and it will; it will try to get rid of it any way it can. You are going to have diarrhea, you are going to be puking, you are going to be sweating. Your body is going to be saying I want this drug out, now. And once you start purifying yourself, it's hard. I think that we get a lot of information that says recovery is wonderful, it's miraculous. . . . God, it's a pain in the ass. It's a pain in the ass for the first year and a half.

But I think that once we get the alcohol out of our systems, get the drugs out of our systems, the point of consciousness is so much more rapid because it's all accessible. So on that level, I feel that we don't have to make recovery a burden. And there is a lot of pain in the beginning but I think a lot of that is chemically induced. I think much of the pain and so forth is caused by the fact that we are taking risks and that we don't have guarantees. And with our addictions, we did; we had instant guarantees.

You just have to ride with it and know that there is something on the other side. And that is the risk in sobriety, to wait out the effects of the drug. We have to remember that we are comfortable in our addiction. Then all of a sudden (at least that's how it feels) to be conscious and to reach that clarity, it's spooky. It seems so overwhelming and we tend to see ourselves as weak. But I think that's bullshit. . . alcoholics are the strongest group of people I know. Basically, the overwhelmingness is just a measure of how deadened we've allowed ourselves to be. Through the use of alcohol, we have systematically cut ourselves off from our own life force. In recovery, we are going to find all kinds of ways that we have learned *not* to cope. It is frightening when you come to the total impact of what you've fallen into. So I tell women that we always have a choice between life and death and whenever we are choosing alcohol, we are chosing death. And I don't think most people want to do that. If they did, they would just go out and die.

So we heal ourselves in a three-fold process. First, we quit pretending that our lives are working. Second, we look at how we set ourselves up, and third, we get the information and create something that is not based in that self-hatred and in those addictive ways of being. It is a lifetime process. We can only use excuses for a certain period of time and then we have to get on with it. What we get with sobriety is life, nothing more, nothing less, and essentially that is enough.

Physiologically when I am frightened, the sensations I feel are the exact same ones I feel when I am excited. My stomach churns, I get nervous, I sweat, I may start to stutter and I feel somewhat paralyzed for that moment. Now as a drunk, it is much easier to say, well I'm frightened, so I stop. And if I have to say, well I'm excited, then that's a commitment I have to move on. So you have to look at what the set-up is and how you choose to go with it.

So with anger, and in that first year with anger we have to not internalize it, as we have been taught. It has to be okay to be angry. There is a lot of shit out there that is worth getting angry about. The thing is to channel it. To say, "Okay, yeah, I'm angry," and move with it. For me that tends to be more political, I tend to go after systems. The thing is now I don't deny my anger, I don't try to stop and figure out where it is coming from and I don't try to be a nice girl. I now allow myself to be angry and experience that. I have to learn what those feelings are about. A lot of my anger is based on hurt and sometimes I don't know which is which. I'd much rather be mad than admit that I'm hurt and need something.

That's one of the first things I'd tell a woman in recovery. You are not alone; go find someone for support. Because we do need each other, we need each other desperately. And alcohol only isolates us so much more. So a big part of recovery is to say "I'm not alone" and to make connections, however you need to do that. If the only thing out there to hang on to is a faggot white boy, hang on to that. I did and it saved my ass.

Don't be like me and be politically correct and hang on to your bar stool and die. Go out there and get the information and get the support because as we all recover, we'll start finding each other, I have faith in that.

**JS:** So how can recovery programs be made more accessible?

**CC:** Well for one, by being there. There is a scarcity of programs. What needs to happen is that programs need to be more community-based and they need to get out to the community they are specifically serving. Alcoholism is still a very scarey thing for people. And maybe in the process of creating community centers, we could have an alcoholism component, that would make things more accessible and specifically safer since people could say they were just going to the community center.

Programs certainly need to be representative of who they say they intend to serve. The staff needs to be, the peers need to be. There needs to be a lot more word-of-mouth that happens; there needs to be more of a push from all of us, getting the word out, bringing it up as a subject to talk about. It needs to be talked about like cancer. Not drinking needs to be just as readily sociable as drinking. There is a whole push to de-glamorize drinking and some of that is starting to happen, especially in the acting community.

But getting back to programs, programs need to value who they are serving and be truthful about it. I don't think that any treatment center can truthfully serve all women. It is horrendous to say that you are going to serve the lesbian community and then have an all straight staff because that is not the lesbian community. Programs need to be realistic about what they can and can not do and call out for support from the community if they need it. Always my philosophy is to be united in our diversity and to talk about it. It is okay to be diverse and as alcoholics, we are diverse.

In the women's community, and in the lesbian community, I think that we need to start creating centers where it is okay not to drink, where it is not okay to be drunk and using drugs. We need to be calling for chemical-free space, just as we call for lesbian space, just as we call for women of color space. We need to start taking those stances and we can. It is an equally important issue that we support women in recovery and that we will no longer support women in their addictions. I always insist there be alternative drinks at community functions. I think we need to talk about alcohol and drug addictions as women's issues because they are.

For third world women, the problem that essentially comes down is that alcoholism is a white woman's health issue. That's bullshit. As women of color we are dying more. I think that on some level, white lesbians could put that message out. Some women of color will totally dismiss it, but some women will hear. And for that one woman that hears it, you cannot afford not to say it. Just as a woman of color, I will never stop confronting racism, I will never stop confronting this and I hold that as a true responsibility, and I will never deny my own recovery. I will try to be as visible as I can, all the time, as a third world recovering drunk. I don't get to split my identity. Not as a Chicana, not as a woman, not as a drunk. If people are uncomfortable with it, tough shit.

I don't have a magic formula for recovery but we have to come out of the closet as drunks. We have to start questioning our friends, our families, and start educating and start talking about why is alcohol so primary.

**JS:** So what would your community look like if it were clean and sober?

**CC:** It would be wonderful. In essence, my community now is clean and sober. A lot of the women I'm with are in the process of getting clean and sober and it's wonderful. It's risk-taking; it's not boring. It may be dramatic, but it certainly is never boring. My community is always growing and healing. It's creative and magnificent. And it is a real pain in the ass, it is real, there are real pains. It's life. It has everything, all the shit and all the glorious roses.

So that's how I view my community and it's how I'm creating at the same time. One of the things I always tell women is to never make sobriety a fucking dream. Make it real, own it today. Own the fact that you are sober and you are clean. It's here right now. If you hold it as a dream, it's going to be a dream and you are going to lose it. I want to be able to look at our addictions as things that have passed, things that we have learned great lessons from, and that we have learned the tools for our own healing. It no longer holds us down.

And whatever heals us is valid. There isn't any one system, not any one way of being a drunk, and not any one way of recovery. Whatever system of support you get, use it and then we'll find each other. There are lots of us.

# It's A Wonder We Have Sex At All

### An Interview with JoAnn Gardner-Loulan

JoAnn Gardner-Loulan, 34, is a therapist in private pratice in Palo Alto, CA. She has been counseling for more than six years. She also facilitates quarterly weekend workshops on lesbian sexuality, where lesbians come together to work on issues concerning sex. She is one of a handful of women who do this kind of work in America.

She is a small attractive woman, white-skinned, dark-haired, full of life. She looks like Hollywood would like us to believe a young all-American mother would look like. But there are differences beyond the visual stereotype that quickly become apparent. She is an out lesbian. She became a mother two years ago through insemination. Now she and her lover and the baby live together and the baby's father participates in the raising of the baby on a limited basis. Her energy appears to run on high most of the time. She talks fast, gestures in the air to make her points and her eyes give off light.

She is also a co-alcoholic in a recovery program. The themes of chemical abuse, sex and recovery from chemical abuse are common with the clients she sees in her counseling practice. The lesbian sexuality workshops she conducts are chemical-free.

This interview took place in December of 1982 on the converted porch of her home, overlooking trees and California winter greenness. I felt quite safe while I was with her.

**JS:** So tell me what you do.

**JGL:** Well, I am a psychotherapist who does counseling and as an offshoot of that, I conduct lesbian sexuality workshops. These workshops are also lovingly called sex camp. They are usually made up of twenty lesbians and two facilitators and a woman who does a massage workshop. We basically come and talk about sex. I feel lesbians need some sort of support and information about sex. We don't have any books to go to; I mean we have two or three to go to but it's not much. We just don't have the information and I feel like the best way we are going to get the information is talking to one another. Constantly, when I work with women in my office, they'll say "Well nobody else feels this way" and I'll say "Hey, come to sex camp. I've heard three hundred women talk about their sex lives and I'll tell you, there are a lot of women who feel that way."

**JS:** How did the sex work and recovery come together?

**JGL:** I was talking to a woman whom I met at sex camp. She was a month clean and sober. She was talking about that for a while and somehow the conversation got off on to my father and she said "Sure sounds to me like you have an alcoholic/co-alcoholic relationship with your father." I said, "What do you mean?" And she said "Well, your father's an alcoholic." I said, "Well, you know, I sort of thought that and sort of didn't. I think he's got a problem with his drinking, but I don't know about alcoholic. Everybody in the family knows he has a problem with his drinking." She said "Well it sounds to me like you are co-alcoholic, the way that you talk about him and how you are preoccupied."

That's how I got to a co-alcoholic recovery group. I felt sort of elated that there might be some place to go with it, something to do with it, because I felt like a lunatic. I talked more about my father, who lives 3500 miles away and whom at that point I hadn't spoken to in two years, I talked more about him than people talk about their lovers who they live with. I used to be that way, and I say used to be, because I have been really helped by working the program. I am really not preoccupied with my father anymore. That was never true in my entire life. Now I feel like I've got more understanding of how to take care of that in my life and how not to run my life around other people's lives.

Just this morning, Susan (my lover) who has been sick, said that she was going to go down to town. She was insistent. I was suggesting that we cancel an appointment that we had, and oh no, she could do it, she could do it and I'm getting into this whole thing. This woman is 41 fucking years old. She's gotten along fine before she met me and she's still alive, which is a miracle as far as I'm concerned, since I act like she can't live without my help.

So I used some of the program this morning. I said to myself, JoAnn, mind your own business. You can't control this person. She will be okay, she will live. I mean she has a cold, big deal. It's this whole thing where I get into running people's lives instead of taking care of my own.

Learning to mind my own business is one of the major things about the program that I've learned. To learn to bolster my spiritual belief, that I'm not in this by myself, that I am just part of the universe. I used to be the center of the universe. I was in control of whether it faded or made it. I was in charge of anyone around me. Now I am more and more taking my place. I am just one more part of these trees and birds that are around. The fact is that I can't control the universe. I am powerless over the universe. I am just a part of the universe.

That was a major revelation for me as a child from an alcoholic home. It was imperative to be in charge all the time. I had to be in charge of whatever situation I was in. My father wasn't physically abusive, but he was emotionally abusive, yelling and screaming about the smallest things. I never understood his mood swings. One day I could say the sky is blue and he would just go ah-uh. The next day I could say the sky is blue and it would be my head against the wall. He never did that to me physically, but that's what it was like.

I also learned to overachieve. The challenge for me now is learning that there is nothing required of me. I get into believing that I have do something to be on the planet earth and that's not true. I can just be here and take up space. Growing up, I felt that I had to have straight A's, do everything and do it the best. My brother tried to do it all wrong, hoping that would get something. None of it worked for either of us. I was the nice sweet one that everybody loved. I attribute that to being in an alcoholic home: being better than anybody and still not good enough.

Co-alcoholism is a deadly disease. My mother died of cancer when she was 53. I swear the breast cancer was about co-alcoholism. I want to say something about disease. The Chinese interpretation of disease is a lack of freedom. That's what I consider co-alcoholism, alcoholism and addiction: a lack of freedom. I'm not free. But I'm freer than I was and that's what matters to me.

I had been in therapy off and on for ten years. In all of that I never dealt with the alcoholism in my life. Most counselors don't know anything about addiction. I've been in a co-alcoholic recovery program for three years now. This is absolutely the only type of therapy that ever touched my relationship with my father, which I am free of today.

A whole lot of what this recovery program has taught me is simply accepting reality. Let's just talk about reality. Let's not say how it should be. Let's not pretend it could be another way. Let's not make up the past. You know, let's not make up the future. I would like that tree that's blocking the window to be moved over a foot, but that isn't the way it is. Let's deal with what is happening in the now and what's real about the now. In my whole life, all I was taught to do is live in the past or live in the future and fuck the now, because now is too painful. But what's important is now and what's important is reality.

I was counseling a woman for sexual issues in a short-term therapy situation. Well, it became apparent that the woman was smoking dope daily. I said "You know there's no way we can work together. To me, you would be throwing your money and your time down the drain." It was just not going to work. There is no way to work on a reality basis on your life if you are stoned or drunk or using some sort of drug compulsively. You are altering your consciousness because you are in pain. If you didn't use, you would have to deal with your pain some other way. You'd have to deal with your pain, or kill yourself. In my mind, using drugs is killing yourself.

What I try to emphasize in my work around sex and sobriety is reality and living in the present. I think it's real important because sex in sobriety is a very painful and loaded topic. In all the recovery meetings I've been to, even lesbian meetings, sex is rarely one of the topics. Everybody's scared shitless to talk about sex. Most alcoholics and co-alcoholics aren't having sex or the sex they are having is scary and uncomfortable.

I attribute lack of sexual functioning in sobriety to both physiological and psychological reasons. Let's start with the physiological. I don't care what chemical it is, they all affect your metabolism in similar ways. They all throw your pancreas, liver, stomach, kidneys and adrenal glands off-kilter. If your chemical of choice is alcohol, you're taking in tremendous quantities of sugar. Other drugs throw off your metabolism. Your liver and kidneys are trying to filter all the toxins out of your body. Your pancreas is forced to push out more insulin than your body requires because of the sugar overload. Your stomach is affected not only directly by the chemicals being ingested, but also by the reality that most addicts don't eat properly. They often just fill their stomachs with crap to get to the next day. In addition, your adrenal glands are constantly being drained by forcing out larger than normal quantitites of adrenalin. This is in response not only to the artificial stimulation of the drug, but the high drama that characterizes most addict's/co-alcoholic's lives.

The adrenal glands and the kidneys, according to Chinese medicine, are the organs where you physiologically store your energy for sex. You have depleted those before you get sober. When you get sober, you don't even have the artificial stimulants hyping your body up and so your body sort of goes "mbbblblbl" like a deflated balloon. It just sits there for a while because it is sick. It is physiologically depleted. There is no energy available from which to get any sexual charge.

The other complication here is that people are absolutely exhausted in early sobriety. When I say early, I mean the first two years. Part of that is not having the artifical hype of the chemical anymore, and the other part is that your whole organ system is totally zonked. When a person is getting sober, they are usually trying to get their work together after a long period of making chemicals first. Then there is sleeping and eating. Sex is extra. I don't care what anybody says, eating takes precedence over sex. So you've got three things that come before sex, period. I don't care if people say they have to have sex to survive, they don't. They might not be having fun, but everyone can live without sex.

The co-alcoholic is just as depleted as the alcoholic. Co-alcoholics live for adrenalin hypes; we live for the drama. We are also eating on the run, eating crap. We have the next drama to go to, or we gotta take care of somebody, or we're up all night getting coffee in somebody. We are depleting our adrenal glands because we are constantly hyped, running around for two people (or more if we can find them), and under unending stress.

So what you've got is two people who are like deflated balloons; they haven't got anything to give anybody. They're just trying to keep it together. So sex, forget it. You're energetically depleted, physiologically depleted and everybody is angry.

Anger is the primary psychological issue to be dealt with in sobriety. Everybody is angry when they go into sobriety. They start paying attention to feelings they never paid attention to before and having feelings they didn't have for however long they were using. The co-alcoholic is having some feelings for the first time also. If these two people are in a relationship together, and they were in a relationship while using, and now they are trying to get clean and sober, whoo, that's just pure dynamite.

And even if they come together after sobriety, and they didn't go through the active using days together, there still is anger and rage coming out at one another. It's the old tape. You are attracted to the same kind of people. You're pulling all the same strings and pushing all the same buttons. Doing that over again is very frustrating and very difficult.

**JS:** So how does one have sex in sobriety? Okay, so your body is rested and better after awhile, and then what happens?

**JGL:** The desire comes back but it can take a long time. Some people's desire doesn't come back for years and that's not meant to be discouraging, that's just meant for people to know that's okay, however long it takes to come back.

Usually, people who are getting sober have never had sex without using some sort of chemical. While using, your body is anesthetized and so you can't very well tune in; you don't feel what's going on anyway. I know lots of people talk about peak experiences on drugs and I feel this is a misnomer. People are having experiences, but they have little to do with our own sexuality. The body is falsely stimulated and the person is not experiencing their own bodies. If your central nervous system is anesthetized, it's often going to make it very difficult to have an orgasm. A lot of people have sexual response trouble when they are using. They often don't know it, or are unwilling to admit it.

Persons in the co-alcoholic category, have usually had sex with someone who is using chemicals. Therefore, their sexual experience has been under the influence of chemicals also. Everybody's pretty scared having sex for the first time. This is for the first two years, maybe more, of having sex without chemicals.

When we ask these two people what the primary problem is, they are more than likely going to claim that one or the other has problems with orgasm: either not having any, or not requently enough, or not in the right way, or, on and on.

I think we need to demystify orgasm. An orgasm is simply a muscle spasm. Nobody wants one in their leg, but everybody wants one in between their legs. My belief is that orgasms are not that important. People make them very important and I think that's bullshit. You can have a perfectly satisfying sex life without ever having an orgasm. I think we've gotten indoctrinated by the whole male idea of orgasm and coming. You know, going on for seven pages in a D.H. Lawrence novel about it, Fourth of July and getting hit by a Mack truck and all this other crap.

We have this idea that we are good people if we can have an orgasm. We have this whole fantasy about orgasms. Orgasms in real life have little to do with movies and books. We are so influenced by anything that isn't our real experience. I often find women who are "pre-orgasmic" and find after discussing in detail their own experience that, in fact, they have had orgasms. They just never called the feeling "orgasm" because they weren't a big deal.

But if we are talking about recovery of sexual functioning, there are some ways to help reverse the physical and psychological reasons for lack of sex drive. One of the things I tell people first is to start eating right. If people can, cut down on caffeine, cigarettes and sugar. Unfortunately people usually increase all these in sobriety. They continue to deplete the system. It's important to get your system as clear as you possibly can. Eat what you feel good about eating, but eat a balanced diet.

The second way to help is to just let yourself rest. Let yourself sleep and hang out and rest for as long as you can do that. If the co-alcoholic is going to get her act together, she's going to look at being less frantic also. Rest is in order for both sides of recovery.

The third part of changing the sexual reactiveness is to practice. I think people should practice sex. Do it with a partner who's willing, or by yourself if you are single. First practice holding hands. Practice getting held. Practice spending sensual kind of time together that doesn't have anything to do with genital contact. Practice kissing, practice hanging out in a hot tub together (if you are in California). Practice sleeping together with your pajamas on. Practice sleeping together without your pajamas. Do everything gradually. Have steps that you follow.

Start with the thing that you feel like you could do, like hold hands. Do it very gradually, step by step. Give yourself support for whatever it is that you are doing and get support from other people. Practice and don't go beyond a stage until you are comfortable with it.

If this means you are going to be a year sleeping in pajamas together, if somebody is willing to hang out with that, terrific. If you need to do it, do it. If she can't hang out with you around this issue, you still need to keep doing it. You've got to be comfortable with what you are doing sexually.

A fourth suggestion I have is get counseling. This can be in the form of a trained person. Or you and your friends can counsel with one another. It can be counseling in terms of going to groups, simply forming a rap group that talks about sex, with lesbians.

I think it is very important to do it just with lesbians. I don't care how hip straight people are, they've got homophobia. I don't think that a lesbian who is talking about her sexuality needs to deal with everybody else's homophobia, as well as her own homophobia.

A fifth suggestion is that we deal with our own homophobia. By homophobia I mean an inordinate fear of homosexuality. When I say deal with it, what I mean is talk about it, with other lesbians. I think it's very hip to say that we are not homophobic and it is the straight people who are homophobic. I don't think that's true. I think we are homophobic. We live in a totally homophobic culture and I can't believe that we don't carry that homophobia with us. When times are tougher, we have more of that going on inside of us. When we have two people together who are homophobic, who are lesbians, who are sober, whose bodies are exhausted, who are physically and spiritually depleted, who are women who aren't supposed to know anything about sex or being sexual to begin with, I mean it's an absolute wonder that we have sex at all, in the best of conditions.

If you are in a recovery support group, bring up sex as a topic. You are going to find out that most people aren't having sex or if they are, it is very scary and difficult. Getting support, hope and strength from peers is very important.

The main ingredients that I suggest for a gradual recovery in your sexual functioning are: eat right, rest, practice, practice, practice, get some form of counseling, deal with your homophobia, and get support from your peers in recovery and the lesbian community in general.

And eventually your sexual feelings are going to come back. You may have to get a new girlfriend or you may have to have an affair if you're single; you may have to go out and have an affair if you are married and if that's an option in your relationship. You may have to go out and do all kinds of things that you didn't think you were going to have to do. You are going to have to rewrite your own history. You are teen-agers again and it's a pain in the ass, but you are.

If one woman's desire comes back before the other woman's, it's like everything else that one wants to do more than the other. You have to be patient, masturbate and accept reality. You can't make it be different. You can kick and scream and yell and make her make love to you, but that won't make her sexual desire come back. So you have to deal with the reality of the situation and get your needs met within what is real. The main thing is to deal with what's real instead of wishing it were some other way.

**JS:** I know that lesbians use sex as a weapon like everybody else does. And I know that there must be pyschological scars from days of using and co-ing of when sex was a weapon that was used with the drug use. What do you do about that stuff?

**JGL:** That's when you have to get to the couple's anger, that constant anger and resentment that most of us have around sexuality. You have to deal with that on some level, with somebody, at some time. You need some sort of forum to talk about that and to put the anger right there out on the table.

I think we use sex a lot as a weapon. We use sex as a weapon, both against ourselves and our lovers. Sexual weaponry is usually non-verbal. I think that we've given sex an inordinate amount of power in our culture. I think that everybody makes sex a bigger deal than it is. I mean it is for fun, sometimes it is for procreation, but mainly it is for fun. We do all kinds of things around sex to make it not be fun. Mainly, we have it symbolize a lot of things. Our culture says sex means somebody loves you, somebody thinks you are worth something; or I'm good, or hot or attractive. Sex doesn't necessarily have a fucking thing to do with any of these or with being in love. It may be one way that people who are in love want to express themselves.

Sex doesn't have much to do with what our culture has made out of it. The culture wants to organize it, keep control of it, make certain things legal and certain things illegal. Our culture has defined sex as something that it isn't. I think we need to bring sex back to our own definition.

I have to come back to accepting sex as part of our experience. We have this culture that says that lesbians are over-identified sexually. They say we are lesbians because of our genital contact. We know that being a lesbian is a lot more than our genital contact. The sexual part of our life is relatively small compared to the rest of our lives and we are lesbians all of the time. Our culture identifies us through our sexual activity and because our culture says sex is gross, we have a lot to deal with.

There is not a heterosexual that I've ever come in contact with who questions whether they are heterosexual simply because they haven't had sex for a while. If lesbians aren't having genital contact, they often think maybe they aren't lesbians. If lesbians *are* having genital contact, they think they are doing it wrong!

My idea is to make sex not a big deal anymore. Try to make sex part of our every day experience. We act like sex is from Mars or something. We can have sex or not have sex; it's okay, either way. We can have orgasms or not have orgasms, and that's okay. Let's make sex into a regular part of our lives, instead of some bizarre foreign rite that we do.

**JS:** So can you tell me what you think recovery is?

**JGL:** For the co-alcoholic, recovery is learning emotional sobriety. Learning to be sober around your emotions, learning that there are no more big deals. I guess it's growing up, gaining some level of emotional maturity. I think it is accepting what is. Accepting relationships for what they are and not asking them to be something that they aren't. Not asking yourself to be something that you aren't. Accepting that there is nothing required of you. . . just that you be on the planet simply because you are breathing. It's a constant process to learn that. That's not too different from recovery for an alcoholic.

**JS:** So do you think that as a community we can make ourselves clean and sober?

**JGL:** Yes. We have great potential. The gay ranks of A.A. and Al-Anon, if you just want to talk about those recovery groups, have been growing tremendously. I think people really have to start recognizing what effect alcohol and drugs have on their lives, and how it really and truly has fucked up their lives. It is such a disease of denial. Alcoholism has such a bad rap and a "lesbian alcoholic", who wants to be that? It's two of the worst things you can be according to the majority culture. To admit that is really scary. We need to give support to one another to admit it. I believe our community can do this.

**JS:** How can our community institutions foster recovery?

**JGL:** Always have a clean and sober section, no matter if it is a concert or at a festival. Sponsor clean and sober activities; come up with alternatives to working through the bars. Be supportive of people being clean and sober, both verbally and actively. Serve non-alcoholic beverages. Have fundraisers not based on alcohol. Do outreach to get lesbians into recovery. Wouldn't it be great if there were lesbian alcohol recovery beds in more than one place in the country? That can be done if our community organizes it.

**JS:** If our community were clean and sober, what would it look like?

**JGL:** It would look like women really struggling to try to do something together and being supportive, struggling to be grown-up. I don't think we'd have near the bullshit controversies that we have, if everybody were sober. I think that we would be making a culture that was truly counter to the culture that we've been raised in, and not just counter because of our genital contact. I think it would be not buying into what the majority culture says is okay and hip. I feel like buying into the culture of drugs and alcohol is buying into instant pain release and that is a load of crap, it is the ultimate capitalism. Capitalism says if you buy this, you'll feel better, as opposed to doing your healing work on your own. There isn't an instant relief for anything. The sooner we accept that, the more we will be able to live in reality and really heal ourselves.

# There Is A Jewel In This Process

## Issues for Lesbian Couples in Recovery

### An Interview with Marty Johnson and Mary Bradish

**M**arty Johnson, 37, and Mary Bradish, 41, are both therapists working in the Bay Area. Marty is smaller, dark hair, luminous eyes, talks with her hands. She is a therapist in private practice and has been counseling women and children for five years. Mary talks more with her eyes, alert warm eyes in a face of classic Celtic beauty. She currently works at the Iris Project in San Francisco, one of the nation's first poly-drug abuse programs for women. They both have Master's degrees in Clinical Psychology. Together, they are planning to start a group for lesbian couples in recovery.

They are a lesbian couple in recovery. Marty identifies as a recovering alcoholic; Mary identifies as a co and an adult child of an alcoholic. They have been going through recovery together and have bonded strongly in the process. Throughout the interview, they both made themselves deeply vulnerable, and often they touched hands over the back of the couch to reassure each other. They talked slowly and their words came painfully, but they offered a wisdom and solace based in their own hard-won love experience: insights not only about lesbian couples in general but also about lesbian couples in recovery. I didn't feel as though I were sitting at the feet of experts, rather it was as though a friend of a friend had heard I was in a similar place and she had come to see me, just to share with me what she knew from her own heart and to sit in community with me. I felt they had given me something very valuable and dear to them, something they trusted me with, and I felt less alone and began to wonder if this wasn't the way we make community after all.

---

**JS:** How do issues for alcoholics and co's come together in lesbian relationships?

**MJ:** I tend to see that the alcoholic is often much more of a loner, much more separate. Part of being the loner is the relationship that she has developed with alcohol, a relationship that has really blocked her from learning about being intimate, being attached, being close, being dependent on others. Her dependency needs have been expressed and relieved by the bottle.

**MB:** And she protects her relationship with alcohol by staying separate from people. That's why isolation is such an issue with alcoholics.

**MJ:** As an alcoholic, I don't know how to express myself intimately with others. I think I have a perfect friend in the bottle, an ally who's always there, only a half-an-hour away. And this friend always responds and I don't have to say anything and my friend the bottle never refuses. So what I fail to learn or develop is how to assert my needs.

The co on the other hand, has also not learned to express her needs. Neither one does a good job of it. But the co has really learned how to take care of other people, to scan, to pick up what other people need, at the expense of learning how to be separate or express what she wants. The alcoholic is not really separate, but presents a veneer of being able to be alone and to handle being alone.

**MB:** The alcoholic is very dependent and very needy at the same time. She hides this, and feels it is a very bad, evil, sinful secret, to be that needy. A co is also very needy and dependent and secret. She hides that secret by giving all the time and not feeding herself. So you have two people who don't know how to express their needs and two people who are tremendously needy and two women. You have two women who have been socialized not to acknowledge their needs. They have also come to believe — and in fact it's often true — that they are vulnerable if they are alone and safe only when they are with others.

**MJ:** Also, with two women, you are recreating the primary relationship between mother and child. There is a recreation just by virtue of your sex.

**MB:** If you are in a heterosexual relationship, the man is separate and different from you. I'm in a relationship with Marty. She is a woman, and this time around I'm going to get everything I didn't get from my mother. She's going to read me perfectly and she's going to be able to give me everything I want or didn't get. And so we have enormous expectations.

**MJ:** These expectations are not even verbalized, because the assumption is that because we are both women, we will both want the same thing. As women, we assume we have similar feelings and similar reactions and similar ways of processing.

**MB:** And any time that's not true, any time I experience Marty having a different feeling, I feel threatened by the difference.

**MJ:** So differing needs is an ongoing issue in lesbian relationships, and problematic. As a lesbian in recovery, another issue I find us dealing with is attachment for me and separation for Mary. As an alcoholic, part of what I need to learn is how to attach to other people and how to break my relationship to a bottle. The co has usually been attached to people and has developed skills in relating to others. My job in our relationship is to learn how to connect to Mary.

**MB:** And my job is to learn how to be separate. And that's terrifying. That's where both of us experience a lot of rage and fear. Marty says "I need this, why aren't you giving me this right now?" and I feel a pressure to give her what she needs *and* I want to say "No, I don't want to."

**MJ:** Mary's job, as a co, is to learn that I will survive, even though I've put out a need and she is saying no. She needs to learn how to survive her anxiety and fear of not taking care of me.

I find, for me in our relationship, she gets inordinantly rigid when she says no. And in a way it is absolutely essential that she be able to swing out to that end of the pendulum to say no.

**MB:** And the same is true for Marty, as she learns how to attach. She is 13 years old sometimes, saying I need you, be here.

**MJ:** And terrified. I think what happens to couples is that they get real scared when they are touching core, vulnerable places. They are very awkward and bumbling. They connect in very insensitive ways at times. I mean you don't have sensitivity for those skills you've never learned.

What we lose sight of, at times, is the process. We are a couple in the process of learning the skills of attaching and separating. We will survive this moment of difference. Even though we are blowing it and I feel like it is never going to work, this is one moment in time and not the whole relationship.

**JS:** So out of your experience, what advice do you have for lesbian couples in recovery?

**MB:** I would say, have a third person to talk to, to remind you of the commitment that is bigger than the moment, and to remind you about the process and to be aware of the issues for each person. In some ways, our issues are different from those couples where alcohol was more a part of the relationship. Marty stopped drinking soon after we got together.

I think it would be much more difficult for us, if we had a whole bag of resentments in the relationship, from alcohol being a a third member of the couple. It would be tremendously more difficult if there were years of old "stuff" that was ready to be used as a weapon. For couples who do have old resentments, it's important to create cleansing rituals.

**MJ:** You need to express the resentments, but you also have to be willing to give them up. You have to verbalize it and give it up. Some people would need to do it with their partner and some people wouldn't.

Part of that cleansing ritual may be related to abstinence. I feel a question that a couple needs to face is are they both going to be abstinent.

It can be part of the cleansing ritual. You clean the relationship, you clean the house...

**MB:** And it's affirming. It gives strength to us as a couple to have a household where when people come, we say "no thanks, we don't drink." People bring wine and we say "Thanks, but take it home with you because we don't drink here." We went through a whole process of figuring out what our rules were.

My decision not to drink has helped me to better understand Marty's relationship to alcohol. The longer I'm abstinent, the more I notice alcohol in the world. I cash a check at the grocery store and there are all the liquor bottles around me that I never noticed before. The longer I am abstinent, the more I see the impact of saying I will not ever have another drink. In the beginning, I think it was just that I was so relieved that Marty wasn't drinking, that I would have done anything to support that. Now, it's much more my struggle than it used to be.

**MJ:** Another struggle for us as a couple in recovery is around Mary's issues of being a co. By focusing on alcohol, it has also focused us on the issue of how she takes care of me at the expense of her needs.

**MB:** Yeah. A couple of things happened at the same time to make me look at my being a co. One was getting clear about Marty's alcoholism. In my therapy, I started realizing that I was tired of not getting my needs met. I also was taking a class on family systems where I needed to write a paper about my family of origin and its system. Essentially what it did was make me look at how my family was an alcoholic system. I see myself having a lot of the same co-ing behaviors as my mother, (that's where I learned them). It's been very helpful having a partner who calls me on my co-ing a lot, and whom I've come to rely on for calling me on my stuff.

**MJ:** And it has helped me in terms of recovery to be in a relationship that supports my learning how to be healthy and not self-destructive, and to be in a relationship with someone who is outside of all the systems I grew up with.

I grew up in a family where you weren't allowed to be close, weren't allowed to need or be intimate. Now I'm in a relationship where, most of the time, I feel safe to express my needs. I have a hard time doing that and create all sorts of mishegoss around expressing needs, but I am with someone I feel I can learn to do that with.

**MB:** I think we fall in love with people who have something to teach us. And sometimes that is a hard lesson and sometimes it's a safe and loving lesson.

**MJ:** Another lesson we are learning in recovery is that we need to learn to play. As a recovering alcoholic, I don't know a whole lot about play, about nurturing myself, about that softer side and about relaxing. I also don't think Mary knows a whole lot about playing either, since she is always taking care of others, always paying attention, always focused outward.

Also there is a certain level of intensity for alcoholics. Alcoholics tend to live on a real edge and the alcohol feeds that kind of edge, a sugar high, a psychological high of grandiosity, of just pushing yourself, seeing how far you'll go. When you stop drinking, you don't have any way to express that edge. So the ways you tend to do it, are to be complusive about work, compulsive about going to A.A. meetings, compulsive about your sobriety: you get equally intensely involved in stuff.

So a step in the couple relationship and a step in sobriety is learning about letting go. Learning how to play, how to relax, how to turn off the intensity. We work real hard at figuring out stuff, work real hard at processing. I think there is a dilemna in that figuring out, because what we don't focus on is how to have an "easy" time. We need to learn how to alet go and not take care of each other, when to process and when to play, whether it is separately or together.

I don't think that is as much a primary issue for a couple in early recovery.

**MB:** Because then you are dealing with heavy-duty, immediate kinds of things. The immediate issue is stopping drinking. Most of the couple's energy is focused on not drinking. It's only later that they have time and energy to learn to play.

We've learned some things about this that work for us. It is very important to go away, to get out of the house and out of the routine. That new structure, the structure of being away, gives us permission to let down and play.

**MJ:** There are several levels to play. There is just the physical level of playing and relaxing. And then there is the psychological level. I am still learning how to say, "Look, we've processed enough today. We don't have to figure this out right now." We can trust the relationship and let whatever we are dealing with go and come back to it later.

It's a step-by-step process. And most couples aren't going to do it right immediately. It may start with something like how to have time-outs and have both people feel okay about it, and finding out what each person would need to feel okay about it. This is what we are working on.

What happens for me as an alcoholic is I get anxious when I can't figure it out. I am used to instant gratification.

**MB:** Marty needs to learn some coping mechanisms that allow her to back off from stress and tension and anxiety. Alcohol gave her permission to sit down and relax; when she was stressed, it was a way to diminish her stress immediately.

And so part of recovery is learning coping skills about how to tolerate anxiety and not have to take care of it right away.

**MJ:** And this brings up another issue that is true for many lesbian couples, in recovery or not. One of the things that is a real safety valve is a commitment, a sort of container for all the struggle over time. Both of us have made a commitment to each other to be together for the next forty years and we have acknowledged that publicly and are taking legal steps to do everything we can to make this a permanent relationship.

The healing process we've been talking about takes time. The thing that I think is the most helpful is knowing that there is a container for the relationship, knowing we are committed to working this out and that basically, we can't walk out the door. I think we need a framework that says both of us are here to work this out, because it will take time and we will be sloppy at times. Sometimes we need a third party to help us figure out what's going on and what we're feeling inside, someone to help us name our worst fear.

We would like to do a group with couples in recovery, with lesbian couples in various combinations: some with both alcoholics and some with alcoholics and co's. Basically, I think that all women are co's to some extent. If you are an alcoholic and a woman, you are often acting as a co, too.

**MB:** So it would be for lesbian couples who have alcohol as an issue in some way.

**MJ:** Part of my desire to do a group is to find answers to the questions that no one has written about. But part of it is from our struggle as a couple working in recovery that there was so much we didn't know. The relationship issue that I talked about earlier, about being separate and together is specifically a recovery issue and I don't know many people who are working on that issue as it relates to couples. I'd like for it to be a support group for lesbian couples, where there is a place to come and find that you are not crazy in your relationship. . . that the stuff you are doing other people are doing, where other people can use each other as teachers.

**MB:** A place where there can be someone who says in so many words: expect this, this might happen, I've tried this.

**MJ:** I'd like us to teach couples to observe each other, but also to work with themselves, about what they are bringing to the relationship from their past. Who are all the ghosts in your relationship who get evoked by the different things your partner does that really have nothing to do with her?

**MB:** I want to do a group for all those kinds of reasons, but also because I want support. I want to be with lesbian couples who are dealing with the same kind of issues that I'm dealing with.

Commitment for example. I've learned a lot about commitment, about marriage. One of the things I've learned is that in homosexual marriages, words are cheap. It's easier to leave than it is in a straight relationship. Our relationship — like all recovering alcoholic relationships — has been tested.

There was a point at which we made hard choices: Marty made choices about alcohol that were hard choices. She made those decisions for herself, but also in part for the relationship. And so did I.

After we had been together for about three months, I went to a weekend workshop about working with couples. Up to this point, Marty was still drinking and we had not talked about that or the issue of alcohol at all. So I came home and told Marty that I wanted us to work with lesbian alcoholics, that sometime I wanted us to talk about alcohol and us. I was terrified, but I was also loving her a lot. I mostly wanted to know how alcohol was a part of her life. It was a way to open a door for us to talk about her drinking. I knew she was an alcoholic, but we weren't talking about it.

**MJ:** So my worst fear was now out on the table. I'd been wanting and dreading this moment because of my fear of Mary's reaction. I left, and went and got a glass of wine and looked at the ocean and thought "What am I going to do now?" I had to decide if I was going to run away, or come back and face the music. I came back and said, "Okay, you have one hour to ask me any question you want to ask me." Five days later, I had quit drinking and I have not had a drink since then.

**MB:** I was terrified. This was something I didn't know anything about. This was a part of Marty that she had kept separate and hidden. I'm not a confronter. In that moment, though, I loved her a lot. She was a very vulnerable, frightened woman who had come back to face her worst fear. Basically I just wanted to know what she felt. I didn't have a lot of judgments about it, I just wanted to know.

I knew Marty and I loved her and I saw weaknesses in her that she wasn't acknowledging and they were part of what I loved. It wasn't that I was afraid she would leave me, or the relationship. It was more that I was afraid to bring out something that was so hidden and so scary. So I asked her how long she had been drinking, how much, and I said, just tell me about it, tell me about being sixteen. I just loved her a lot. It took a lot for her to come back through the door.

**MJ:** I was terrified, but I also felt there wasn't a whole lot of judgment. Mary never made the intervention in an accusatory way. It was done with concern, saying I want to know and I want you to know that I know and I want to start naming what I know, so we can stalk about it.

Sometimes people make interventions in an accusatory way, or in a judgmental way, because they are angry and because they are real frustrated with someone they love who keeps hurting herself.

What happened inside me was that all my critical voices were called up and so I become defensive and frightened. When I came back I was feeling relief that we were finally going to talk. It seemed like Mary really wanted to know and she wasn't judging me as harshly as I had judged myself. I felt like the worst possible thing that Mary could know about me was out on the table.

It also coincided with a period in which I really wanted to quit. At that point we didn't talk about Mary's abstinence. And we didn't lay down any rules in the context of a couple relationship. Three weeks later, we confronted that other side when Mary went out to eat with friends and had two glasses of wine and then came home and kissed me.

And my reaction was, the smell of the wine made me sick to my stomach. I felt repulsed and betrayed and I got mad and upset. I was surprised too. Up to that time, I thought that alcohol was *my* problem. But what got real clear was that we as a couple had to deal with abstinence.

**MB:** I was shocked and hurt. I did feel at that time that it was her problem, but I had the wine at dinner without thinking about it. And I felt guilty, too, because Marty couldn't. At the same time, I felt deprived, because I really like wine and I don't have a problem with it; so why couldn't I have it? But it became clear to me that is not important to me; I want to spend my life with Marty. It was my choice, because alcohol cannot be a part of us, and us is Marty and me. The other piece is that as I become more in touch with how alcohol was part of my family system, abstinence becomes more of a personal choice for me. So part of me said, yes, that makes sense: though alcohol is not a problem for me, it is an issue for me.

Our experience with alcohol — the choice that we've made — has been a real gift. And out of our choices has come our commitment. And being a couple in recovery has allowed us to test our commitment.

**MJ:** I think for me, another part of commitment that I've learned, is that saying "I love you" is not enough. In fact, that is the easiest part at times, yet it is only words. Relationships are real hard work. Commitment is hanging out in the winter fallow periods of the relationship, when we are not talking the same language and we feel like we are on different mountain peaks and being able to maintain some kind of commitment through those periods until we can get to the good times again. I think I grew up with the illusion that if you love someone that is enough.

But part of commitment and being in recovery is learning how to go through those hard periods, and just going through them. And at moments it feels like we are never going to get through this moment and I think what I'm learning is that you do. There are enough moments/tests of doing it and getting through.

Sometimes we hate each other. We don't like each other and can't stand to be in the same room. Getting through that stuff, getting through the anger is, in a way, more of a commitment than the warm fuzzy stuff. The question is, how does a couple build a container which makes space for both the love and the anger — which allows space for differences as well as closeness.

**MB:** A container for the relationship is crucial, whether a couple is in recovery or not. And it's hammered out over time, to meet the partners' changing needs. Couples need to ask themselves about their bottom lines. What are their needs? What are their limits?

That's one that an alcoholic couple faces. The partner may say my limit is that I will leave if you don't stop drinking.

**MJ:** When that person stops drinking, what is the next limit? What are the rules if someone slips? Lots of feelings are going to come up: rage, betrayal, disappointment, fear — sometimes relief. If alcohol has been a part of a couple's life, and has been removed, sometimes it's a relief to face the old, known enemy rather than all the new feelings. What happened? What went on? What's important is that you start talking about what's going on inside.

For the couple, what was going on inside both of them? What was going on in the relationship that contributed to the drinking?

We have just drawn up a contract ourselves that says that we have to go into therapy if Mary or I starts drinking. It's a set-up to say you'll leave if someone drinks. The commitment is to working out the relationship, not to leaving. Part of the set-up is that if you set the limit way out there and then the person does take a drink, the partner is confronted with how to uphold her limits. We need to look at what limits we can back up in this moment.

**MB:** What we worked out is that if Marty or I slip, the relationship is endangered and we have to do something to confront that danger. It also takes the onus off the person who slips and puts it back onto the relationship. The onus is taken off the other, too, to have to leave. If Marty slips, there are going to be a lot of reasons for that and some of them, I just know, will come from the relationship. There will be something going on that is not healthy or feeding us.

**MJ:** And for myself, I have some self-destructive internal voices. For me, nurturing causes more chaos at times to my internal system than not getting nurtured. Not getting nurtured is a real familiar place for me. I grew up with that system. And part of me wants to self-destruct anything that is positive, because then I am back in familiar territory. If someone says to me, I'll leave if you drink, I have a wonderful way to act out all those voices that say, I don't deserve. For most of us, we initially don't know how to deal with the good/positive stuff, so when someone sets a limit like "if you drink, I'll leave," then there is a way out of all this positive aliveness that satisfies the internal voice which says "you don't deserve to be happy."

**MB:** Another big part of the process that I've learned is the power of naming. The power of naming, of talking about alcoholism and putting things out on the table instead of leaving them covert and unspoken and ambiguous. If you name something I don't think it's as terrifying as if it's unnamed. In the process of our recovery one thing that's happened is that we can sit here tonight and talk about being an alcoholic and co-alcoholic. In the beginning of recovery, we couldn't do that. Part of the process is learning how to say those terrible words: alcoholic, co-alcoholic, drinking, drunkenness. They are very uncomfortable for many of us. But naming takes away the incredible power something has when it is unnamed.

**MJ:** Now we are at a second stage of naming: learning to name negative feelings about the relationship and each other. To name and put them out on the table and learn that they will not destroy the relationship.

In my individualistic way, I hate naming, I hate labels, I hate jargon. What I hate is when words/names are used as weapons, as a way to avoid struggling with the process. It is short-hand. . . which is wonderful except when you only use the short-hand and forget that people are unique and have their own style which they bring to the situation. But the power of alcohol lies in its being a secret which is unspoken, unnamed. When you can begin to own/claim the name "alcoholic," the secret becomes a manageable reality.

I have a terrible fear that if I name something I don't like, the other shoe will drop and all I have in this relationship will disappear. That may have been true when I was a child but it's not true now: naming things doesn't mean that the other shoe will drop. I think there is a whole process for couples about learning how to name, a whole process of learning how to talk about your insides. All of us learned how to talk, but none of us learned how to do it well when it comes to expressing our insides.

Learning to talk about your insides doesn't happen overnight. To expect that things will change overnight just because alcohol is removed is crazy. We need time to learn how to connect in growthful ways. I figure we have 40 years to get this down. As an alcoholic, that's a hard thing for me to accept this notion of needing time. I'm just beginning to learn, just beginning to appreciate time.

And sometimes we get stuck. One of the wonderful things Mary does is to identify my voices from my family. When I get stuck, she helps me name my voices and we are able to joke a little about it now.

**MB:** I'll say (if it's her mother talking): "Get her out, get her out of the bedroom!"

**MJ:** And when Mary gets stuck as a co, I try to get her to be more direct, to really say what she wants.

Mostly, I think it's learning each other's process. Like with words. I tend to use words loosely, just to describe the moment. Mary's careful with her words, and she goes inside and carefully describes what she really thinks. That makes havoc in our communication sometimes, because our way of using language is so different.

Sometimes, when I get stuck, Mary just stops me from talking and she connects with me in some other way like holding me. When I get scared, I tend to push away. Physical contact can bring me back.

**MB:** And that's just something that we learned by being together.

**MJ:** What I've learned about Mary is just to tell her not to take it on. . .

**MB:** . . . to remind me that I haven't been bad, that I don't have to do anything to make it better. . .

**MJ:** . . . or that what I'm saying is not about her, it's about me.

The part I wish I was better at is to encourage her anger, to say to her: it's not me, you need to do it, I want you to do it. But it's hard and I get hooked and I get real defensive. I guess it just takes time to learn to do that. But we have lots of time.

One of the most positive things about being in a relationship where alcohol is an issue is that you get a chance to start all over again. By removing the substance, you get to focus on how to deal with each other.

**MB:** It's been a real jewel for me, a turning point in my life to have a part of Marty be alcoholic and to have to look at that in her and me. It was a gift I was given that day when she sat down and said, okay, you have one hour.

**MJ:** Alcohol made us look at how we are inside. You get to start your life again. You don't get to relive your life and you bring your life with you, but you get to choose how to live your life now.

And I would want anyone who is going through recovery to know that there is a jewel in this process that is the gift to each person. You really get a chance to say how you want to live your life, how to create a relationship that's life sustaining. It's a choice that takes a lot of courage: hanging out with how do I want to live my life and that I want to live.

If my community were clean and sober, we would have to make that commitment to life, to being alive. If the therapeutic community were clean and sober, there would be more compassion and more integrity, an owning of one's own addictive/self-destructive processes, rather than focusing on someone else's processes.

In general, if my community were clean and sober, the pace would be slower. In order to stay sober, you have to restructure your life and find other ways to deal with stress. There would be time to connect, time to learn to connect. People would maintain the integrity of their feelings. Relationships would develop over time and people would feel free to say their feelings. There would be playfulness and fun. And lots of animals.

If my community were clean and sober, I'd never have to hear another drunken conversation. And I'd never have to watch someone numb out, that is something that is painful for me to watch now. I choose not to be around people who drink or use much anymore. I can't be around that because it brings up all of what I did to myself.

If my community were clean and sober, it would be much more connected than our communities are now. It would be a place where you didn't have to numb out and people would strive to connect.

**MB:** If my community were clean and sober, it would be more alive.

If my therapeutic colleagues were my community, and they were all clean and sober, my community would have a lot more integrity, empathy and understanding. If my community were my friends who are not yet clean and sober, they would be more alive, more beautiful and more honest.

If my community were clean and sober, it would be life-affirming.

# PART III:
# THE POLITICS OF OUR ADDICTIONS

# Four Poems In Search Of A Sober Reader

### by Catherine Risingflame Moirai

I.

We have a history, yes
and it is full of women
who died
because some man
decided we
should be stoned
or burned       or shut up.
I carry with me visions
of women screaming
as the flames rise
as the doors close
as the rocks fall
and they are visions
of us.

We have a history,
she and I.
We both know the feel
of locked doors
our fists against the wall
the words no one wanted.
We have a history
and we know       either of us

could have had electrodes
strapped on       lit up
could have had stony streets
turn harder.

But we survived, yes
and I was proud       of that
and of our love       proud of her
I drank her like the coolest water
and every act of love
was also praise.
But it was not enough:
our lovers' knot couldn't
bind her to peace.

She's gone to live with a man
and on the walls
are cartoons of women.
She spends nights smoking
in the bars; she tells me
she will sell
what's at hand. She wants to prove
she's normal
and I am left to mourn
her       still living.

This is a social disease
the desire to be
normally dead.

II.

The woman in the mill, sweating
while her husband drank her wages
had cause to be mad.
Hunger and beatings breed
hatred       and another nine months later.
Rage came easy, too, for the woman
without a vote, watching
the man stagger from a saloon
where he cast her future,
his wishes. And the woman
helpless to save her daughter

from the man in her life
was foolish like a bird
beating against the bars.

We have forgotten why
women went with hatchets
to destroy the demon
drink. Our books show cartoons
of ugly faces beneath absurd
hats; we say those women were foolish
and neurotic. We are embarrassed
by this evidence of women
who moved against the flow of reason.
Those were simple stories
too hard to tell in school.
But when men laugh, listen
closely. We of all movements
should know the power of bad press.
Ridicule is a powerful brew
and served to us for reason.

## III.

When everything is connected
the smart man makes a profit
on the links. Consider shipping rum,
New England to Africa. White men
bought dark bodies and piled them
tight as caskets in the hold.
The cost was low: a woman
for ninety-five gallons, a man
for thirty more. It was best
to mix the captives, never taking
many of a common language
lest they remember each other
into freedom       and revolt.

The middle passage was the hardest.
The cargo died inconveniently
or mutinied against the chains.
Some starved themselves; others found release
through nets spread above the sharks.
At least ten of every hundred died.

*119*

A month before the end, the women
were bathed in salt water
and given to the crew.

In the sugar colonies
sale was quick. Demand was always high;
a third of the arrivals died
within three years. Survivors
worked the cane: planted, cut, milled
and boiled. Yankee traders
carried home the sugar
and molasses for making rum
and so it began        again.

This is historical fact.
The slick magazine, feminist
to the core, has pictures of the beautiful
people who drink
Puerto Rican rum. The best
of course is white,
very expensive. So are the people.
I imagine they speak
perfect English.

## IV.

When I ask for free space
the woman over there
says we must keep our meetings
accessible: Fay, black,
has more pain, and needs her drugs
to continue        and Angie, poor,
remembering rape, can not go on
without her bottle

pounding the walls
til my hands are bruised
I want to drink
to forget

my mother, stumbling down the hall
did not drink because she was Catholic
divorced       on welfare       or because

my father abused her
and left

my mother, vomiting on the bed
drank         because she did
not stop

watching a woman kill herself
by inches of a bottle
is not
a revolutionary act.



**CATHERINE RISINGFLAME MOIRAI:** lives on a farm in East Tennessee with other sober dykes. She is learning to be happy and aspires to become a middle-class land-owning capitalist.

I'm blessed because my immediate community of four *is* clean and sober; our farm is alcohol/drug free. Our job now is to go heal the old wounds and learn to laugh more. But when we go into Knoxville, looking for a larger community — then we see what it is still like in the "real world." If *that* community were clean and sober, we'd have some place besides the bar to dance. We could go to a lesbian performance without having to be the ones to provide healthy beverages. We wouldn't be called "divisive," "racist" and "classist" for wanting alcohol-free space. We wouldn't be told alcohol is only *our* problem. Organizations would survive and grow, not fall apart because people are too busy partying to do the work. Most of all, we wouldn't have to watch women we love killing themselves — and hating us for seeing what they are doing. If our community were clean and sober — we'd actually *have* a community.

# Creativity, Politics And Sobriety

## by Abby Willowroot

No one wants to be an Alcoholic. It conjures up images of old men in alleys, of pain and shame, or images of wimmin falling off bar stools and lying on floors. These are real images of real Alcoholics, but they are just the tip of a very large iceberg. These stereotypes, like all stereotypes, perpetuate half-truths that keep us all unclear.

I am an Alcoholic, an Artist, a Mother, a Womyn in her late thirties with a future. I am an Alcoholic and today I am Sober and Drug-free. I have been clean and sober since December of 1980.

For the past 13 years, I have worked as a feminist jeweler and symbol maker, designed matriarchal pottery and shown graphic works. There was always a little nagging feeling that I wanted to do something I didn't even dare to look at. Today, as a direct result of my sobriety, I'm doing it. My jewelry designs are being produced by a fine craftswomyn in the community and I am making large sculptures in a variety of media.

After more than two years of continual sobriety, I am watching my skills return, and it is an indescribable relief and joy. My judgment improves every day, as well as my physical and mental condition. There were many times when I was loaded that I would fantasize making all kinds of things, but I was always too loaded to put my plans into a concrete form.

There is no end to the popular stereotypes about artists, living in a humble garret, little money, good friends, cheap wine. But the truest old line about artists is that "creativity is 1% inspiration and 99% perspiration."

I have created more solid designs and pieces in two years of sobriety than I managed to do in fourteen years on chemicals. The images and forms that I have created in sobriety are both stronger and softer than my earlier work. I live my life and my art one day at a time now, and it works beyond my wildest fantasy! I feel that the pieces I create are artifacts of wimmin's culture and now I create them with *all* the skills the Goddess gave me, not under the influence of patriarchal poisons.

I used to believe that drugs and wine would "make me more creative," free me to explore my deeper self. The truth was that I hid behind drugs and alcohol because I was afraid to *really* look into myself, on any level. As an artist, I never felt good enough, and I judged my work by someone else's standards, looking outside myself for approval of the things I created. The harder I tried to please people with the art I created, the less it pleased me, and the harder it was to look inside. The less I looked, the more I relied on alcohol and drugs to create that false sense of creativity.

For a long time after I quit drinking, it didn't seem as if I would ever make anything again. But as time passed and as my body began to heal itself, creativity came out in ways I had never experienced before. When I began to work again, the things I made surprised me. I tried lots of different media for the first time. Sobriety has put joy into my art again. I no longer worry about whether anyone will like it finished. I don't even worry if I'll like it finished. When I create things, I'm much more involved in the process than the results. If I put all my energy into the process, the results will take care of themselves. Working this way keeps me curious and pushing my limits, in imagination, in technique, in vision.

Perhaps the most important thing that has happened to me in my sobriety along the lines of creativity is that I am creating a womyn who values all life enough to live. I am able once again to combine the two most important facets of my life. . . creativity and politics.

I have worked in feminism since 1970 and the most revolutionary thing I have ever done was to put down the drink and the drugs. I have worked on committees to save wimmin, stop nuclear power and other issues, but every day I spent money to kill the only womyn over whose life I had any control: myself. When I put down the alcohol and drugs, I saved the life of a womyn who deserves to live. Every day that I do not take a drink or a drug, I am demonstrating my caring for wimmin by caring for myself. My life has value and so does the life of every other womyn. Alcoholism is just another word for womyn-hating, in my life.

It is believed that alcoholism is a disease. I would disagree; I think that our culture is the disease and that alcoholism is a symptom of that disease.

Cultural conditioning keeps wimmin from valuing themselves and each other. Much of the message is designed to keep wimmin consuming in order to feel better about themselves and boost the economy. Happy people are lousy consumers. When wimmin feel good about themselves, they are not looking for external fixes.

Alcohol and drugs are recommended to help wimmin relax. . . have a good time. . . forget your problems. . . feel more glamorous, prettier, more chic, happier, invisible. Advertising encourages us to "escape", to be anything but ourselves. All our lives we have been taught that technology has a new and improved life just around the corner.

We have been fed on illusions of style, charm and sophistication being achieved through the use of the "right" wine or scotch. They tell us we can achieve tranquility and happiness through tranquilizers, joy through the right drug, energy through the right brand of speed. We have been taught that discomfort is unnatural and that we can get rid of it with a pill. Stress and anger are seen as the appropriate reasons to pick up a drink and swallow our rage.

This culture is designed to keep us barefoot, pregnant or loaded. The politics of addiction are painfully simple. Women in this culture are encouraged to kill themselves and dope and alcohol do the job quite thoroughly.

The excessive use of alcohol and drugs has always been used as a tool for the decimation of potentially powerful groups. In this country, we have seen it used to annihilate American Indians and subdue Black Americans and Mexican Americans. It is in use today as the club used to keep the Irish in line by the British, as well as in many third world countries.

Alcohol and prescription medication are being used in the same way on all kinds of American wimmin. Dope and alcohol make us more manageable. Separating people from their ability to act and think rationally makes them easy to control, especially once the addiction has been set up and they "need" those drugs or alcohol, once they can no longer see life without them. It is said that alcoholism is a dis/ease of Denial. Alcoholism is the disease that tells you you're fine while it is killing you.

When John Lennon died, I thought, what a waste. And then I looked at my life and I was killing myself with Drugs and Alcohol. At that moment in time, I could not deny that fact. I realized that creating life-oriented art and staying loaded all the time was about as political as scraping waxy yellow build-up off my floors.

It was clear to me that I was not trapped in a formica kitchen. Feminism had helped me escape all that, but what I had done with my liberated life was to build myself a counter-culture prison of dope and alcohol. I was no longer a slave to a man or a menial job, but I was a slave to a mind-altering chemical and I was dying as surely as I was years before when I took Valium and drove car pools.

It seems that somewhere in the sixties we got the illusion that the government didn't want us to use drugs. The truth is that if the government didn't want drugs available, they wouldn't be. Drugs gave us the illusion of choice. For me, the realization came that the government wanted me loaded, safely neutralized in the little box marked "manageable. . . out to lunch". This may or may not be true, but it was enough to get me sober and keep me sober for over two years.

When you are sedated as with alcohol, prolonged cohesive action becomes impossible, staying focused becomes fuzzy. Many wimmin are proclaiming the values and customs of our foremothers, reclaiming wimmin's power, researching wimmin's oppression, and then going to the bar for a few drinks. Many wimmin are writing lyric poems of wimmin's power but needing to get loaded before they can be "inspired". They do not make the connection.

The journey inward back to our heritage, back to our power and back to our mother is hindered by the use of chemicals. In the wimmin's community, the activities often center around bars and alcohol. This is a holdover from the time when we had to hide ourselves away and punish ourselves for being bad. I have watched wimmin drink to hide from themselves, and when they succeed, they kill a womyn who deserves to live.

In all the ways we feel that we are not enough, we turn to a chemical that we think makes us better. It doesn't. And the same low self-esteem, that causes us to turn to drugs and alcohol, is what makes recovery so difficult. Women seem to recover in direct proportion to their willingness to look at reality. Women who want to hold on to their illusions and refuse to look honestly and curiously at themselves and their lives do not have a very high success rate. Many of them choose alcohol, drugs and death over sobriety and self-honesty.

The reasons for this lie in their conditioning and their pervasive fear that if they look deeply, the person they find will be less than worthless. These feelings of worthlessness are so deep-seated that wimmin are terror-stricken at the idea of *really* looking at themselves. The feelings are sometimes so strong that as one womyn said, "I'd rather die than look at my past!" The sad truth is that she probably will.

Looking at all the ways in which we have accepted illusions, made mistakes and abused ourselves in our lives is not ever easy, but it is essential if we want to be free from our past and its pain. We all do what we think we need to do to survive. We are not bad because we have chosen to do things in a certain way in the past; we just did what we thought we had to do. We did the best we could at the time.

Sobriety means learning new ways of doing things, forgiving ourselves and others, and going on with our lives. For many wimmin, the fear of looking at themselves keeps them trapped in the past, in the old patterns, and defending old behavior. The belief that they deserve to be sober, happy and free is very difficult for some wimmin to grasp and hold onto. You cannot stay sober until you can trust that you deserve it. For many wimmin, their self-esteem is so low that they believe they deserve to die, because they are not good enough.

Sometimes, the fear of seeing myths about wimmin in our culture is greater than the will to survive. The fairy princess myth is a terminal condition; it takes millions of wimmin's lives every year. We have a hard time naming this condition, as the instruments of death are different: alcoholism, drug addiction, tranquilizer overdose, car accidents, cancer, heart failure, anorexia nervosa and many more. The condition remains the same with symptoms that are startlingly similar: low self-esteem, fear of life, fear of not being acceptable, fear of failure, fear of success, an inability to accept life as it is, an unwillingness to examine past beliefs, a secret hatred of all that wimmin are and an unwillingness to claim power. But disease or symptom, the results are the same: recovery or if left untreated, death.

In order to face recovery, a womyn has to want to live more than she wants to die. Recovery is a lot more than not picking up a drink or a drug. It means changing old ideas so that the desire to use alcohol and drugs is no longer a part of life. Being sober is letting go of the illusion that alcohol brings escape or relief. Recognizing the ways in which we have relied on chemicals to make our joy and take away our pain takes time. . . sober time.

Sobriety for me is living in the solution, not in the problem. I am alcoholic; that will never change. What has changed is how I am living with my disease. Living with the solution means that I must stop living in a fantasy. As long as I am willing to accept things as they are, I stay clear and move forward. By accepting, I don't mean abandoning the desire or drive to change certain things. I just mean accepting that certain facts exist. Once you have accepted reality as it is, you are far better able to move towards changing that reality, in positive ways.

When I feel down because I'm broke, the solution is to earn some money. I used to think the solution was preaching revolution. When I am irritable because I'm hungry, the solution is to eat something. I used to just wait until it got so bad I couldn't eat. This all may seem simplistic and I guess it is, but when I was loaded, I couldn't grasp the obvious. As a practicing alcoholic, I lived in my illusions of what things were; today as a sober alcoholic, I have some clarity.

As an artist, a great deal of my work is responding to the environment around me and creating images that communicate what I see and how I respond emotionally to what I see. Sobriety has affected this process greatly. I now perceive things with all my senses and without the haze of chemicals. I am much more aware of the beauty and pain around me. My awareness has expanded in such a way that I no longer need to create artificial images and fantasies in my work. There is a new appreciation of the beauty in simplicity and the character of every day experience. I always thought I appreciated these things, but my sensitivity has grown and deepened.

Creativity comes from within as well as through the artist. There is no creativity in a vacuum. Alcoholism eventually creates a vacuum around the alcoholic. The ability to be selective about detail requires an awareness of all the detail present. Sober, I have this awareness to bring to my work. We all create out of our experiences of the world. With alcohol and drugs, my experiences were distorted. The distortion and the disconnection from feelings made the communication of true experience difficult, if not impossible. Today the things I have shared through my art are more healing and connected than they have ever been.

Sobriety also unites one with feelings that were previously cut off. It is precisely these feelings that are the starting place for all creative works which have the power to touch deeply and truly speak to another person. The business of art is to communicate honestly. This demands a high degree of control of both feelings and skills. The awareness of what those feelings really are makes it much easier to communicate than if you are aware of only their shadow.

Like many artists, I "channel" much of my work. By channel, I mean that ideas don't come out of my brain, but pass through it. This is not how all my work takes form, but it is the way much of it happens. When I design something, it builds in my head, detail by detail, changing and growing until I am ready to begin. When I channel something, it feels different in my head; it comes from a different part of my brain. When I am channeling, a design pops into my head fully formed and complete. This is one of the great joys of being an artist.

In sobriety, channeling is both frequent and clear. When I was using alcohol or drugs, this process was infrequent and distorted. I have watercolors from early sobriety and watercolors from the end of my drug and alcohol career. There is a startling difference in both quality and feeling. The subject in both watercolors is the same but one is fuzzy, muddled and clumsy while the one done sober has clean lines, clear colors and shows the skill with which it was executed. When I was loaded the first picture looked pretty good to me. Now I can see that it is just sloppy ramblings in paint. I can see that because I am sober.

Today the process of creativity is a beautiful and challenging adventure of both reaching out and reaching in. As a sober alcoholic, I am just now beginning to find out who I am, what my visions are and the many, many different ways I can express those visions. Womyn energy is by nature creative; it flows and ebbs and flows again. In sobriety there are no unnatural blocks to that energy. As a sober alcoholic, it is possible for me to sit still and let the process happen, go where it takes me and not judge my work until I have completed it. The old impatience and self-consciousness are gone. The manic highs are gone; the illusions are gone. What is there is a strong drive to see what comes next, a zest for sharing feelings and images.

My experiences as a womyn in this culture deserve to be shared with honesty, courage and hope. Sober I am able to do that. When I was a practicing alcoholic, I created images to help heal other wimmin's lives, but I was dying in my own. Today, my images contain the new life that sobriety has given me. I believe with all my being that wimmin do have the power to heal, to heal this planet, this culture, and especially to heal each other and ourselves. Today I know that the first step towards being truly political and truly creative is to stay clean and sober. Before I can value life in the world, I must value life in myself.

**ABBY WILLOWROOT:** grew up in Ozzie and Harriet America and lived to Sober Up. She began her drug career at the age of 11 on her doctor's advice. She's the mother of two sons, two plays and 10,000 matriarchal images. She is currently working on large sculptures and staying sober One Day at a Time, with a wonderful sober womyn lover, and many sober sisters.

There is a place where wimmin's eyes are clear and alert. In the evening, conversation and sharing have replaced chemically-induced oblivion, cruising and loud music. Wimmin work on all kinds of research and productivity in a quiet acceptance of each other's differences. Wimmin here accept and love each other, because they've learned to accept and love themselves. Change here is constant and healing as wimmin touch each other's lives in positive ways. The Goddess is alive and well and working in our lives.

# Alcoholism: Violence Against Lesbians

## by Nina Jo Smith

*"Redefining violence and weaving together forms of violence into a total system of social control are implicit in the adoption of the term 'violence against women'... if we conceptually link all forms of violence against women, then our fight, too, must be against the whole web."*[1]

- **A**lcohol is involved in nearly two-thirds of all violent incidents[2].
- Nationally, alcoholism ranks with heart disease and cancer as a leading cause of death[3], but remains a low funding priority for national health care spending.
- Alcoholism is the primary health problem in the gay community, causing more deaths than any other disease[4].
- One out of three lesbians experience addiction to alcohol and other drugs; at least two out of three of us are addicted and/or are adversely affected by the alcoholism and addiction of our friends, lovers, co-workers or families[5].

This article is written in the hopes of expanding our definition of violence against women to include the violence we experience in our lives as a result of alcohol. Alcohol is a potentially addictive drug which, alone or in combination with other drugs, is used by us and against us.

As women and lesbians, what happens to us when we and those around us drink? What does alcohol have to do with violence against women?

As women, we suffer the violence of rapes and assaults, most of which involve an assailant who has been drinking. Many of us experience arguments, fights or beatings with relatives or lovers at home, strangers on the streets, friends in the bars. And as women, we hide our alcoholism as we hide other forms of violence against us: rapes, battering by lovers, sexual harassment on the job or in the street. We are assaulted by images of drink, violence and coercive sex in advertising, film and pornography.

When we are alcoholic ourselves, we also suffer the isolation, denial, invisibility and stigma involved in being a woman with a "drinking problem." When we are intimately involved with an alcoholic, we are likely to experience anger, verbal and physical abuse from our roommate, lover, child or parent who drinks.

The onset of violence in my personal life corresponded exactly to the onset of drinking in my family during the years immediately before, during and after my parents' divorce. This period taught me that drinking was the source of releasing strong emotions, especially pain and anger. Events of this period later led me to live for nine years in hiding from my father, convinced that he would kill me if he discovered my lesbianism. In later years, my mother's drinking wove a web of silence around our past, all emotions, and drinking itself.

At the age of twelve, my first drunk was a release from the silent pain of experiencing the disintegration of my Baptist family in our small town. Later, I drank during times of crisis and emotional pain, and when trying to "fit in" in social situations which occasioned drinking. When I became old enough to sneak into the bars as an eighteen-year old lesbian I drank to fit in, and to provide a barrier (a glass) between me and others. I drank for self-protection. I drank because the only place I knew to meet other lesbians was once a week in a gay bar on women's night. In my sobriety, I ask myself, "In whose interest was this?"

Alcohol has been used as an instrument of colonization and control to quell resistance of native people throughout the history of the invasion of this continent. It has been used to undermine organizing in poor, black, latino, gay and women's communities. Notice the number of liquor billboards, bars and liquor stores in poor neighborhoods, around housing projects, in the gay ghetto. The "Miss Black Velvet Latina" contest is a case in point. As women have been "targeted" by the liquor advertising industry in the last ten years, people of color have been designated as the target population for ad campaigns over the next ten years[6].

Women and gays are rising. Alcohol is a depressant drug. The liquor industry spends over $400 million *annually* to advertise its products[7], and as noted above, appealing to the growing "women's market"[8]. Who does this serve?

We live in a culture which is bathed in propaganda, myths and rituals of drinking. As lesbians, many of us do not know how to separate our lesbian identities from our identitites as drinkers. Liquor advertising appeals to our need for diluting our alienations, to our need for sexual fulfillment and for taking control of our lives. They sell us the butch image and the promise of letting go of it, dissolving into softness and affection as the evening progresses. For many of us who came out in the bars, alcohol has been the key to our sexual liberation (so we thought) or at least to our sexual expression. To a great extent, alcohol has been synonymous with our sexual identity.

So how does drinking — ours and others' — do violence to us? Alcoholism, as well as homosexuality, are considered abnormal or worse yet, subnormal. Both are seen by society as psychological diseases or signs of moral depravity, especially in women. For our survival, many women who are lesbians or alcoholic have adopted a strategy of hiding. A flawed woman in this society is lost. We hide our drinking as one of our flaws. Even those of us who are out as lesbians bear scars from the emotional violence of years of hiding our lesbianism from ourselves and others.

In this hiding, we forget how not to hide our feelings. Parts of us remain in the closet at the same time other parts step out into the light. As lesbian alcoholics, we experience the double pain of isolation, an unspeakable violence.

It is one of the devastating betrayals of alcoholism that through drinking we may seek a way out of isolation, but isolation insidiously becomes the essence of alcoholism. Silence and isolation do a great deal of violence to the spirit. Being a lesbian alcoholic meant I became encased in an isolation within isolation.

During the last few years of my drinking, I became a student of Tae Kwon Do, a Korean martial art. This began to give me a way of working out some of my anger — a way which did not necessitate drinking. Eventually my study, combined with the rapid deterioration of all my closest relationships, brought me to the realization that in order to survive and to stop abusing the love and friendship of those I cared most about, I would have to stop drinking and learn to break out of my alcoholic isolation.

To some extent, all women are isolated from one another. Lesbians are often extremely isolated from each other and from the mainstream. To the extent that we are isolated, we are vulnerable to many other forms of violence including alcoholism.

As isolated women, we learn to hide our illnesses, because we know the treatment may feel far worse than the disease. Meanwhile, the disease progresses undiagnosed and untreated. As lesbians, many of us are reluctant to subject ourselves to the probing hands and prying questions of physicians we distrust due to their (usual) antagonistic sex, class position and sexuality.

Likewise, many alcoholics become casualties of the so-called health care system of this country, suffering and/or dying from alcohol-related diseases: liver damage, malnutrition, arthritis, diabetes, anemia, menstrual problems, difficult or early menopause. Alcoholics have a suicide rate 58 times higher than non-alcoholics, and have a life-expectancy of ten to twelve years less than non-alcoholics[9]. Alcoholism, though pervasive in the society and a leading cause of death, is rarely diagnosed, due to patient and provider denial and societal stigma.

Especially in the mental health care system, women are often treated for our supposed neuroses instead of our alcoholism. As lesbians, we experience alcoholism treatment programs which are racist, sexist and/or homophobic. Some "health care providers" want to cure us of our lesbianism before they will treat our alcoholism. There is currently only one residential recovery program in the U.S. which welcomes lesbians, the Alcoholism Center for Women in Los Angeles, and only one outpatient program for lesbians and gay men: Eighteenth Street Services in San Francisco, which has only two funded staff positions[10].

This limited professional support for lesbians in recovery is sometimes matched by limited personal support. When I began to share my recovery process and alcohol problem with the women in my life, most of them responded at first by surprise and denial. Perhaps some of them didn't want me to blow their cover. The aspect of isolation brought on by my alcoholism meant that those closest to me did not really know me and were unprepared to help me deal with my recovery.

The violence of alcoholism and the violence of oppression as a lesbian created a gap between me and myself, and between me and my community which could begin to be bridged only after great struggle and great loss, and only with the support of a growing movement of women to become clean and sober, strong and free.

In the three years of my recovery, I have received a great deal of support and healing from A.A. It speaks to the isolation and despair of an alcoholic. Its members share strength in knowing that we have survived great physical, emotional and spiritual violence. My continuing study of Tae Kwon Do offers me the opportunity to teach other women self-defense and martial arts skills. This is the greatest gift of my study and my sobriety.

In studying self-defense and a martial art with women I have found the strength within myself to face the violence I have known. Through participating in a movement to liberate all women, I am part of an effort to end male violence against women, and establish a society in which women can live in safety and dignity.

When we speak to each other about the violence of alcoholism within the lesbian community, we can begin to relieve the isolation of lesbian alcoholics, which makes us prisoners within society and prisoners within ourselves. Together we can do what we could never do alone. . . .

*Special thanks to Ruth Mahaney for supporting and loving me through the hardest of times; to Cynthia Hales for the gift of life in the martial arts; to Joan Nelson for encouragement to deepen and share my analysis of alcoholism as violence against women.*

## References

1. Flint, Susan, quoted in Schechter, Susan, *Women and Male Violence: The Visions and Struggles of the Battered Women's Movement,* Boston, South End Press, 1982, p. 134.
2. Final Report from the California State Commission on Crime Control and Violence Protection, *Ounces of Prevention: Towards an Understanding of the Causes of Violence,* California Department of General Services, 1983.
3. Alibrandi, Tom, *Young Alcoholics,* Minneapolis, MN, CompCare Publications, 1978, p. 14.
4. Norman, Pat, Lesbian and Gay Health Services for the City of San Francisco. Interview, 9 February, 1983.
5. Balcer, Suzanne, Eighteenth Street Services, San Francisco, CA, Coordinator of Women's Services. Interview, 11 February, 1983.
6. Balcer, ibid.
7. Alibrandi, op cit., p. 13.
8. Sandmaier, Marian, *The Invisible Alcoholics: Women and Alcohol Abuse in America,* New York, McGraw-Hill Book Company, 1980, p. 284.
9. Alibrandi, op cit. p. vi.
10. Balcer, op cit.


**NINA JO SMITH:** I was raised in a small town by gentle and strong oakie and midwestern working people. I have the good fortune to love and be loved by women. As of March 8, 1983 — International Women's Day — I have enjoyed three years free from the pain of using alcohol. I'm grateful to have met the challenge of alcoholism and have great faith that my spirit will continue to embrace life.

In my vision, a clean and sober lesbian community will be healthy — emotionally, physically and spiritually. We will be vibrant with life and compassion, fighting for justice in our lives as passionately as we have fought for life itself. I fully believe this is an attainable vision, for so much more is possible today than I even imagined a few years ago.

# A Way To Fundraise That Works

### by Alana Schilling

I am a member of the Board of Directors for a women's health clinic in San Francisco, the Lyon-Martin Clinic. We have been in operation since 1980 and I have been involved since the clinic's inception. Things are changing a little for us at the clinic, but before we discuss that, perhaps a little history is in order.

The creation of the Lyon-Martin Clinic was inspired by a four-month project that Dr. Patricia Robertson conducted in the fall of 1978. Dr. Robertson was, at the time, chief resident in Obstetrics and Gynecology at a local teaching hospital. She became concerned with the lack of medical research on lesbians and by the apparent high incidence of anti-gay feelings among other physicians. Traditionally, it was felt that lesbians did not use health services available to the general population due to the homophobia of their providers, as well as the lesbians' fears surrounding issues of anonymity, non-biological families and special health issues.

In an effort to study these issues, Dr. Robertson organized a short-term clinic to compare the health risks of lesbians to those of heterosexual women. She wanted to examine the interaction of lesbians with their past health care providers and to determine if an on-going health facility was needed to serve the Bay Area lesbian population.

The response of the local lesbian community (approximately 100,000 women, based on various statistics) to this clinic was overwhelming. Within a month of the clinic's opening, there was a three-week waiting period for appointments, testifying to the need for such a facility.

After a period devoted to fund-raising and staff organization, the Lyon-Martin Clinic opened in February of 1980 in response to the need expressed by the short-term clinic. The permanent clinic was named for Phyllis Lyon and Del Martin, two devoted lesbian organizers who helped us with initial funding. We wanted to provide health service to all women, regardless of sexual orientation or current financial situation. We wanted to be able to provide general medical treatment and to provide health education and nutritional counseling as well as health screening and health care. Since the beginning, we urged our clients to participate actively in decisions regarding their health care and to take responsibility for maintaining their health. As part of this effort, we have a long Medical History form with a wide range of questions pertaining to where lifestyle and health issues meet.

Unlike many clinics, we are not subsidized by government grants. In order to meet our objectives in terms of health care and accessibility, we have had to do a large amount of fundraising to supplement our low client fees. Several times each year, we have fundraisers: sometimes direct mail appeals or major donor solicitation, sometimes dances or raffles. These have all been successful in making more women aware of our facility and in increasing our patient load.

Within this last year, however, our staff and Board of Directors have become increasingly aware of the extremely high incidence of alcoholism and drug abuse in the lesbian community. Our Medical History form has always had a section to determine problems of substance abuse, including alcohol, drugs and cigarette smoking, and our health care providers discussed these issues with our clients. But our attitude towards substance abuse with regard to our fund-raising was coming under increasing scrutiny from inside and outside our organization.

In the past, we have held various fundraising events at local women's bars, such as a spaghetti dinner at one, a Christmas party at another, a dance at another. For raffles, we have asked various women-owned businesses to donate prizes for the raffles and they have generously done so. This past year, we had a fall raffle where we offered as a major prize a case of champagne and wine, again donated by a business in San Francisco.

A woman wrote a letter to Lyon-Martin to question our offering alcoholic beverages as raffle prizes. The letter was brought to a Board meeting and discussion followed, with some women questioning how a progressive feminist women's health clinic could respond better to issues of recovery from substance abuse. Other women questioned ways to fundraise, without that traditional fundraiser, alcohol. The debate continued for some time.

Before our Christmas fundraising event, I ran into a woman I know from work who also was a client at Lyon-Martin. We were discussing the joys and sorrows of the season and I told her about our coming Christmas event for Lyon-Martin and asked if she would be going. She said no. The woman is a recovering alcoholic and mentioned that to me. She said she had seen the advertisements and various flyers all over the women's community and she was concerned that the flyers prominently advertised an alcohol cash bar, with no alternative for those who didn't drink.

She suggested that we make the event alcohol-free, and in the event that we couldn't do that, she suggested we try to provide some alternative to the alcohol bar. She suggested we set up another bar, with non-alcoholic beverages in a different part of the room from the alcohol bar and that we sell juices and mineral waters. She also suggested that we not focus the event on selling alcohol, but on selling beverages and on the dance, not the drinking. If we decided to do that, she said, we should have our advertising say that, so women for whom alcohol was an issue would know the event was accessible to them.

I took her ideas to the Board. While we were not able to implement her suggestions for the winter fundraiser, we did deliberately plan our annual spring "Butch-Femme Soire" with those suggestions in mind.

The Butch-Femme dance was a huge success. We made much more money on the juices and mineral water than we did on the alcohol. We had contacted distributors of mineral water for donations and they made several cases available to us at no charge. The profit we made from the dance helped pay our rent for the next few months.

But the dance was successful in other ways too. For me, personally, it was the first time in a long time that I had been at a dance and not seen anyone lurching about, being drunk. The entire tone of the event was different. Women congregated around the non-alcohol bar and talked and danced. There were no fights, no raised voices, just women dancing and having a good time.

I want to say to others that it is possible to raise funds without alcohol. I am very glad the women who came to Lyon-Martin were able to point out that although we were covering substance abuse fairly well from a medical perspective, we were not serving the community very well from another perspective. I am glad we had a chance to remedy that and am sure that we will continue to do so in the future.

Now that the issue has come up, it has affected me in a personal way also. Though I am not a substance abuser, I have started to attend Al-Anon meetings because I have so many friends who are. I would like to learn all I can about it now, and I think that many other women on the Board and staff are investigating the health problems associated with alcohol abuse and how it affects every aspect of our lives.


**LONNIE SCHILLING:** I work as a word-processing supervisor at the University of California at San Francisco, and am very involved in lesbian and gay organizing in the Bay Area. In addition to my work on the Board at Lyon-Martin, I serve as the vice-president of the UCSF Gay and Lesbian

Caucus. We have just finished sponsoring a successful day-long conference on lesbian and gay health issues, in which there were afternoon-long workshops about substance abuse and recovery.

> If my community were clean and sober, it would be a lot more together. Alcoholism tends to make us have a false strength about ourselves. As lesbian women, we aren't working together on issues that are of importance to all of us. We aren't able to. The alcohol puts space in between us. If the lesbian community were clean and sober we would be able to use our real positive strength to be closer to each other and to be a community of women to each other. We would be able to have a good time by really relating with each other. If there were less alcohol in our community, we would be more aware of our sisters' inner love that would create a strength to help us overcome the issues that face us today: work, children, life and death. We could be there for each other when we really needed each other.

# Killing Us Softly

## by Margot Oliver

**M**any of us as feminists work in refuges or health centres or schools or other jobs where we come into contact with women who appear to us to have problems with drugs, or whose life problems appear to be made worse by their drug use.

Do we just keep quiet or do we say something?

Keeping quiet isn't really a very good alternative, but saying something can be pretty difficult too, even counterproductive, and I think the reason is because confronting someone else about their addiction means you inevitably have to look at your own drug use if you want to be honest with them.

And it's so much easier to be honest and objective about someone else's behaviour — to actually "see" it, than it is your own. . .

You are either (1) a non-user, (2) a controlled user or (3) an addictive user yourself.

If you are a non-user, it should be fairly straightforward: "Look, although I don't drink, it appears to me you've got a problem with the booze. Do *you* think you have?"

What you do from there depends on whether they deny the problem or admit they too are worried about it. If they admit they are worried about it, the best thing you can do is to help them get in touch with a self-help recovery group. Whether they take or refuse the help offered is up to them, but take care, if you find yourself worrying, planning or obsessing about their recovery or lack of it, chances are you may need support too. After all, you're the one "carrying" the problem. . . more on co-addiction later.

If you are a sister-addict, but no longer using, and are recognizing a problem in common, you will be able to talk of your own experiences in getting off — and no doubt be very helpful to the other woman. If you are a sister-addict, about to try giving up, you can support each other — a happy co-incidence.

But when you are a controlled user — problems. In my experience, this is what happens:

The controlled user at heart believes that it is possible for everyone to control their use (after all, "I'm no different than anyone else"), *therefore* it's all a matter of individual desire or will power, *therefore,* there really is no such thing as addiction, or if there is, it's not a problem, or doesn't really matter (or at any rate, not compared to "the important issues"), or is something that happens to people who are always, mysteriously, outside our acquaintance.

Such attitudes lead to the classic "pull yourself together" line, or trying to be tolerant, or, to extracting promises from the woman that she will change...

None of these is the least bit helpful to anyone caught in the grip of addiction.

The two things successful controllers refuse to contemplate is (1) stopping altogether themselves, and (2) that they themselves might be addicted.

This leads to all sorts of weird double messages being given to the woman you're trying to talk to — even though these messages may not be spoken directly in words. Far better indeed if they were!

(1) I think it's o.k. for me to drink/smoke, etc., but not for you. Your life would obviously improve if you weren't out of it all the time. I just like to get pissed occasionally.

If this were actually said in words, at least it would be honest; more often I think it is told in actions, with words saying something else (all the more "reason" for the person to keep using because you're such a hypocrite...) Even if it is spoken in words, I don't think we should be surprised if the other person does not respond and reads it as: this woman is telling me to do as she says, not as she does... pretty poor feminist politics indeed!

(2) I think *you* have a problem with drugs, but I won't talk about my drug use one way or the other...

In other words, the classic victim/expert, us/them politics that radical feminists have sought to avoid.

The above situations are a bit much for a lot of feminists and in my experience they are often resolved in a way that is even more disastrous — by denying that the addicted woman has in fact got an addiction problem at all, often becoming quite literally unable to "see" the addiction. After all, if you can't see someone else's behaviour, you don't have to look too closely at your own: "Yeah sure she drinks (etc), sometimes too much, but then so do I/so does everybody else/it's not really her real problem and you can go on to provide her with the same sort of rationale you provide yourself: need to unwind/just feel like it/go crazy if I don't/had a horrible life/under a lot of stress, etc, etc, etc, etc.

Denying another woman's addiction is potentially fatal to her (denying your own may be potentially fatal to you, but at least that's your responsibility).

There is another related and I think equally disastrous piece of thinking about addiction that I think feminists are particularly susceptible to. I believed for years all the while my drinking and smoking dope were increasing and my life (particularly my emotional life) was getting no less chaotic. It goes something like this: "Social conditions cause addiction because they cause people to be unhappy, oppressed, etc. — therefore to cure addiction we have to change the social conditions. . . "

**Obviously in the long term this is true.**

In the short term, while we're offering "society did it to her/me" rationales, women are **dying,** either the death of the body or the death of the spirit, which is worse, or ruining their health and sanity — the very women we need alive and well to change those very social conditions that are so destructive to our lives.

Obviously, in the short term, users do use more when we are unhappy — breaking up a relationship, lost our jobs, are broke, get kicked out of our houses, feel isolated; and fixing those things, if it is possible, often makes us use less — but the fact remains that there is always something bad about this society and our lives (it's a patriarchal nightmare, let's face it.)

Indeed, let's face it:

**The point for an addict is to learn to face it without the drug —** without the blot-out that ultimately adapts *you* to *it* and certainly does nothing to change anything.

**. . . Social conditions may cause addiction but the only way to cure it is to stop using. . . !!**

It is, in the present state of affairs, still a revolutionary thing to say to a woman (including oneself): Yes, I know that all those things are wrong with your life/head/heart, but did you ever stop to think that they might get better if you stopped using/drinking/smoking dope. . . Do you think you have a problem with drugs?

Are the drugs helping or are they digging the hole you're in even deeper than it is already?

The answer can really only be provided by the person concerned, but what I am trying to say is that there are ways of talking to other women (and ourselves) about drug use that will assist them, rather than maintain them in the denial, deception and illusions that are so much a feature of drug use.

But it does require that first we make the connection between our own drug habits and theirs. It's something many feminists are not prepared to do — and I think there are two main factors in this:

(1) The prevalence of drug use of all kinds amongst feminists, particularly lesbian feminists. Addicts usually seek out a social scene in which our behaviour appears normal, and there's quite enough drug use around in feminist circles to make being "out of it" appear perfectly normal. In fact, you're far more likely to stand out if you *don't* drink/drug, etc.

(2) The degree to which many women are protected from the consequences of their drug use by other women.

Which leads us to the topic of *co-addiction* — a whole issue in itself!

**My lover/friend/sister/mother's an addict — what do I do?**

If you're worried about the drug use of someone you're emotionally involved with, chances are you're already doing a whole stack of things which both help maintain that person in their addiction and — *far more important to you* — are making you as sick emotionally, and possibly physically, as they are with the drug. *Only can you see it!!??*

Co-addiction was first recognized in the 1940's by the American women who formed Al-Anon: "Al-Anon... offers a self-help recovery program for the families and friends of alcoholics, whether or not the alcoholic seeks help or even recognises the existence of a drinking problem..."

Men no long predominate in addiction groups — it's on the up and up with women (isn't equality wonderful) — but women still predominate by far in groups like Al-Anon devoted to the co-addict. Why?

"Co-addiction" itself is a relatively new term: up until fairly recently there was no word to describe this whole syndrome, and I'll use it here till we get a better one. A definition is another matter, but here is one: "A person who assists in maintaining the social, emotional and economic equilibrium of the addict."

For a relationship or household to continue to function with untreated addiction, it is necessary for someone to step in and assume the responsibilities abandoned by the addicted person. The person who "steps in" is the co-addict, and since this lessens the negative consequences of the addict's behaviour, to themselves and others, the result is to *prolong*, not shorten the addiction.

*But more important for you,* the person who pays the price — in buildup of resentment, frustration, depression, guilt, self-hatred — the whole nasty range of negativity — is you.

It is my observation that the way women are expected to be in this society — always taking care of things (particularly men), being motherly, coping, smoothing things over, helping out, taking responsibility for the whole home scene — is so close to the role of the co-addict as to be virtually indistinguishable from it.

When co-alcoholic wives start to recover in Al-Anon, it is often the first time in their lives they have been able to develop any sense of separate identity from their husbands and families — quite a revolutionary experience, needless to say.

For those of us who choose to give our emotional energies to women, we perform the co-addict role for each other — often under the guise of sisterly support. It is a revelation for us to learn we are playing out such a familiar old role in such apparently "new" relationships.

Paradoxical stuff, and what a trap. What I have learnt about my own behaviour as a co-addict is that I play a pretty active role in it. I've come, in fact, to think of myself as an emotional or relationship junkie — as capable of getting hooked on a relationship (particularly with an alcoholic, after all, they need me) — as the addict is of getting hooked on the drug.

"She was addicted to the booze,
I was addicted to her..."

I'm perfectly fine, well, I do o.k. at any rate, when I'm not in this state of emotional addiction — but when I am — head, heart and actions go completely crazy. I am literally "under the influence" — willing to hand over to someone else the responsibility/power to look after my emotional well-being, so they continually have the power to make me feel bad or good (the "hit"...).

Of all the people in the world to give this sort of power to, an addict would have to be the last rational choice... It is similar to the power and responsibility the addict hands over when they are out of it, or can't get it together, which the co-addict is more than willing to assume. At least then *something* will be in control... and there it is, the closed circle of the deadly addict/co-addict relationship.

And all in the name of love, of course.

More and more I have come to view both states as stemming from a fundamental lack of self-love and self-worth. But then, when you live in a woman-hating society, it is pretty difficult to develop a genuine sense of self-love — in fact, you're not supposed to, *that's* what it's all about.

Which is why women are such good candidates for co-addiction *and* addiction.

Which is how oppression works. *They* don't have to get us directly, we will do it ourselves in the end. So much more convenient for them.

I think we can make the mistake of thinking of "oppression" as some abstract notion. We forget — we are *supposed* to forget — that it's literal. Depression kills, drugs kill, the soul if not the body.

I know we are all living under the threat of the crazy boys (and a few girls) who run this world blasting us all to smithereens — but in the meantime, while we're waiting for the Bomb to drop, women are killing themselves with overdoses or living the living death anyway.

Whose hands are behind these private and individual acts of desperation? (And how like the private and individual desperation of the backyard abortions so many women die of each year, unnoticed — privately and individually, of course...)

How many of the rich and respectable citizens of this country fatten off drugs — alcohol, tobacco, pills, junk, dope, pills, pills, pills. They, of course, are not the ones who get their prison sentences for stealing or dealing to maintain their habit, they just get the money.

**W**hat is to be done:

(1) Let's talk about the whole subject of drug use as if it were real, reality happening and as real a personal and political issue as any of the others.
(2) I personally think that abolition and/or government regulation makes things worse (given who is/would be in charge of such things, i.e. more of the same boys of psychotically criminal bent, who are in charge of everything now).
(3) Try being straight — i.e. actually drug-free for a while. See how long you can manage it. You might even get a kick out of it!

    That is, look at your own addictions: "First change yourself..."

    In the end, it *is* yourself who uses or doesn't and it is only yourself who can say **no.** Saying no for me has been very tied up with taking back my Self, and refusing to be a victim anymore.
(4) Find a self-help support group with women who are also trying to get off whatever it is you are trying to kick. For myself, I have found good support from the Al-Anon lesbian group and the women's A.A. meeting. If you can't find an exact group, any group devoted to addiction will possibly help. A.A. and Al-Anon are the most numerous and geographically widespread.

    Try and do it alone if you like, but since emotional isolation was one of my problems, this was not a good idea for me. Also, statistically, your chances are much better if you can find a support group you feel comfortable with...
(5) Join or start a political action group.
(6) And so on! Take it from there!

**MARGOT OLIVER:** I am a white, Australian lesbian, with no children, biologically speaking. Was raised and still live in the urban environment of Sydney. At various times have worked as a teacher of chemistry and physics, as a film-maker and distributor, and as a swimming teacher. Currently finishing work as co-author of *For Love or Money,* a history of women and work in Australia, and as co-producer of a film of the same name, both to be released in the second half of 1983. Feminist politics are fundamental to my life. I grew up in a family affected by alcoholism, a fact of which I was unaware til I confronted my own addiction and co-addiction, a confrontation caused by difficulties in my relationship with a sober alcoholic girlfriend. Alcoholics Anonymous and in particular, Al-Anon, helped open my eyes to what was going on in my life, in the community around me, and in my family of origin.

It seems significant to me that I find it a lot easier to articulate the negative and (in my opinion) still largely unrecognised effects of addiction and co-addiction in the lesbian and feminist communities, than to envision what a world without addiction might be like.

My hope for the future is for a world where the values which were highly regarded and sought after would be: trust; harmony; community, co-operation and sharing with others; tolerance of difference; egalitarianism; honest expression of feelings; love and an awareness of the effects of one's actions on others — and where women and 'the female principle' of creativity and life-giving would be held in highest regard.

In my view, it is the lack of these things in our society — most of the time — and the prevalence of their opposites, that leads large numbers of us to want to deaden or change our feelings through drugs and other addictions. . .

To me, it goes without saying that a society which had high regard for the values I have described would be one in which women were not enslaved by men; where each person felt equally worthwhile and valued; where there was freedom of sexual expression; where each person was enabled to contribute socially useful labour and had the right to a livelihood; where decisions would be made by consensus and conflict would not lead to destruction; where militarism and all its attendant horrors would not exist; where rape and pornography would not exist. There would be no rich and no poor, on either an individual or national basis. It would also be a society which would aim for the minimum disruption of the natural world of which we are a part — and on which we ultimately depend for our survival.

And I think that calling these hopes 'utopian' (implying 'impossible') is part of the patriarchal con to make sure they don't happen. . . .

# PART IV:

# THE WAY FORWARD

# Untitled

### by Cathy Arnold

This kettle of fish
that feathery fire
I busily name
each whim and distraction
mucking about
in channels where
the swell and flame
were born

**CATHY ARNOLD:** 4/29/58. All I ever wanted was more. I've been addicted to immediate gratification for as long as I can remember. Recovery has put my passion into perspective, but not on the back burner. Recovery 4/2/79 and still in progress!

(For Cathy's vision, please see the next story.)

# The Meaning of Rapture

### by Tricia Larkin

January 31, 1983

Dear Gatherers of herstory:
 We are two women who are in the process of recovery from alcoholism — I for five years, she for four. We met nearly five years ago and our lives have been entwined since.
 At that time, I was beginning to come out — as a person, as a woman, as a lesbian. Recovering from the non-living of addiction brought forth feelings I never knew existed. My world expanded with each day of sobriety — which was often equally confusing and exhilarating! The confusion came with the pain of going through emotional puberty in an adult body. The pains of growing up were often worse than the withdrawal from alcohol.
 Initially, I tried coping with this by getting high — only to find that I would return to that non-feeling, non-living existence. What they told me in my self-help program was true: a drug is a drug is a drug and alcohol is the first drug. So, I began bringing my feelings into focus — a little hurt, a little anger, etc. until I was able to finally look at the hidden Tricia. Growing up Catholic gave me a lot of rules, and I learned early to deny in myself that which did not conform to what was expected of me. My alcoholism reinforced this pattern and the walls became larger — hiding who Tricia really was.
 When the time came for me to see and experience my feelings about other women, I was (and am) grateful for my sobriety, for it allowed me to have a gradually unfolding, beautiful experience. Of course there was pain and anger as I fought through the years of blockage and training, but being sober allowed me to hold onto the feeling of rightness (however small) I

started with. Living sober provided me with the tools to have awareness, to accept what was true for me, and to process and grow from that truth. There were many times when I was afraid and stopped in my tracks, willing to settle, but sooner or later, I gained the courage, or someone came into my life — and I began tentatively to move again.

Cathy came into my life at one of those times. The first time I saw her, I felt a connection with her that frightened me. As she was new to recovery, people in our group pushed her towards me because I "was young too and could identify." I watched her come around with a hunger for which I was beginning to learn the name. I kept a distance between us but helped her get to places and meet people who could help her get and stay sober. She would often challenge me and say, "I know you have more sobriety but why are you so stiff with me?"

I knew the answer, but would never say it aloud; instead, I intellectualized around the subject and never really answered her. She knew I wasn't answering her, but she trusted some small feeling in herself that said: stay close. From a safe distance I watched her sober up, struggle through relationships, become responsible for her actions, develop and grow.

One day she started asking about feelings she had which confused her — feelings for other women. I told her to speak to someone older, wiser, more sober. I didn't reveal myself. She continued to explore, experience and own all the parts of herself as I watched from behind my shrinking walls.

Finally, we began to speak to one another and awkwardly probe each other's feelings. Often, I wonder what our friends thought as they watched us sparring through our recovery. I know they smiled a lot; I had a knot in my stomach and couldn't.

One night we were celebrating the anniversary of another friend's fifth year of sobriety. She was a lesbian who was "out." It was beautiful to me to see her being whole and proud. Cathy and I went back to my apartment to talk because of the tension that permeated our time together.

And that night, at the ripe old age of 25, I experienced my first love. I had been involved physically and emotionally before this, but never both at the same time with the same person. While I was drinking and getting high, drugs were a necessary part of the experience. That night, for the first time in my life, I could identify with the word rapture. Everything came together and I glowed from the inside out. Even today I can summon the shivery feeling of our first kiss when the walls crumbled to rubble and the truth was set free.

Cathy and I loved and fought our way through two and a half years, continuing to use the tools of recovery to grow through our experience without using alcohol or drugs. We moved to a large city and met many other women, many lesbians, many recovering alcoholics and addicts who added their strength, hope and experience to ours. Just as in sobriety, health in any area needs support from others; that's why women have been intrinsic to our recovery. There are so many women who have helped us to be here today and to be healthy and whole — I don't even know all their names.

This letter started out because Cathy asked me to write a little bio to go with her poems. Although it seems to be about me for the most part, today I know that it is about her, and each woman who reads another woman's words, sees herself and is glad she is not alone. Cathy and I are no longer together as lovers, but through sobriety, we continue to share our individual growth. And, knowing the importance of other women and connecting with them for our own healthy woman identity, I rejoice in her writing. It is another step towards claiming a part of herself that she has hidden — afraid to expose it, but eager to see if others would say "yes, I know!"

**TRICIA LARKIN:** 8/29/54. Led a quiet, tense life 'till college, when alcohol and drugs helped to overcome a feeling of not being a part of things. I became a part of everything! Since getting clean and sober 3/8/78, I have found things I enjoyed and worked at developing them. Some have worked out, others haven't — so it keeps me busy looking for new goals and continuing to develop old ones.

March 22, 1983

Dear Jean:
We are pooling our resources again — something in sobriety we have come to depend upon. The blending of our spirits always creates a perspective that is more honest, more loving, more possible than any that exists within the range of what we alone can envision.

What has been true for us is that our community, as well as our lesbianism, has been an outgrowth of being clean and sober. The emergence of ourselves as we shared with other women — who were coming out of closets, bars, rooms and destructive relationships — was a process.

Often, with all of us out there reaching and envisioning all over the place, it has looked like the aftermath of a wild round of "Twister." But we believe that the storm of doubts, detours and pain that comes from our involvement with each other is a messy but vital part of the picture.

A clean and sober community must anticipate, encourage and in fact *call for* this evolution and upheaval. The past is filled with judgments, fragmentation and separation from our souls, our value as women, and our ability to express/accept our lesbian identity. Both individually and collectively, as recovering lesbians, we must turn away from the painful isolation and risk to be part of a community in the process of growing. The combined energy and experience is life giving.

# Refrain

## by Cathy Arnold

I replay a portfolio
of growths
to observe
a bobbing sea
of hapless shapeless duffleheads
their impotence
a mimicry
of the sad sweet
sustaining tenor
echoing the depth of my love

I know no salve of permanence
trust no cohesive thread
time yet yields assurance
with this I must be fed

# Sobering Thoughts

## by Alice Aldrich

There is always one point at which you can recall becoming conscious of an action. So it was with me. Imagine, if you can, a woman with a baby face and white hair pacing the floor while drinking beer. The phone rings and it is her long distance lover calling to see how she is. Words are exchanged at first pleasantly, then guardedly. During lulls in the conversation, the woman takes gulps of beer, which fuels her voice. Tension mounts. Finally she is yelling and crying and banging the phone into the wall.

The other occupants of the house — two cats, a dog and a woman — recognize the rage. The cats disappear under beds, the dog leaps through an open window and the roommate runs out the front door. The woman who drinks, hangs up the phone and stumbles through the house. In the last two weeks she has tried to put the phone through the dining room wall, the den wall and the kitchen floor; but the only destruction is the crack in the plastic sliding shower doors. For the first time in years, she wonders if this behavior is "normal".

What can I say to convince you that after years of heavy drinking, numerous blackouts*, many pass outs, frequent memory lapses, suicidal thoughts, constant rage and occasional violence, I did not know there was a problem? At times I suspected a problem existed, but I did not "know" it. At work I would promise to jog that evening; instead I found myself at home with a glass in hand "sipping" my sherry. I swear to you that I never could remember pouring that first drink, nor could I remember pouring the

---

*A "blackout" refers to a period of time, hours to days, that a person can not remember after drinking.

others that inevitably followed. But, I can remember the warm glow of the first swallows, the flush, the relaxation, the safety and sometimes, the beginning numbness. I was home and this was my best friend. It released me from remembering, eclipsed problems and gave an escape from me.

After the scene above, I modified my pattern. Since it seemed impossible not to drink, I would drink with consciousness. Now, when I came home at night I would say, "I hereby choose to drink this poison" and proceed to drink. Rages were confined behind closed doors. I would only get slightly drunk in the early evening, sober up after Walter Cronkite went off the air, and at nine or so would retreat to my bedroom with my bottle (I was too embarrassed to make the frequent trips to the kitchen and was afraid roommates would comment.) I would prop myself up in bed with pillows, take my Valium and drink till I passed out. No one ever noticed.

On the day I admitted the link between my drinking and my actions, I surprised myself by writing in a journal that I had hidden my drinking from employers, family, friends, lovers and, perhaps, myself. "How droll," I thought, "I am to be a typical female alcoholic hiding bottles under the dirty clothes." After years of striving for my own particular uniqueness, this realization of my human commonness stung. The specter of being just one more out-of-control drunk drove me to quit drinking.

The first week wasn't all that bad. I did feel jittery and sleep was difficult without wine and Valium. At times I was irritable, but I did not have any severe physical withdrawal symptoms. This was the longest I had been without drugs or alcohol in five years; in fact there had only been two days during that time without drugs. Because I didn't feel good, yet didn't feel bad, I decided to withhold judgment on this action until later.

I have very few memories of the next several weeks: a sober blackout, so to speak. The "fog" moved in to protect me from the constant blare of reality and wrapped an opaque curtain around my fragile self as I re-entered the world. I lost ten pounds and bags formed under my eyes from too little sleep and too vivid dreams. A fog in the daytime, but I had very clear dreams by night of running down long, unfamiliar hallways and attempts to survive in foreign countries where I did not know the language or customs. At times there were the nightmares of "accidently" picking up the wrong glass only to wake drenched in sweat, not sure if it was real or not. Or, if it predicted the future. During the day, I sat at work, tired and unable to concentrate. Sobering up felt like slow torture, but I was desperate for my life to be different.

After five weeks, exhausted and confused, I attended my first A.A. (Alcoholics Anonymous) meeting. I don't think anyone forgets first steps (like first loves) and my first A.A. meeting stands out. Typically, I arrived late. The meeting was in progress as I slipped silently in and worked at invisibility by pulling my hair over my face and slouching down in the chair (which is difficult on small metal chairs in a brightly lit church basement).

I was scared, terrified to be exact. I do not remember what was said, but I do remember the laughter. In fact, they laughed so much at so little that it irritated me. In remaining true to my own sense of individuality, I vowed that I would never be that silly and I certainly was not going to be brainwashed. I was cautious of replacing the crutch of alcohol with the crutch of A.A. Therefore, it was best to be on guard from the beginning.

I went cautiously and seldom to meetings. In fact, I attended only one meeting a week or every other week. Talking was difficult as my words came out disjointed, my thoughts unclear and all the while, I was blushing furiously. I could not remember what I said, but the words of others struck deep, often agitating me and providing me with materials for hours of pacing thoughts. The specifics were often forgotten but I retained the sense of life and struggle (and even laughter) that these sober lesbians* shared with each other. They said it was hard but not impossible; it was a struggle but with laughter. It was corny, but it worked.

For me sobering up in A.A. is necessary since I do not want to do it alone, but it is, at times, difficult. As a lesbian and a feminist coming into A.A., I was to run into ideas and institutions that I had abandoned ten years previously. Unfortunately, the lesbian feminist community does not always understand alcoholism or how to help. And all too often the alcoholic is ostracized without explanation, and once sober, never quite forgiven. We can be a fairly rigid and judgmental community; no different, I suspect than any other community.

I had chosen to become a part of the lesbian feminist community, had received support for many of my ideas, but had become isolated from other types of people. Joining and staying with A.A., therefore, required some adapting and adopting a philosophy of accepting what I needed and discarding the rest. I was told what to expect before I attended my first meeting but it was still a jolt when everyone stood up at the end of the meeting, linked hands and said the Lord's Prayer. I keep my silence, but I use this as proof positive that I am willing to go to any lengths to sober up.

Finally, a dream. A group of women and I are walking at night on a brightly lit street in a city. Very slowly, I begin to rise off the ground and float in the air above my friends. "I'm flying," I shout down to a bewildered group and float higher and higher. I learn to control the direction and speed of this free-form flight and, emboldened, begin to turn somersaults in midair. I am ecstatic and the dream provides energy for weeks to come.

At the end of my second month of sobriety, Thanksgiving appeared. An ominous time, I feared, since holidays are equated in my mind with depression and drinking. In an effort to avoid the usual celebrations, three of us

---

*Alcoholics Anonymous has many different kinds of groups: straight, mixed gay, women only and lesbian only.

agree to meet at our house in the country for a Thanksgiving retreat. I insist on attending my lesbian A.A. meeting before leaving, to fortify myself against the holiday, but everyone at the meeting seems off center and I am left feeling further unsettled. It is late when we start for the country, so we omit dinner and drive for two hours in a light rain. When we arrive, we find the house cold, dark and dusty from disuse, but we gather our energies to unload the truck, get firewood for the wood stove, and fetch water to drink from the spring. As I begin putting groceries away I am momentarily alone, and as I open the refrigerator, I am confronted with three bottles of very cold, very beautiful beer. I am tired, hungry and lonely as I lean on the door staring at the "solution". No one would ever know. Instead, I slowly close the door and go upstairs to cry myself to sleep. It is clear that I need some other modes of coping.

I did not suddenly embrace all the concepts of A.A. nor learn all the tools of effective living, but I did slowly start to accept things. For the first time, I allowed other alcoholics to help and relieve some of the burdens and I began to open up. Becoming sober is a process which only begins with the not drinking. I put down that last drink and began, in many senses, a new life. Or at least, I began a reclaiming of what was rightfully me.

And things were different. It's not as if I had never done any of these things before, it's just that I had never done them while being consistently sober. There is a difference. Take tea, for example. Tea, like spring water, was for dullards or health nuts (neither of which I aspired to be). Now, I began to enjoy the ceremony of preparing the tea and curling up in my favorite chair to read. And, reading. I not only understood what I read, but I could remember it the next day. And, I was reading something besides Ann Landers and the comics, a sure sign that some of the depression was lifting. And, fruit. Since fruit never went too well with beer, I just never bothered to eat any. I was surprised that I not only like fruit but that I actually craved strawberries, apples and pears. But there were things I had not yet tried while sober — like running, or dancing, or sex. This worried me.

Spring came and I celebrated nine months of sobriety. I had become a regular at several A.A. meetings a week, had a sponsor (a person who agrees to help guide the newcomer through the perplexities of sobriety and/or A.A.) and, in general, had worked very hard. I began to wonder, however, if nine months was long enough to be cured from my disease and I began to compare my experiences with others in A.A. There were many differences. I had never been jailed, hospitalized, detoxed or fired from a job.

In fact, on the surface, my life had been in pretty good shape when I quit drinking. Perhaps, I could do controlled drinking. This thought hit hard one very hot, humid night. It was midnight, the air conditioner was broken and I was depressed. Only a beer would help. I ransacked the kitchen, and finding nothing to drink, went to bed feeling dejected and deprived. For the next week, I badgered my A.A. friends with all my arguments of why I, unlike other alcoholics, could do "some" drinking. After all, maybe I had made a mistake and I wasn't really an alcoholic. No one was impressed and no one believed it. However, one of their arguments did cause me some concern: "If you are not an alcoholic, why are you so concerned about drinking?" I did not have an answer. I took Anatbuse* to buy myself time.

Spring passed into summer and I slowly began to accept fully that I, too, was an alcoholic. Full acceptance is never a single cataclysmic event, although at times I wished for the lightening bolt or burning bush routine. But with acceptance, there is hope. Now hope is a funny thing. Without it, one must opt for death and must only decide on a slow or fast form. My mother, being creative, chose both routes; for years she drank herself into a stupor and at the age of 50 took a gun and shot herself in the heart for one last grand and angry gesture. For years I thought this to be my legacy. Mind you, I never sat down and said "I will become an alcoholic and commit suicide just like Mommy did," but by the time I was 16, I was an abuser of alcohol and by 35, wished constantly for death. And now I was at 36 with the coping skills of an early adolescent having to decide if, and how, to live.

I chose living and once that decision was made, my mind and body woke up. Colors became bright, smells were sharp, sounds were everywhere, and textures emerged. And my sexuality resurfaced. At the end of the first year, I fell head long into lust and love. I was very attracted to a woman, but scared since I seldom had been sexual without alcohol and/or drugs in the past (a fact previous lovers had always noted and I hotly denied). I didn't know what to do with these feelings, and to make things worse, sexual feelings are rarely acknowledged in A.A. groups. Considering that A.A. was founded in the 1930's by white middle class men, this makes sense, but for a lesbian in 1982, it posed problems. Reluctant to talk to non-A.A. lesbians for fear of their lack of understanding or laughter, and unable to go to A.A., I muddled through on my own.

I didn't know how to initiate, felt uncertain about my body being able to respond and was downright skeptical about getting relaxed enough without drugs to enjoy sex, let alone consider an orgasm. How was I going to face all of these problems without a drink? Overriding these fears was a very deep and compelling attraction and since it was clear that she was not going to initiate, I was forced to. As we sat in her car in front of my house, I leaned over and kissed her full and long. I thought I might die. We spent an incredible night touching and holding which ended in a very nice

---

*Antabuse is a medication prescripted for alcoholics as a "deterrent." If you drink after taking Antabuse, you end up with a pounding headache, flushing, nausea, vomiting and other physical discomforts.

*156*

lovemaking. It wasn't orgasmic, but it definitely felt good and I began to think life was worth loving, at least, if not living. The softer parts of me emerged.

The hope kept getting stronger that there was something for me besides alcoholism and suicide. I took many risks, sometimes lost, but always grew. As the second spring approached, my lovership ended calmly out of a mutual decision and I learned to cope with pain and anger. I learned to cry and laugh and through these, to release the layers of insecurities and fears that I drank to numb. I began to venture out alone and discovered the difference between aloneness and loneliness and learned to deal with each. Maybe the best part is simply that I learned to like who I am.

During this time, I made a decision not to "confess" my alcoholism to the world in general or, specifically, to my co-workers. This left me unprotected in many social situations where drinking was expected. One afternoon I joined a birthday celebration with my co-workers at an expensive restaurant and everyone except myself ordered a drink. There was no problem until one of the women insisted I take a taste of her saki. I declined; she offered, again. This ritual of urging, with my declining, was repeated three times. Finally, out of fury and frustration, I picked up the damned saki cup and took only enough to wet my tongue and at that, only the very tip of my tongue.

Two days later, I recounted the incident to two of my closest A.A. friends and was met with intense reactions. One woman was concerned that I was setting myself up for a "slip"* and advised that I examine my behavior. The other friend had a delayed reaction that surfaced a day later when she angrily confronted me: "What the fuck do you think you are doing playing with alcohol?"

I was confused and angry. I had no intention or desire to get drunk, but had felt trapped by a social situation and did not know what to do. I had taken it to A.A. for clarification and felt that attack unwarranted. We screamed at each other and intense feelings held at bay for a year of sobriety surfaced. I imagined smashing her to bits; anything to get her to accept my point of view. We managed to calm down, but damage had been done to the relationship by the anger and mistrust. Meanwhile, I remained confused over the incident of the "sip" and slowly came to realize that Alcoholics Anonymous may not have all the answers.

Two weeks later, I brought up the incident to another group of friends to obtain their point of view. Like the A.A. women, they were angry, only this time at my co-worker for her display of covert hostility. With this additional input, the situation came together for me. Contrary to the A.A. fears,

---

*A slip occurs when a sober alcoholic goes back out to drink.

*157*

I was not going to get drunk from one sip and I felt resentment at such a fragile view of sobriety. However, it was clear I needed better coping skills for social situations.

The incident of the "sip" also brought out in the open my battle with anger and there would be others to follow. Once sober, I no longer needed to act out my internal violence and, in fact, I put a lid on *all* anger. It was just not to be trusted. I had been raised in a home where anger was decreed non-existent by my father; instead, it seeped out as sarcasm, withdrawal or alcoholism. As my drinking accelerated so did my anger until it became my predominant emotion.

Anger was fear, loneliness and insecurity. Having been so explosive with my anger while drinking, I was afraid to feel or deal with any form of it while sober. It did not go away and the lid blew at work after a year and a half of control. The initial trigger was actually from the night before when I faced the fear of losing a close friend. The next day, a male co-worker and I started trading digs as we had in the past, but this time, the digging went deep, fast and we lost control. We had worked together for a year, actively disliking and distrusting each other. We were just too similar; both alcoholic (he still drank), both insecure, and both with the same set to our shoulders signaling defiance or defeat. The fight erupted in the hallway but ended in my office, as we screamed profanities and slurs at each other. Staff and faculty from two other departments in the college peeked in to see what was happening and fortunately the students were gone for the day. As the insults peaked, a secretary interposed her body between the two of us to prevent him from hitting me with his fist. It was an intense fight but I did not even have the sense to feel fear, just more anger.

Although the Director considered it, neither one of us was fired, but we were both advised to seek counseling. By this time, I had become frightened by my anger and the inappropriateness of its expression. Through a short time in therapy, I realized anger remained my safe emotion. In this case, the anger was a mask for the fear stimulated by the similarities between this drunk co-worker and my sober self. It was the two halves of my personality in a quarrel over which was to be and the fears that I could not leave my alcoholic persona behind.

Since then, I have been able to get to the point where I look for fears when I feel anger. As I feel better about myself and more sure of who and what I am, I rely less on anger. Other emotions can and do get expressed.

I was still actively involved in Alcoholics Anonymous, but was feeling dissatisfactions. Since the incident with the "sip", I was aware that any deviation from the A.A. program could be viewed as a prelude to getting drunk. This stems, in part, from a lack of understanding of why the program is so successful for so many people. It does work.

However, the structure, as outlined in the 1930's, is not comfortable for all people and the organization has a strong reluctance to change. I was angry that there was pressure, although subtle, not to proclaim lesbianism in straight groups nor to proclaim feminism too strongly in any group. There just did not seem to be any place where I could fully be myself: alcoholic, lesbian, feminist and sometimes, activist. I could not have sobered up and stayed sober without the support of A.A., but I was beginning to need and want more both from A.A., and the lesbian feminist community.

Accepting my alcoholism was a hard-won battle, but accepting the reactions of the lesbian feminist community was another. For months I was not able to admit my discomfort over the drinking patterns in this community. My need to be liked eclipsed feelings that surfaced when women drank around me, but especially when they drank heavily at parties. This is a potent issue in a community that drinks heavily.

After several months of sobriety, I attended a party. It started off well-spaced through the house and in the yard. The food was good, the women friendly and the talk interesting and clear. As night approached, we all moved into the house, crammed into several rooms. I was aware people were drinking, but I was very involved in a good conversation so the effect was diluted. Slowly I became aware that I was having trouble concentrating on our discussion.

The room had become too hot, too noisy and too crowded. The center of attention was a drunk woman repeatedly throwing a pack of cigarettes on the floor while proclaiming something nonsensical. It was funny once, but the seventh time was boring. However, everyone participated and encouraged her each time by their laughter. I abruptly left the party.

It wasn't until months later that I realized how much I disliked that atmosphere and behavior. Some of these women were my friends and what would I do if I could not stand to be around them? They all seemed willing to accept alcoholic behavior as the norm and I wondered if there would be acceptance for those of us who chose not to drink.

Slowly, a group of non-drinkers emerged. Some were women who had been in trouble with alcohol; others simply chose not to drink (a fact that still astounds me). I have been surprised to discover how relaxed I feel at chemical-free parties. At drinking events there is always a background layer of tension to monitor your glass so you don't accidentally imbibe someone else's alcoholic drink. Being sober also means that I am acutely aware of the drinkers whether they are slightly tipsy, throwing up, falling off porch rails, picking fights, or slowly passing out. It is not always attractive.

At a non-drinking party, women begin to talk, dance and laugh from the moment they arrive rather than waiting for their chemical of choice to take effect. I enjoyed getting to know sober women, having long talks, dancing slow, sexy dances and going home being able to remember who they were and what was said. There are enough women who enjoy chemical-free space that I no longer seek out those who depend on drugs. I have not been disappointed.

"So," you ask, "where is this woman now?" Imagine, if you can, a small woman with a baby face and white hair sitting at a typewriter carefully telling her story. She pauses to think and stretches to relieve the tension in her back from typing. She looks content. Nearby, her cat sleeps under the desk lamp to be ready for pets. Her roommate walks through the room and they talk for a moment, obviously at ease and liking each other. "Dull and corny," I hear you say? Maybe true, but for the woman who no longer drinks, it is her choice for living.

**ALICE ALDRICH:** is a health care worker presently ensconced in Baltimore, MD with her loyal and trusting cat, Fatso. She enjoys good women, good food, good conversation and good sex. She is looking for other sober dykes to work with.

If my community were clean and sober it would look like a brilliant piece of crystal: sharp, clear and dazzling.

# Confessions Of A Not-So-Ex-Alcoholic

## by Red Arobateau

In the fall of 1976, our Oakland M.C.C. church went up to Sacramento for a conference. The M.C.C. is the Metropolitan Community Church, a national Christian church made up of lesbians and gay men. At the conference I ran into a woman I'd known from the gay bars in San Francisco six years previous — another dyke like myself. I never fail to marvel how God sends certain people into our lives at certain times. S. told me she was an Alcoholic, and gave me a few pointers on the subject. She had been dry for six months and going to one A.A. meeting per day. First off, S. said, "There's no such thing as an ex-alcoholic. Don't kid yourself. If you're truly an alcoholic, you're always one. You just have to quit, period."

Sheepishly, I pulled a bottle of wine I'd brought to the conference with me, out of my tote bag. It was empty. I had just gone brazenly into the kitchen of the church & poured myself a drink in a punch glass when I thought nobody was looking. Now, I held the empty bottle up to her. S. just looked at it, and smiled a short dry smile that showed it wasn't funny.

We sat among the rest of the sisters & brothers who nibbled hors d'oeuvres & drank punch before the main dinner; which was to be roast beef, fruit salad & broccoli & hot rolls with butter.

Two important things she told me. Alcoholism don't get better, it gets worse. And my nine years of being dry — not drinking — had not cured me. No. They were just nine years on the wagon, not touching a drop. If I was to start drinking now, it would be stepping right back into hell.

I guess I had to find out the hard way.

S. took her first Communion with me. I was coming around the aisle to line up to approach God's table, & receive the healing blood and body of

Christ, when, out of the crowd S. popped up and grabs my arm — she was nervous and wanted somebody to go up with her. Praise God!

Ironic how God brought us together again in the Communion line. Later that evening, after a delicious dinner, S. told me she'd send me every pamphlet on A.A. she could get her hands on. Meanwhile, I decided, sort of, maybe I would quit drinking. Ten days later, the package arrived, but that week, after drying up since the conference, I took my first drink anyway.

I didn't hear her then, but now I hear her. "There's no such thing as a cured alcoholic." The only cure is, no alcohol.

---

A little herstory about my problem, which is not a rare one: I had last sworn off drinking back in my hometown Chicago, at age 23. I had remained on the wagon all nine years. No exceptions. I had given up once before that, in New York City, at age 19.

Those years passed, in which my compulsive nature fitted nicely into the framework of mucho cups of coffee, and Coca-Colas. My running-in-the-street in those days was fed by caffeine and sugar. Oh yes, I love to run the streets, to dig on people, to groove on places. But now, more sanely. My diet started to get a little bettter too. Yoghurt, health foods with no preservatives. Wheat germ. Vitamins.

I sustained myself on welfare; living in one hotel room, or crashing with friends.

---

In some ways, giving up alcohol for the second period in my life, (and for the 4th, 5th or 10th time, I can't remember) was more difficult then when I was young. When I was 19, I knew it was stopping me. That alcohol was my cover-up for shyness — I'd get drunk instead of looking for a job. I knew I was its slave, period.

This time, it was insidious — not so much in my body, the craving, but more in my head. I'd lost that drive to do or die — that I'd had as a teen. For one thing, many of those books of my life's ambition were piled on my shelf, written, bound in their different-colored jackets. Distributed and read by my friends. As a teen I'd known I'd never write those books as long as I hit the bottle. Dousing the creative flame in a drunk. Strung-out on alcohol instead of stringing words together with a pen. Now that work, much of it, was behind me. I'd dissolved the mystery of what it means to be an artist for myself. I'd learned how to write. No, it was nothing mystical, just work.

Work. Do it. Writing was less glamour, and just a job. Rewarding yes, but still a job. I had to sit at my desk, alone for as many hours per day as I needed to produce.

But now that was mostly done and I was drinking out of boredom. Success in real estate, plus investments from some money left by my dad when he died, took away the daily desperate need to work a job. It was easier to give in.

Also, in this last year off the wagon, I had made a startling discovery — now I could write and drink at the same time! Again more insidious. In fact, alcohol seemed to help me concentrate — for instead of tugging at the bit like a work horse, wanting to get up from my desk and fool around, go play with my dogs, or eat, or sleep; instead, liquor kept me "fed." "Happy." Sitting right there working — but getting drunk too.

This was a far different reaction from the younger woman, who doused her creative flame in liquor. Who used drink as an excuse to abandon a job and run the streets. I had to realize, yes, I probably *can* drink and write — do my life's work, but, I'm simply killing myself also. Period. I have to face the music. Red can't drink one glass of wine, not one half glass, not take even one teaspoon of alcohol!

Oh how I'd like to damn the people who know so much! Who've told me in many a bar, that the beer they were drinking is healthier for the human body than the Coca-Cola I sat there sipping. Yes, Coca-Cola and coffee are poison to the system, but poison is better for the body than a beer is to me, an alcoholic — because it's not addictive. And that's the thing. That one beer is part of the long process of addiction.

Anyway, after being on the wagon, almost exactly nine years, last October, I started back on liquor.

I figured one little nip — half a glass or so of wine a day wouldn't hurt me! — in fact, it was like a medicine!

Other people got to enjoy themselves, didn't they?

It all started insidiously enough. Months before I actually went out and bought a bottle of liquor, a certain item on the medicine shelf in my bathroom had begun to pave the way back to hell. I have an allergy to animal fur, and I have three dogs who stay outside. And, in the foggy sea air of Pacifica where I lived at the time (a real estate investment) many nights found me wheezing. The Vicks Company had put in my mailbox some time before a product called Nyquil. For want of anything else, I took it. It seemed to relieve my breathing. But also, one day I noticed by reading the label that I was no stranger to one of the ingredients. The fact was, this medicine was 25% alcohol! Soon, in a matter of months, I associated my medicine with relief. Had a swig for all purposes: tiredness, headache, de-depression, menstrual cramps. A swallow before I went to sleep — and inevitably I'd get up and have another swig or two. A drink of this thick green liquid when I got up in the morning. Whatever — soon, closer and closer drew my association of medicine & alcohol and relief. Every night I had a swig.

Soon, my mental association of medicine, alcohol and relief had become complete.

This may seem like a joke to many. I can see folks rolling on the floor in laughter. Wow! One swig of medicine led to the path of destruction! But this is a testimony of truth.

Now laugh on, friends, for the truth is stranger and funnier then fiction. (That's why I am strictly a reporter of life, and not an inventor of tales — my imagination could never compete with the facts!) Yes, it was only one brief step from this 'medicine' to Manischewitz wine. Somehow, with its kosher labeling, and Hebrew script, it gave the impression of religious wine. I associated this liquor, then, not with alcohol and getting drunk, but with a religion. Something to ease you after a hard day's work. And indeed, I'd been doing my work. Working my butt off for the past four years overtime at the office, and the past fifteen at my typewriter. Maybe that was another part of my problem too. And this was a blessed wine. Logically, it must be safe.

Coming from a non-drinking family of black on my mother's side, and Latin American on my father's, I remember my grandmother always had a bottle of Manischewitz wine in the refrigerator — but in her case it was the same one, lasted maybe six months. So this bonafied it for me.

But from here, it was one month's step to drinking dry red wine, that had always been my thing, instead of sweet. Red wine and beer, which had been my nemesis.

In that year, I went from taking two or three swallows of wine (which at first gave me a warm rush, & made me high) up to maybe five drinks a night. Some days, even weeks, I didn't drink at all. I was on a teeter-totter. Gone was the memory of my addiction. Forgotten was the oppressive burden I'd struggled for years to throw off in times past. But soon, ultimately, the ugly cobra reared its head again. Fangs & red eyes glaring back at me. It was evident after a year, my life was becoming re-centered. I was just looking forward to the first drink of the day, get set to get drunk all over again.

So, for a solid year, I drank. Wine. Now, ironic again, God led me to the place of working a temporary job — and it was right in the middle of skid row. Sixth Street. God set me down right into a stage set of derelicts. A few city blocks, in which destruction of mind & body was unveiled. To a more intelligent person, fear again or warning might have sobered them up. But, mornings, as I got off the four a.m. shift as cook, I couldn't wait to drive home to have a glass of wine and freedom off the slave job — as I walked across streets lined with derelict people.

I saw down there, in the heart of skid row, the drowned vessels — people shipwrecked. They lay capsized, up and down the streets. Victims of that disease — Alcoholism. When I walked on by, nights, I saw the Alkies along desolation row: their ruined clothes, bloated skin, hair matted. A Mexican in a phone booth, passed out, a streak of piss down his leg where he'd let-go his bladder, slumped in a pool of urine — with a half-empty wine bottle beside him. I see the irony. This person, though in poverty, was not in starvation for alcohol, but in excess. More than he could drink, in that half-full bottle on the ground. A sort of reverse starvation.

Twisted like a pretzel, laying on a window ledge of the City Hall, was a white man, his face cut open in a red gash. Hairy white legs that haven't seen the light of day for 13 years, showing, one shoe off. Alcohol is no respecter of persons. Race, class or creed. But society traps us in different ways. Few female Alkies in the street — all in one room somewhere in subterfuge. Grimly the scene impressed itself upon me night after night.

A realization dawned on my feeble mind: that there is infinitely more to drink out there than a person can ever drink.

Let me explain. All my life I haven't had enough love, enough companionship, enough peace of mind. For many years, I couldn't afford enough to eat; didn't have enough money to spend. For example, walking 20 blocks to a gay bar and 20 blocks home in the dead of night, in the cold wind, to save 25¢ in busfare to shoot a game of pool! Things like that. I could easily, when invited to a party, or a church buffet (I was an atheist in those days, but believe me, I'd be the first through the church doors to get to that food! Praise God!) — I could easily just eat and eat. Gorge myself. Three heaping platefuls and wait around for more and I'm only 5'2". Plus, take food home with me, all tucked in my pockets in napkins 'n thangs. When around other sisters; and friends, I'd party-harty! Dance my ass off! My spirits soared — extra high, because, an artist must spend so much time in isolation. In a factory gig you're interacting with others. I was like a bird let out its cage & as a gay person, cut off from family ties by my homosexuality. I mean, I could just gobble-up good things! So, to me, consumption had only one limit — when the good things ran out. When the party was over, when my coins were spent, then, I'd starve.

Now I was 32 & had money. A fact slugged me — on every corner is a liquor store. Gallons and gallons of booze! I was over 21, I could go in and buy at any time! And it hit me, there's more out there than I could ever drink. You can drown in a sea of it.

Now, my drinking certainly wasn't like the days of my youth. Compared to those old wild days, I was much more controlled this time. But the tip-off was my great love for the wine. The process had to be examined also. Fact is, I'd started out a year ago saying I'd have a few sips out of a tiny glass — which greatly affected me — and which grew swiftly to more and more.

Seven glasses of wine or beer at a weekend party. Staying out with friends. That was my tip-off. Do I need it to get worse before I quit? And give up that first drink forever — and put that first drink in the hands of God?

---

After seeing S. I decided I better quit. No more alcohol. For about the sixth time that year, I poured out all my bottles, and half-drunk bottles of wine. That itching in my throat. That unquenchable thirst. That bottomless cup.

Giving up liquor was different from before. After nearly ten days of not drinking, the desire was still hanging on. It was because I hadn't fully made up my mind. In the old days, after four days without a drink, my desire for alcohol had left. — Because I positively knew I had to quit! But today, older and tireder; seeing so many of my friends — church folks — drink two drinks, just relaxing, then stop, without getting loaded. Have a beer with lunch, a cocktail at dinner. My desire to enjoy my life for a change, instead of work, work, work and little pleasure — and alcohol is such an easy pleasure to get a hold of. You can buy it — this coupled with realization that a lover, a happy home may never come to me. I just wanted to feed myself joy I was missing.

About two weeks dry, after my talk with S: after receiving the A.A. pamphlets she sent me, I was relaxing in bed, the Bible by my pillow. I had closed my eyes, and suddenly, I had a vision before I realized it. It was of glasses. Empty drinking glasses, as many as there are days — into infinity. A calendar, with a glass sitting on each number of a day. The glasses were all empty. Clear, sparkling, and, in the bottom of each one was a penny — some kind of copper coin. Oh wow! God had told me — there is a reward for me, each day of my life that I don't take one single drop of alcohol!

Our Creator loves us. We are God's children. I don't think God wants us to be addicted to anything. Not to love — an idol, or drugs, or money, or anything. "Put no other Gods before me." This is definitely for our own protection, not God's, who is Almighty.

I realized it isn't a matter of me consuming as much as possible, while it was available — which is compulsion, because now I have money. I can buy all the alcohol I want and then some. Ugh!

The matter is, to take away my desire — to separate me from my desire for it.

The color of my skin reminded me I had too many strikes against me already. White looking, but mixed-race black. Female, and homosexual — to take on the disease, Alcoholism, would be a heavy addition.

I thought "I have to give it up permanently." My father hadn't taken a drink in his life — surrounded by brutality of drugs & drink among the third-world people in the ghetto, his fear was wise. Soon I was thinking "His teetotaling was good enough for him, it's good enough for me." That's another thing that helped me quit.

About this time, I'd begun to realize there was this higher, vaster intelligence out there — God, and it was really blowing my mind.

I mean, I was beginning to see God working in my life — the proof, after praying blindly to something I couldn't see or feel, for nearly a year.

I began to see this great and loving intelligence, this God, moving in my life. This great, great heart. I *felt* the Holy Presence. A God who really did walk and talk with Her/His people.

I turned my problem over to God: please help me stop Jesus. For good. Forever.

This dull emptiness inside me was now being filled, slowly by a mighty & gentle power. A mighty God, a Holy God. Life was easier in the simplicity of Christ.

The years dry had been a sort of race. To achieve what I could, before I might die. I had not thought about alcohol — not once. Even though the majority of my nights were spent in some gay bar in some city, surrounded by drinking women, as long as *I* wasn't drinking, I didn't miss it. It's not the sight of others drinking when I'm dry; it is the close familiarity of just having had a drink yesterday that makes me want more. I'd order a cup of coffee, or a Coke, and get high off the sugar rush. Maybe pop an aspirin if I felt chilly or had a headache. It kept me sailing for hours.

Coffee. Drinking the Java heavily. Some liquid to sip; the years had been a race to get-over. To make it — my way — in a most unusual fashion, on welfare, with no thought of money, just my ambition to write. To reproduce stories of life. To learn how to make sentences and paragraphs reveal beauty in people. To record what I saw.

It was a race against death. To make something beautiful before I died. And, being in the streets, taking a risk nightly, just to be a lesbian, death was imminent most of the time! To leave some works behind me.

Today, I'm more content. Now, I realize, I have to fill this space in me, by learning how to live.

I'd been in enough rap groups to know that I must learn how to live — that my Alcoholism, my compulsive nature, my need for instant gratification, was tied up in my life, in me not knowing how to get enjoyment.

God began to work in my life. I tuned, accidently to some radio programs. In one, an Alcoholic talked about his life & lies he used to tell himself during his struggle. Then another radio talk show came on, about eating six small meals a day, and thus keeping your blood sugar consistent. Cut down on all sugar, including liquor. You see, the human brain takes only one kind of nourishment — that is glucose — sugar produced by the body as food is burned up. If this level drops, loss of consciousness, irritability, eventually even insanity can occur. Such simple things! To eat right!

Slowly, after three decades on earth, I began to realize something very simple — years of city living, cut off from the soil, in a concrete and neon jungle — that, we are what we eat. You eat plastic plus cardboard and chase it down with drugs & liquor, and that's what you become. Starved. A haywire machine.

Thanks to the urging of those 'health food nuts', I began to see how very much my diet had to do with my state of mind.

Eating better, more peace of mind; much of my craving disappeared. But, most of all, I was not stringing it out, tempting myself, by taking that one glass per day. Not even a *whiff* of a drink. It boiled down to it like crystals in a spoon — **death.**

All my old ways had to change. I started by substituting some of my yens, by just simply eating. Steak and eggs. Ice cold milk. Fruits. Cheese and spinach. Greens with vinegar. Broccoli with butter and garlic. Six small meals a day. Roast beef. Chicken legs with hot sauce. Now I had energy. It was easier to lift my weights, do my Karate. I worked in my garden an hour a day.

It's done now. I've learned my lesson thoroughly. No avenue is left to explore — no exit. No excuse for one drink. Not even one. Not even "just a sip" as many a "friend" will coax at a party — "Ah c'mon one sip won't hurt you": they are a lying dog & I'm sorely tempted to hope they rot in their ignorance! — One sip *can* kill.

Beyond my love of talking about myself, or my love of writing, in this ms.,there is also desire for people to know there are others like them who can't have one drink. Who can't have that luxury. Who must always watch, and stay away from any alcohol. People who can't relax and flow with "social drinking" but who must be on guard, and forever raid the milk in the refrigerator, or the coffee pot, instead.

"The freedom God gives us. The freedom just to be." I like that line. Here is another one from our church: "The message of Jesus Christ is a Gospel of liberation. Through freedom in Christ, each person attains their full potential and personhood."

I remember the vision again — of infinity of sparkling glasses. Empty glasses — with a reward in the bottom of each. Our gentle, kind, & understanding Creator does not chain us with chains, but gives us freedom of choice. And through this freedom God has let me prove it to myself. Now, when I needed strength, I began to pray, "Jesus just take this drinking away from me! I can't stand it! It's killing me! Help me!" Now, God is my refuge, my fortress, and I come back running, placing my problems in Her/His Almighty hands.

Now, I don't want to count the days since my last drink. I just want to say — it's over.

**RED AROBATEAU:** has been a street lesbian for 25 years. Age 39, fallen from the bourgeoisie; retaining many of its ideals. A mongrel of mixed-race heritage. A butch. Centered in the female Christ and God the Mother.

Mine is the lesbian ghetto which circulates in drinking establishments, streets, group meetings and parties. If this ghetto were clean and sober and less self-deluded, it would have more energy to take positive actions to help itself, through services, institutions and sensitivities; and make much more fun. Its sisters would be freed for higher emotions and direct their efforts towards their greater consciousness. I mean we could learn to put our arms around each other and really *hear* one another. Be aware of our personal hurts and learn how to get what we need, and how to uplift others. We'd be a holistic people. Instead of blocking emotions, we'd *feel*. That is the most important thing: we'd allow ourselves to *feel* and our ghetto would not be so cold. Not so sharp points of icebergs, not living death. The cut throat, the stab to the heart which we now endure. As freer women, we would really discover what love is, so instead of lonely sisters cut off from each other sitting up at a bar all night, pretending their lives are o.k. when it's a lie; we could experience a genuine healing greater than the bottle, greater than the pill, far greater than the fear.

# Womanrest: Sometimes In Sobriety You Have To Make Big Changes

## A conversation with Karen Voltz

Karen Voltz, 37, now lives "out in the boonies" in the northern Wisconsin woods, where she runs a chemical-free retreat for women, called Womanrest. She sent me a tape of her thoughts about recovery during the winter of 1982/83. I was interested in this woman who had grown up and lived in Milwaukee, the city of beer, who had started and run Sistermoon Feminist bookstore, who had eventually burnt out and gotten sober. I was interested in how we continue to make contributions to the movement after we burn out and I was particularly interested in the story of a hard-driving activist woman who finally sobered up. I wrote her back, asked her questions, wanted to know more about her new life and the beautiful lake she had said was right outside Womanrest's front door. Shortly thereafter, I got another tape in answer and it began to feel as though we were having a conversation, two women who had never met, who could finally now meet in earnest, now that we were both sober. This then is a story I shaped from her tapes to me. At one point during the tape, she said: "This is how I would like to write this, just as though I were talking to you."

---

I stopped drinking two or three years ago... I'm not even sure how long it's been. And often times I get aggravated at myself because I can't remember things and I laugh about being senile and of course you can't be senile and be 37 years old. I've been "being senile" for a long time and I really think my memory loss is related to my drinking.

I grew up in an alcoholic home. All I can remember is loud yelling and violent fights and my father's hangovers. He was an electrician and a milkman and later he ran a bar. I think my mother was a battered woman and she left my father (though she wouldn't divorce him because of her good Catholic background). We ran away from him when I was seven years old. My later relationship with my mother wasn't good and she put me in a detention home my last year in high school because I had been picked up for drinking.

When I got out of the detention center, I was eighteen and I did prostitution for about a year, hanging around in taverns and making pick-ups. When I was nineteen, I met my husband and we got married. We were married for nine years. I was a battered wife. All the violence and abuse happened around alcohol. He was programmed to be the macho man and he was frustrated with his work in a factory, even though he made a lot of money. He was programmed at an early age that women can be used as scapegoats and that alcohol can be used, and he didn't have an outlet for his stress: I became the outlet for his stress, me and alcohol. We do not teach men how to be nurturing, we do not teach men who are growing up in a violent working class background how to release their tension in effective ways and we do not teach them how to deal with alcohol. And as a result we have a lot of fucked-up people in this society. I am not excusing his violence towards me, just saying where it came from.

I started drinking when I was in eighth grade and did hard liquor and beer and drank heavily until whenever I stopped two or three years ago. I'm not sure how or why I got sober, but I think it had to do with loving myself, taking control of my life and doing something to stop the destructiveness in my life. For ten years, my entire life was the movement, the lesbian movement and the feminist movement, running Sistermoon Feminist Bookstore in Milwaukee, Wisconsin and organizing groups and fundraisers and concerts. I was just living in a whirlwind. Before that, I was married and I drank also, but the drinking didn't stop in the movement.

Now, mostly, I'm real happy with my sobriety. It's changed a lot of who I am, how I relate to people, what I do in my free time, who I socialize with, how I relate to my lover of eight years, how I relate to my daughter, in so many ways I am different because I have stopped drinking.

Now, it's is a whole different way of being. And I'm not sure what happened, where the click was when I started deciding to love myself and take care of myself, that I was a valuable person and that the alcohol wasn't good for me. It was hurting me and it was hurting the woman I love and it was hurting my relationships with friends. I started cutting down and thinking about it. Then I went to a workshop for chemical dependency on Wisconsin womyn's land. It was a real good weekend for me, hearing other women who had been drug addicts and alcoholics and how their lives had changed and how far they had come. I didn't drink anymore after that. I stopped.

*171*

That weekend I made the conscious decision: no, I'm not going to slow down and I'm not going to watch it; I've got to stop; I'm an alcoholic. That was several years ago.

It wasn't just that weekend that gave me the strength and the role models to stop drinking. I'm not sure when or where the process started. It seems like a lifetime ago. But I think it probably started with feminism and that helped me to begin to start to love myself.

Now, people can't come to my house and drink. People can't come to my house and be stoned. I don't want to go anywhere where there's drinking and people being stoned. I feel like we are on different levels. I think it's important women have the experience of being sober and not being high together but still having a good time, eating and drinking and playing together and being sober. You don't have to have three bottles of wine with dinner to have a good time.

So people know when they are around me, whether it's a potluck or whatever, that drinking is not something that they do. And so they don't do it. And the ones who do, aren't my friends anymore. A lot of my relationships were drinking relationships and those women I don't see anymore. I want to talk with someone who's sober, who's with me all the way.

When I go out with my daughter now, we have fun. It's not like going to dinner with Mom and Mom's tired or Mom's exhausted or Mom's crabby or Mom's hungover. We have fun and I relate to her more as a friend. And she confides in me more.

My socializing is no longer geared around drinking: not around drinking and dinner, or drinking and women's events. The booze isn't controlling me. So if I'm having a talk with a friend and a meal with a friend, it tends to be earlier in the day. The quality of my friendships has grown enormously because they are sober. It's not "Hi, how are you, who are you sleeping with?" I tend to talk more now too because I'm not so carried away by the alcohol. And I talk more about how we are really feeling about things and how we are both doing.

I have a love-hate relationship with my own community. The community means an enormous amount to me. In the later days, I depended on the community for a lot of things, and it didn't come through for me. We have so many expectations of women, of each other as lesbians and feminists and of course, when the expectations are unfulfilled, the result is crushing.

The community didn't fit into my sobriety a lot. Its events aren't part of my sobriety. One of the worst problems when I got sober was trying to still function in the community, be part of it and be sober. Ninety percent of the community events are involved in alcohol. And of course, I became less tolerant of people's alcohol and drugs and smoke at the events and the lateness. I felt more alienated and more women in the community felt alienated by me and alienating to me because of my stance around alcohol.

In the last year, the largest change I've made is that I've left Milwaukee. I lived in Milwaukee, the city of beer, all my life and I never thought I'd leave my community or my lover or Sistermoon, my bookstore. I never thought I would leave, ever, ever. But I've done it; I've done it to save myself. I could not deal with me, being responsible to that community, being a responsible Virgo, committed lesbian feminist woman, I could not do it anymore in the city and live. The burnout level I had gotten to was immense. And I could no longer dull my pain or my grief with alcohol.

I think sometimes in sobriety we have to make big changes in our lives. In my sobriety I was still depressed and unhappy. Drinking didn't make me depressed and unhappy, it was other things in my life and then I would drink to try to take that all away and of course now I don't have the relief of drinking anymore.

The only time in the last few years that I felt sane was when I would be in the country and be around nature. So that kept saying to me, you have to find a way to be around nature and still live and survive and be a feminist, but not do it the way you have been doing it, Karen, because you're changing, but your environment's not and you're slowly dying.

So my lover and I got a loan and found a house trudging through snow banks in February in nothern Wisconsin and I moved out here to save my life. I felt like the city was killing me, the stress was killing me, the speed was killing me, the responsibility was killing me. I wanted to start changing the way I lived. Of course there are problems up here, but they are there anywhere.

I started a business up here called Womanrest. It's a chemically-free retreat place for women to come and canoe and swim and fish and ski and I cook meals for them. Womanrest is surrounded by trees and water and clean air and peace and quiet. It's a place where you can really feel at peace, a wonderful healing place. I am going to describe it a little so you can feel it.

There is a lake in front of me and you can see the shore on the other side and there is an island in the middle of the lake. You can take the canoe and go down the lake to another lake, on the right. And on the left, you can go down to another lake and it goes through streams and marshes. The lakes are lined with beautiful trees, mostly birch and pine. There are great blue herons and eagles and deer and otters and beavers and you can just relax and feel content.

There are hundreds and hundreds of acres behind us to hike. It's quite wonderful. My vision for Womanrest is that women will come, relax, be healed and get sober.

The process of coming here was desperate, however. I felt like I would die if I couldn't get up here, not just get depressed, but die. The anger and the cynicism was just eating me alive and I just no longer had the escape of alcohol or dope or anything. I couldn't relax, I couldn't come down, I couldn't enjoy myself anymore. I was becoming a vegetable; I wasn't going out anymore. I wasn't going to the store or doing movement work; my depression felt out of control; I was out of control. And the last thing I wanted to do was to feel out of control in my daily life. So I had to find a way to do this.

I went back to therapy for six months and my therapist kept asking me what would make me happy. I kept saying that I just wanted to be in nature, to be with nature. And she kept saying there would be a way. And I kept saying but I don't have any money and I can't find the way.

And I don't know what happened, but I got the idea to do Womanrest and I kept going to therapy to deal with my daily frustration. And I got the idea to make it a vacation place for other women to come to, as well as me. And so I didn't feel that I was running away, that it was only for me. Heaven forbid we feminist organizers do a selfish thing.

I got the idea in January and by February my lover and I were looking for land. And we still didn't have any money, we were saving every penny and I wouldn't let her pay any of her bills, we just kept putting all our pay in the savings account and we wouldn't spend any money. And we found this place after the fourth weekend. And we put the closing off for several months, trying to save every penny. But I just felt like I had to do it now or I would never do it. And I did it.

At the end of June I moved up here with a truck and myself and Holly, our dog. I had two weeks to get ready for the summer season. On July 13th, my first guest arrived and there were women coming and going up until the first week in November. Of course there would be more business here and more women coming if I allowed alcohol up here, but it is a chemical-free space.

I find that I can be more whole and healthy up here; it's just more healing up here with nature. And I feel I have more to give. It's not political, it's not the same kind of life or the same pace as the city. It's a place for women in the movement who are tired. Women can come here to escape the way of the city. And I'm here for them and I provide the space for them. It's a way of nurturing and giving, but it's not the same as before.

Right now, I am in extreme financial stress and I am fantasizing about drinking martinis and I hope I have the strength to not do that. Not only can I not afford the martinis but they would not help me in my daily struggle.

I'm worried about Womanrest, about having the money to keep going. I have some resentment that this place will go slow because it is a place where there are no chemicals allowed. There are women who have talked to me about, well couldn't there be another house so they could come here, women who can't go for a day without dope or booze. And they don't understand why they can't come and have that too, and why I have to be this hard-headed bitch who won't allow them to come and enjoy all this because they have to have their stuff.

My life has taken lots of changes and my sobriety has helped that immensely, just immensely. I'm sure if I hadn't gotten sober, I wouldn't be here right now. My mind is just so much more open and I've been more vulnerable and I'm just changing and growing a lot and that's very exciting.

What I have to learn and what I am learning is that I am more important than the tasks, no matter what it is or how crucial it is. I have to learn to separate my work from my being, otherwise all criticism and set-backs become a rejection of who I am rather than what I have done and this is dangerous to me. I have to learn to accept myself, to stop breeding discontent by the high standards I pursue, to stop being so hard on myself and others and to stop disliking myself for not doing more and more and more. I take life too seriously and I'll never get out of it alive if I don't stop doing that.

How I find nurturing is in little things. With food, I am a fat dyke and I do enjoy food. The thing up here that nurtures me the most is the nature. It is just the pure beauty of her, of the snow on the trees and the wildlife and the water and the woods. It's just like a picture book. It's this nature that nurtures me.

And reading books nurtures me. And my lover nurtures me. I am very task-oriented and I get nurturing from a task well done. If a woman comes here and I feed her well and we go on a canoe trip and everything is wonderful that makes me feel good and nurtured. Another way that I nurture myself is getting massages; I did that twice a week when I was in the city. And I nurture me, but I'm not quite sure how.

I think women need role models. I needed role models when I was coming out of my marriage and when I was coming out as a lesbian and so I have no problem with you using my name or the name of my bookstore. I am not ashamed of who I am or what I did or my struggles. In fact, I am proud of them and I think it's important that women can see tangibly the women who have gone through this and how they've gone through it and the changes they've made in their lives.

The changes in my life have been worth it and the whole move out of the city was worth it and I am on the road to being whole. I am much more whole than I have ever been in my life.

If my community were sober, we'd have dances and concerts in spaces of non-alcohol. We'd be pleased to drink herbal teas and juices instead of old fashioneds. We'd have more quality in our relationships instead of fighting for other lovers and power in a bar scene. We'd have more money for quality food, apartments and vacations instead of spending hundreds on booze. Our bodies would be healthier, especially our livers. It is hard for me to fantasize. My life as a Virgo woman is and always has been based in reality and practicality but I know our movement would be much stronger and better funded if all of us contributed our monies and energies.

*(P.S. If you would like more information about Womanrest, send a SASE to Womanrest, c/o Sistermoon, 2128 E. Locust, Milwaukee, WI 53211)*

# First Tries Don't Always Work

## (Chapter Five)

### by Judith McDaniel

Chris tapped the grain scoop on the side of the bucket to knock out the last bit of corn, then swung the bucket into the pony stall. "Here you go, Duchess. Chow time." The pony ducked its head into the bucket, ignoring everything but the grain. Chris watched for a moment as Duchess lifted her head to chew a mouthful. Her teeth were really worn down. Pretty soon they'd have to start giving her warm mash, the way they had old Grey when her teeth had gone. Chris leaned over the stall bars again, this time to give Duchess an affectionate scratch between the ears. Then she rested her elbows on the top bar and sighed as she stared at Duchess. That was the last chore. She was done for the day and Tad had to do the whole round this afternoon. They'd traded so he could leave early with the other men to hunt. Usually Tad helped in the milking parlor, moving the cows in and out, swabbing their udders with disinfectant, then attaching the milking machine with a swoosh of suction. Chris had all the extra chores, feeding the calves, putting hay down for the heifers, graining Duchess and her mother's horse, Hudson.

This morning Tad had shaken Chris awake as he left, long before dawn, and she and her mother had done the milking together. It was kind of nice, actually. Chris never minded the milking. She liked the big quiet cows, the way they nudged one another as they pushed forward into the milking parlor, their heavy udders swaying a little. No matter what the temperature outside, it always felt warm to Chris when she was standing among the cows in the center of the barn.

Her mother seemed preoccupied this morning. Chris hadn't minded. They couldn't talk much above the noise of the milking machine anyway. Mostly they used nods or a wave of the hand when it was time to move one group out and bring in another. But when Chris had gone into the kitchen to get her hot chocolate and a donut before she started the second half of chores, her mother was sitting at the kitchen table, staring at her cup of coffee. That wasn't like Mom. Usually she was all over Chris with questions — and how was this and what did you think of that — and Chris could hardly stand it sometimes. She felt like she was an old rusty paint can and her mother was prying her lid off, going around each crack and probing for weak spots to lift. Not that she was mean about it. It was just that she asked Chris things Chris hadn't figured out yet, like how she felt about Roger dating Jennie or did she think Gregory was a trouble-maker or what? Liz said she ought to practice up. When her Mom asked her a question like that, she ought to say, "Gee, I don't know Mom, let me think about that." And then figure it out, or at least figure out a good answer — like, "Well, Mom, I think Gregory gets in a lot of trouble, but I don't think he makes other kids get in trouble" — and when she asked again, Chris could be ready. Trouble was, Mom never asked again, because she'd get so annoyed at Chris not answering at all, she'd go off in a huff and then Chris would feel bad and be even less able to think of what to say or to know what she thought about anything.

So when Chris sat down at the table with her mother and still there were no questions, just the two of them quietly sipping from their mugs, warming their hands around them after being out in the cold, Chris decided to ask a question herself.

"Are you o.k., Mom? You're awful quiet."

"Am I?" her mother looked surprised, smiled at Chris, then got up to pour another cup of coffee.

When she didn't say anything else, Chris got worried. Had she done something wrong? Was her Mom mad at her about the car and hadn't said? Had she found the mason jar stashed in Chris' book bag? Chris shuddered inside at the thought. Finally she couldn't stand it. "Is something the matter?"

"What? Oh, no." Mom had run her fingers through her hair. "I guess I just always worry about somebody getting hurt."

"What?" Now it was Chris' turn not to understand. Hurt? Was she thinking about Chris' accident again?

"Oh, you know. When they're all out hunting. All those guns. Not that your father and Tad aren't careful," she looked like Chris had accused her of something. "But there are so many of them out there. Lots of them don't know a thing about guns or deer. Not the local men, but. . . " Her voice trailed off again in her preoccupation.

Chris was surprised. Her dad had always hunted. And Tad had been going with him since he was twelve. Chris had gone sometimes too. But not lately. Standing around in the woods till her feet got wet and cold was not her idea of a good time. But they had always had a deer hanging from a tree in the yard in time for Thanksgiving.

"We've always had a deer," Chris ventured, curious now to know what her mother was thinking.

"And I've always hated it," she looked Chris right in the eye and smiled at her. "But some things you have to compromise on. I was glad you like riding Duchess better than hunting."

"It sure seemed like a lot more fun," Chris had laughed, then got up to come out here to the barn and finish chores.

Now she pushed away from Duchess's stall, feeling like she'd done a whole day's work and it was probably only about nine o'clock in the morning. The rest of the day was hers. Mom had taken the kids into town to shop for the week's groceries and do some Christmas shopping. Too bad Duchess was too small for her to ride anymore. Or rather that she was too big for Duchess. It was she who had grown; the pony hadn't shrunk. But now she remembered that she'd never been allowed to ride at this time of year. All the animals were brought in from pasture — horses, ponies, goats — anything and everything was secured in the barn during hunting season. She could walk through the back pasture and out to the creek though. She hadn't been out there in a long time and she felt restless now, not ready to go into her room to work on her government project.

Why didn't Mom ask her more about the deer the car had killed, Chris wondered. Come to think of it, there hadn't been many questions about the accident at all. Chris wouldn't have minded talking about the deer. It was just that — well — she felt too awkward to bring it up herself. Every time now when her mind flashed on the deer, she got an image of that cop asking her did she have any alcoholic beverages in the car. Her boots scuffed in the high grass as she walked. It would have been a lot simpler — Chris was finally able to admit — if she and Liz hadn't had those drinks. Or if she hadn't been caught with the bottle under the seat. But so what? Everybody did it. She wasn't doing anything everybody else didn't do. Tad. Roger. They all did it. Why was she the one who got caught?

She felt better this morning than she had yesterday in school, that was for sure. But it bothered her that she had a headache so often. She'd heard Tad and the guys joke about having hangovers, but she wasn't sure how bad they were. Sometimes when she woke up — like Friday morning — she could hardly move, her head hurt so much. Like she was being hit with a hammer right on the back of her head if she so much as moved. And there had been a few mornings she'd barfed when she moved. All over the bedroom floor, a light brown stream of Coke and who knows what else. She got it cleaned up before anyone saw it. Thank god she didn't have to share a room with Carol anymore. She wanted to ask someone why she was feeling like that, but there was no one she could say it to. She could hear the conversation now. "Hey, Mom, why do you suppose these hangovers are getting worse and worse?" Chris kicked at the meadow grass with more vigor. Right. Then she laughed. Carol was just at the age where she couldn't stop asking questions. Reminded Chris of her mother sometimes. She figured they deserved one another. Carol was always at somebody with "Hey, what's that? What does that mean? Why did he do that?" Maybe she could program ten-year-old Carol to come out with it. "Hey, Mom, why do hangovers keep getting worse?"

All of a sudden, Chris felt tears come to her eyes. That was silly. She wiped them away. What was the matter with her anyway? For a minute she'd been wishing she was Carol's age again when every question was innocent instead of loaded. Hey, that's easy, came a voice in her head. Just get rid of the stuff. Then you don't have to worry. Then you'd never have to see Gregory again and you wouldn't have to worry about whether people thought you were like him. Chris sat down on a rock next to the creek and looked at the water swirling around a large boulder in the middle of the creekbed. The water eddied, swirled, pushed first to one side and then the other with the current. She *could* get rid of it. It wasn't like she needed it, Chris thought, and in that very thought, wanted a drink with a sharpness and clarity that made her whole body shudder. Well, she could stop having her own stash, maybe just have a beer when the other kids did. That seemed more reasonable. She wouldn't have to start right away. After all, there was still half a mason jar in her book bag. Her secret weapon for getting through the weekend, she called it. When that was gone, maybe she ought to just cool it.

Feeling better, but beginning to shiver from the damp November chill seeping through her jacket, Chris walked briskly back toward the house. She had all afternoon to work on her government project and with nobody else home, maybe she'd spread it out at the kitchen table in front of the wood stove, make a cup of tea and. . . who was that? As she rounded the barn, Chris came smack up against a strange car parked in their driveway. She looked around for the driver, but saw no one. She was irritated. It was her afternoon, who was . . . ? Just then Katie Lynde walked around the corner of the barn from the other direction.

Oh, God, Chris thought. Just what I needed.

"Hi," Katie called casually. "Driving by. Thought I'd see how you were doing."

Chris didn't say anything. But she nodded. You couldn't just ignore this cop, even if she was walking around wearing blue jeans and a wool jacket and looking just like everybody else.

"How are you?" Katie persisted, wondering why she had come. Chris didn't look like she wanted to see anybody at all. Sullen. You came for yourself, not for her, Katie reminded herself. It's your day off and you came for yourself.

Chris couldn't ignore the direct question. "Fine. Why wouldn't I be?" She wasn't going to be pushed around anymore.

Katie shrugged. "You had an accident that would have shaken me up. And killing a deer is no fun. Especially a young one like that. Hadn't even had time to get used to cars and headlights." Katie rested one foot on the bumper of her car and looked at Chris, trying for casual. Why *had* she come?

"Yeah." Chris kicked the hard earth with her boot. She looked up at Katie, trying not to be moved by the memory of the deer. "The guys thought it was funny," she blurted out suddenly. Her big mouth. The trouble with saying anything was then you had to explain it for hours. Chris sighed. "What I mean is. . . "

"I think I know. It was like if it had happened to them they would have bragged about it, right? So since it was you and since women don't prove how brave they are by going out and killing deer, it had to be a joke, right?" She was smiling at Chris, including her in this analysis of how the world was.

"Yeah," Chris said slowly, thinking. "Yeah, maybe that was it. But. . . " She wanted to ask Katie why she, Chris, had gone along with the joke when she didn't feel like that at all. "I guess I understand why they made it a joke. But why did I go along with it? Try and act like a big shot." She sighed. "Like I knew what was going on."

"Mmmm." Katie looked thoughtful. "You asking me? I mean, I bet you know why." God it was awful being a teen-ager, Katie remembered. She forgot sometimes how awful it was — that need to be liked, to be one of the gang.

"Yeah, I don't want them to make fun of me." Then her voice became bitter. "To laugh at me like they do Gregory."

Katie wondered if Chris would be any more able to hear advice this morning than she had the other night. She tried to remember herself at fifteen — it wasn't *that* long ago, after all. Had it ever mattered what other people said? People who weren't your own age, that is? Chris was looking bored, like she had something better to be doing and was ready for Katie to leave.

"So, you going to show me around here?" Katie asked.

"What's to see?" Chris shrugged, her eyes not meeting Katie's.

"I hear you've got one of the newest milking parlors in the county," Katie ventured.

Chris shrugged. More obviously bored. But her Dad showed the milking parlor to everyone who asked about it. No way to get out of that.

They walked through the yard towards the barn in silence, Katie wondering how she could best break into what she wanted to say to Chris, but not able to think of any good openings. She had told almost no one what she was about to tell Chris — if she could find a way through the girl's defenses. Can you tell people things they don't want to hear? Maybe it was best just to begin from nowhere. Out of the blue. She took a deep breath as Chris opened the barn door and began. "I started drinking when I was twelve, you know." Then what to say? Her whole concentration had been on getting out that one statement.

"How should I know?" Chris was looking at her like she was stupid. "What's that got to do with me? I didn't."

"I was drinking because I was afraid of the other kids making fun of me. Because I felt different. I was different, I guess." She leaned on the railing of one of the stalls, just in front of the entrance to the milking parlor. Her hands were trembling and she could feel the strain in her voice. She wasn't sure she'd have the courage to say it all.

Reluctantly, Chris paused with her. "Why did you think you were different?" she finally asked.

"I was born up on the mountain." Katie heard Chris breathe in sharp and look at her with new interest. "I was ten before I figured out who my Ma was." She half laughed and then explained. "Ma took in foster kids — to support us, you know — and I always figured some day they'd walk in and pick me up and take me away, too. I still don't know who my father was."

"Your mother won't tell you?" Chris was curious now.

"I never asked."

"Oh. I thought. . . " It didn't seem quite polite to say it. "I mean. You look, well, just normal. I wouldn't have thought. . . "

"That I was a gilder? We aren't all depraved and retarded." Katie's voice was bitter now. "But that's what the kids at school thought. And a lot of teachers, too."

It had started so long ago, almost no one remembered. The new settlers coming in from Holland, trying to find a place in an area already taken by Scots-Irish-English descendents. Nearly a hundred years ago. The language had been different, and the culture. The newcomers had found a place on the side of a mountain that no one else seemed to want. It had been a refuge then, but sometimes a refuge can become a trap. Services had come slow, up on the mountain. Roads were impossible in snow and spring thaw. Electricity had come only recently.

"Why are you called gilders?"

"I'm not sure. I think it was a dutch word. Maybe for money? For somebody's name? It just stuck. It became who we were known as because the other names seemed foreign, too hard to pronounce." It had come to mean a lot of other things too. Poverty, in-bred retardation, teeth that fell out at twenty from malnutrition. Incest. Things she had learned first as a child, then again from the outside, as a police officer. Some of those things she hadn't been able to see too clearly when she lived on the mountain.

"Anyway, I found out real early that if I had a drink, being different didn't seem too bad. It seemed to knock out that part of my brain that always noticed how people were looking at me, treating me different. When I had a drink, I figured if I could just last in school till I was fifteen, then I could drop out and nobody would ever bother me again."

"Did you?"

"Nope." She paused, hoping Chris would ask the next question.

"Oh." Chris could see the question hanging in the air in front of her and she wasn't sure she wanted to ask it because she wasn't sure she wanted to hear the answer. The answer wasn't going to be that nice. It wasn't going to be easy for her. "Why didn't you?"

Katie nodded. Good. "A teacher grabbed me." She grinned at Chris. "You know how bossy and nosy adults can be sometimes. And there was another part of me wanted to go places. Wanted to be a different kind of person. It liked to read — not just about anything, but especially stories about people who were different."

Chris gave her a reluctant smile.

"That teacher told me I was smart and could do about anything I wanted, but I wasn't going to be smart if I kept drinking much longer. She said some people could drink just normally and some people couldn't and when she saw me bringing home brew in my lunch bag, she figured I might be one of the people who couldn't."

Chris' eyebrows shot up. Lunch bag, huh. Well, she had never done that. She wasn't that bad. Oh, yeah, jeered the voice she'd heard earlier that morning, talking inside her head. Tell me you never went out to the car right after lunch. You were afraid of Liz seeing it if you brought it to lunch. Chris was feeling tired. Very, very tired. She wished this cop would quit talking and go home.

But Katie had more to say. "She told me it was just like some people had brown eyes and some had blue. That some could drink normal and some couldn't. I could choose. I could choose not to have any drinks and be smart or I could drink. But once I chose to drink, then I stopped being able to choose." She could see Chris' restlessness, but she wasn't finished. Not quite. "It was never easy. I tried to stop a few times. But I guess what did it was that I really wanted to be smart."

There was silence for a moment in the barn. They listened to the breathing of the heifers and the soft crunch and pull as a few of them chewed their hay over and over. Chris shifted from one foot to the other. Then she yawned. She wasn't going to ask this cop any more questions. She'd had it. She'd heard enough lectures now to last a long time.

"You know," Katie said, eyeing Chris' distraction, "you and Gregory do have something in common." Her voice was sarcastic as she tried to break through Chris's reserve. Damn kid. Katie could feel her anger rising. She forgot she had come to talk to Chris for herself. She wanted what she was saying to matter to Chris.

And she did get Chris' attention with that statement. She saw her head snap up and — for just a moment — Katie saw the fear in Chris' eyes. Was this what she had wanted? Stop it, she told herself. The kid didn't ask you to come over here today and tell her your life history. She tried to smile at Chris and remove the harshness from her voice. "What I mean," she said, "is that you're the two brightest kids in your class."

Huh, Chris thought, this cop must be nuts. Her like Gregory? That was a laugh. "What do you mean? Gregory's flunked most of his courses this year." She couldn't ask, do you really think *I'm* smart?

"Yeah, I know and it's a waste. His scores when he came to high school were among the highest in the state. I talked to the counselor the other day." She looked quickly at Chris to see what she would think about this. "But he's not much help."

"Help?" Chris' laugh was derisive. "Help? He could help if you wanted to dunk a basketball from 30 feet out. But that's about it." She told Katie some of the stories the kids had all heard about being called into Mr. Parker's office to discuss grades and trading baseball statistics instead.

"Is that it?" Katie looked half-amused. "I thought it was just me he wouldn't talk to."

"What do you mean?"

"You know. The lady po-lice officer." She stressed the word police sarcastically the way Chris had heard Gregory do it. "Lots of people — or should I say some idiots — think a woman can't do this job and so they might as well not waste time talking to me."

"Hmm." Chris wondered all of a sudden if Katie knew what people like Gregory said about her. Suddenly she was scared again. What if one of the other kids saw her car parked in front of Jablonsky's? What if — oh god — what if Gregory heard she'd had an off-duty visit? She could hear the rumors now. He'd *never* stop with the disgusting jokes. "Took her on a tour of the milking parlor, huh, Chris? Oh yeah, I can just bet that's what the two of you were doing in the barn."

"Look," she said, suddenly aggressive. "I'm not like that. I'm not different the way you were." She thought of the large pleasant old farm house she had always lived in. She'd seen the shacks called houses up on the mountain. She was tempted to say, "I know who my father is," but it was too mean. She turned her back on Katie and started to walk out of the barn.

Katie followed. She knew what Chris meant. Chris lived the way a lot of the kids in her class lived. The farm, the chores. Enough food, some time for fun and play. Most of the families had two parents and several kids. Some didn't but most did. And Chris' life was mostly just the way it was supposed to be. Except for the booze. Why *should* Chris feel she had anything in common with Katie? But she does. Katie knew that as surely as she knew she was standing on firm hard frozen ground out here in the barnyard. How could she make Chris know it too?

"Don't you have any dreams that are different, Chris? Different from what the other kids want?" She was insistent. Why wouldn't Chris listen to her?

Chris shrugged. They were standing by Katie's car again and she wanted her to go. "I don't know." She was distracted, staring out at the road, hoping no one she knew would drive by and see them standing together.

Katie tried again, reluctant to give up. "Being smart can make you feel different, you know. Or wanting to travel places other people haven't been. You don't have to have been born on the mountain to be different." Katie got into the car, shut the door and rolled down the window. "See you," she said casually and backed the car down the driveway toward the road.

Chris breathed a sigh of relief and turned back to the house. Jeez, who would have thought she'd have stayed so long. It was past lunch time and Chris hadn't even started her homework yet. See you, the cop had said. She sure hoped not. She'd seen about enough of her.

She stirred up the fire in the woodstove that had almost gone out and put the kettle on for a cup of tea. She felt hungry but her mind kept turning to the half-quart jar now hidden in her book bag. She really ought to get it out of there, put it somewhere safe. Maybe have a little nip of it in her tea. Then she remembered what Katie had said about lunch times. Maybe she didn't need it to get her started on her government project. She wasn't like that; she really wasn't. So she fixed a peanut butter and jelly sandwich to eat with her tea and sat down alone at the kitchen table in front of the stove. She felt incredibly tired and lonely. Like she'd been carrying the whole world around with her for days and days and there'd been no one to help her with it. All she wanted to do now was sleep. Sleep. She had to have something to take grey fog out of her brain, the ache out of her muscles and forehead. She finished her sandwich and decided to go up to her room for a nap before she started her project. After all, she'd gotten up extra early this morning to do Tad's chores for him. She deserved some rest.

When she walked into her room, the first thing she thought of was the jar. She went over to her book bag, unbuckled it and pulled the quart jar of vodka out from among the notebooks, papers, texts and junk. It looked sort of disgusting. And where could she hide it? She looked around her room, then settled for a spot on her bookshelf, behind some books. Not much chance anybody would be messing around there.

Maybe she should just get rid of it, she thought as she crawled under the comforter. Just pour it down the drain and get rid of it. Well, she'd worry about that later.

Don't you have dreams that are different? Katie's voice was echoing in her head as she started to doze. Sure. She and Liz talked about their dreams all the time. Liz was going to be an interpreter at the U.N. and Chris — she was going to be a news reporter for one of the big networks. Or maybe she'd be in government. Not elected at first, but an aide or somebody important. How did people get those jobs, that was the question. She could imagine herself at work, see herself in meetings or holding press conferences, but she couldn't imagine getting there. Not from here. Not from Jefferson County where the most exciting news in the weekly paper was the dairy herd yield.

She turned over on the bed, impatient for her dream to begin. She and Liz could do it. They'd live in New York and have a fancy apartment at the top of a building so you could see all the lights of the city at night. They *were* going to be different — not the way that cop meant. They weren't going to stick around these boring old farms. She knew a lot of girls in her class who just thought they'd get married when they graduated. Even Tad — she'd never heard Tad talk about anything but farming. He was applying to the county ag school for next year. Not her. She was going to have an exciting life. Smart. Katie had said she was smart. She could do anything she wanted to do. She could choose to be smart. She knew she could.

**JUDITH MCDANIEL:** is a writer and teacher who lives in an old farmhouse in rural upstate New York. She was a co-founder of the feminist publishing company, Spinsters Ink. Her poems, stories and reviews have appeared in *Blueline, Conditions, The Greenfield Review, Sinister Wisdom,* and other journals and anthologies.

One thing I think about a lot is how I believe that alcohol use and abuse keeps us from focusing our anger, our recognition of who is responsible for our oppression, on the appropriate targets. Alcohol makes vague statements: "life is like that" or "it wasn't anybody's fault." A clean and sober community might be a community that would turn its full attention on oppression. We might be dangerous then — to our oppressors — and they know that. One night while watching the news, news about how Reagan wanted more bombs and how a black candidate for mayor of Chicago was being harassed and vilified, I counted six ads for wine and beer in a one hour period. Six. That's what it takes to get through the news these days without caring who is doing this to us. Without getting up to do something about it.

# Recovery:
## The Story of an ACA

**by Jean Swallow**

San Francisco: January... February... March. It is the winter of 1983. Rain sweeps in from the ocean. Every day, the rain sweeps in slashing from the ocean. Roads wash away; houses slide off hills. The pain in my legs shudders through me in the rain. I am drenched in the three blocks I walk to the subway and work all day in clothes that stay wet.

We try to get to the farm in Albion on the weekends, even though the road washes out about once a week. We are planning to go tonight and I am afraid the road will be washed away just before we get to the stretch that threads through the redwoods. Highway 1 is out ten miles above Fort Bragg and somewhere below; I'm not sure where. The highway conditions tape drones on and I have a hard time remembering which roads we can take to get there. Finally I remember I can ask Sher to help. I'm not going alone. Sher. The farm. The roses.

You sound like you're a long ways off. Can you hear me?

March. Saturday. San Francisco. Usually the rain stops for a few hours a day, but not in any pattern. We want to make a plan to go the beach with our friends Sim and Jay for a picnic. We ask them. Sim laughs and says... in the rain? It has been raining for six weeks up at the farm. Pammie who lives there and ought to know, says 60 inches in that time, some every day.

Not so bad in the city. Not 60 inches here. But still it rains. Every day. Today the clouds streak grey and white and in between, the sky shows blue. The rain hovers over the ocean. We are trying to get to the farm tonight because the new roses came from the nursery this week. We need to get them into healthy soil with good air around them; we need to plant them soon or they will die.

I look out the car window to the ocean and feel the wind through the seams. The air turns cold again and within a half-hour, the sky is a solid gray. The lighthouse blinks on and off. And I am crying. I am still here, crying again. My legs hurt in the rain. My knees buckle and swell and give out. Each time, when I can barely walk, I go to Misha. Misha says the evil chi is trapped, stuck in my knees. She pushes needles into my skin and tells me to relax. She massages my head. Before she leaves, I have shut my eyes and the tears begin to seep out from under my eyelids and roll down into my hair. The tears are not from pain from the needles. The pain is not from the needles.

## Outside the rain begins, and it may never end

When I was a child, we lived in the city during the winter and in the country during the summer. This went on until my father "decided to change jobs" or "went bankrupt" depending on who you talk to. This went on until I was nine. This went on all my life. Listen to me, can you hear me? Things are not as they seem. We stuff the truth behind our eyes and then see as we are told. My father drinks. My father has been worried about his drinking for the last thirty years. My father has been worried about his drinking since before I was born. Things are not as they seem.

I was raised upper middle-class by decorum and expectation. But only sometimes did my family have the requisite amount of money. Sometimes we just didn't have the money. But always, my father made money magic. He could find it when he needed it. He could spend it how he wanted. He could make it do as he wished. Like the rain.

He could make the rain stop. He would snap his fingers and the wipers would scrape noisily against the windshield as we sped through the tunnel. He would snap his fingers again and the rain would splatter on the windshield and smear into the glass and then the wipers would work and we would be able to see the trees on the side of the road outside the tunnel again.

I would tug on his sleeve and jump up and down on the seat. Do it again, Daddy, make it stop again, I would scream. And he would just smile and say he could only make it happen if I would be a good little girl and sit down on the seat and be quiet. Then he would make magic again. And I would try, I would try so hard to be quiet. I hardly ever knew when it would happen again, or what exactly I had done right, but when it happened, it was like the illegal fireworks he shot off over the lake on summer nights; it was like a floating shower of stars.

For a long time, he was able to make magic. I adored him. When there was trouble, he would ask what did money mean? What good is it? It's only money. He would snap his fingers, take his cigarette out of his mouth and pick up his drink, his eyes bright and loving on me. It's only money, not love. And it is love that matters, he would say as he gathered me into him. He is small for a man and handsome and heavy. He would hold me in his arms, gathered up over his belly and kiss me on the forehead with his whiskery heavy cheeks.

Now he lies in his bed for weeks at a time, exhaustion or stress. He lies in his bed in Carolina where he lives and he watches the rain just like me. March in Carolina: the rain pours from the sky in sheets and the soil slides off into the sides of the road and runs in ditches the color of blood. I know March in Carolina. It was my home too. The wind and rain come up from further south and bend the trees backward, pounding in the air like the hands of God. After the storm, the redbud covers the road like a woman's shorn hair on a cold floor.

My father travels all through Carolina, through those storms on his trips to the mills, and he's gone there more than he is home. Except when he can't get up. Sometimes he just can't get out of bed anymore and the sadness washes over him as though it were the ocean and he could not pull himself up any higher on the beach. He is still handsome but his eyes are not bright. He still is there, drinking. They say I am the only alcoholic in the family. And I can not make the rain stop.

I haven't seen him or my mother in three years. I haven't talked to them for a year. I haven't talked to them over the telephone for a year. What would I say? What would I say to them? It rains here too. The rain turns the air cold and moist and I learn to wear my boots from the farm here in the city.

But the roses came this week. One night last fall, after a hard weekend, Sher and I sat in bed and picked the roses. We picked out rose bushes from a special catalogue and took the whites and lavenders and blues. Eight of them. We sat in bed that night and held each other. And though we were terrified, we decided to put a little something down on the future. We waited for them all winter and this week they arrived: small spindly little things. We need to plant them within a day or two, or they will die in their plastic sacks. We are trying to get to the farm tonight. I hope the roads to the coast stay open.

## Things are not as they seem

When I was a child, I lived in an old hunting lodge during the summer. I lived there with my sister and my brother and my mother and when he was home, with my father. The lodge had been turned into a house and sat on a hill just above the lake. A path led through lilies of the valley and pine trees to a steep drop-off and then the lake. The lake spread out in front of me as though it were the ocean. I would sit on the porch of that old house in the middle of the northern Rhode Island woods, in my little white cane rocker and read my books from the library. It would be warm and sunny and a breeze would blow and pretty soon my mother would come by and say it was time to start walking down the long dirt road to meet my father coming home from work in the city.

We waited for him all day. And when he got home, his tie off and collar thrown open, they would have drinks on the porch. After a while, we would eat dinner, though often they didn't eat with us. And it wasn't like I got more attention when he was there, except right at first when he saw us standing by the road, waiting for him. He would stop the big Oldsmobile and haul us all in and there were kisses and questions and he would run his big hands through my hair. He would be sweating, his white starched shirt wilted in the heat. He and my mother would exchange glances, they thought over my head, and then they would kiss. No, it wasn't that he or my mother would pay attention to me when he got home. It was more that they were together there and I knew everyone was where they were supposed to be.

And though I was frightened when I heard them arguing and crying on the porch after I had gone to bed, and though I sometimes got up and watched them laugh as they drank from beautiful glasses in the moonlight, it didn't so much matter what they did; it mattered that they were there. It always seemed to me they might not be there. And even that seemed normal to me. I reckon it seemed normal to them. It was the way it was supposed to be.

And sometimes it was wonderful, like being on the porch in the middle of the afternoon with a warm breeze and my books and a profound sense of peace. Why as a child I was able to appreciate that sense of peace and rest and order, strikes me as odd now. Why I forgot how my legs hurt all those years strikes me as odd too. But now, the feelings return. The ache returns and I wonder if I've moved at all.

In the night, when I was a child, my legs hurt when I lay still in bed. They would throb with the hurting and I would cry out and after a long while, my father or my mother would come in from the porch and rub my calves with horse linament and try to get me to lie still. It hurt worse when I lay still. I couldn't sleep. I couldn't sleep. They would be out on the porch drinking, talking and I would hear their voices rise in anger and know that I shouldn't say anything, shouldn't call to them. And my legs hurt and I would look into the darkness in the bedroom and see faces, always the faces of the devil and the sounds of evil and I would twist into a clenched knot and finally, after a while and maybe from exhaustion, I would sleep.

## Outside the rain begins

In the fall, my mother and I would go for one last weekend to pack the house up for the winter. The air would turn cold. My mother would wear her red wool cardigan and I would wear something cast off from my brother and we would clean up the house. At lunch, we would sit in the sun and my mother would take her cardigan off and run her long fingers through her hair and shield her eyes to squint at the sun. Then sometimes she would stretch her legs out a little longer in her slacks, warming herself just a little longer as though ten more minutes would carry her through the rest of her work, as though she could memorize the warmth, as though for one minute she could just rest.

My mother doesn't rest. My mother lies awake nights, has lain awake nights for years. I don't know what she does in the night. I know she has wanted to die; I've known it since I was a child and watched her try to drown herself in the lake one night at twilight. I wished then I knew how to save her. I wish now she would want to save herself. I wish that my loving her made a difference.

When I was a child, I knew my mother was the most beautiful woman in the world. Nothing was ever out of place. Like her rose garden in the city, carefully tended, each bush a beauty and all the flowers growing beneath the tall climbing roses, each in a special place. And then she had to move and leave them. My father went bankrupt or changed jobs, depending on who you talk to. This changing jobs and moving went on five more times, up and down the Eastern Seacoast. She never grew another rose. She never works in the yard now. They don't have a yard now to keep anything in place. She just holds herself.

She holds herself like a metal spring welded in a tight coil. New Englanders only look cold from the outside. She loves me. I know she loves me though it is hard to believe from here. And she loves him. Who she doesn't love is herself. For a generation, the manifestation was psychic, not physical. It wasn't her parents who drank. It was their parents. They just passed it along. And the death is coming, the death has been lingering there since before I was born. They've both been trying it, ever since I can remember.

I remember the lake. I remember autumn days when the wind picked up over the lake and the sky turned grey and the smell of wetness seeped up from under the leaves and we shut the house up and went away. One fall we went away for good. And then we just kept going away from places. Now it is a Saturday in March. I am in San Francisco. It is raining as usual.

*191*

We are trying to get to the farm. Sher and I go to the farm on the weekends, to what is left of the farm she spent ten years building, to a small cabin set in a circle of redwoods, where we sit by the wood stove in the rain. We talk. We talk and hold each other and remember things. We walk through the fields and the wildness that has grown in the five years since she's been gone. In the cabin, it is warm with the fire. We go there whenever we can.

And though the perennials were killed and the garden is overrun with thistle and blackberry vine, we can fix it. We are going to plant the roses this weekend. By the end of the summer, we will live there. Sher is going home too, but that is her story and you will have to ask her for it. She will tell you, if you ask, but her voice will scream and whisper and you must listen to the night if you mean to hear the whole of it.

## You sound like you are a long way off. Can you hear me?

About two weeks before my legs started to give out this winter, we were at the farm and the devil came back. We were at the farm, come to cut fallen hardwood for the fire, but just at that moment, it was stormy and night, a full moon. We were outside, and Sher said, I just love this weather, don't you and I said No. Actually. Not at night. Not on the full moon. And we went back inside and the devil face swam up in the window before me and I saw how the light could fall just right on her face so that it might become his and I tried to hold on. I have been sober two and a half years, but I have always seen him.

That night he was six feet tall and thin as a wisp and in his full regalia. I could smell of him, the burning smell of sulphur and rancid meat. He was there, in the room, almost next to me. He was waiting. Been waiting.

She stared at me, her eyes held steady with effort. I watched her. She watched me and measured her voice. I was gone too far; she said she didn't know if she could help me. Try to hold on, she said. Try to talk to me, she said. She sat on the chair, her arms on her knees, inched forward. I tried. I wanted to trust her. I love her more than I have ever loved anyone and I trust her more than that. She does her work. She does her work, but that night, in a room where we had made promises, there was almost nothing to hold on to. The room was warm. The light glowed in a small circle around the stove and outside the wind tore at the underside of the roof.

I tried. I began. I could feel the muscles in my leg start to spasm. I looked at her and held on to the stool and said he would catch me if I was outside and draw me up by the side of my wrist and make me lie. I could feel the claw of his hand on the soft side of my arm and I lowered my eyes, away from her.

I could not look at her then, and I began to shake and I could not stop. If he got me, he would make me tell people things that were not true. And it would hurt them and confuse them. Nothing would be real, except him, but most people would not know that. They would spend their lives as I had, one foot nailed to the floor. And they would be lost and hurt and confused. And I would have to spend the rest of my life doing that, in league with him, smelling like him, with him.

Maybe I had already done that. Maybe he already had me, had a right to me, had bought me somehow and what had I done, what had I done? The pain in my knees began to throb and I could feel it rise up in a panic into my face and my voice died in my throat. And I knew if for one moment I showed that I was afraid he would have me completely.

I could feel my face grow wild. I am twenty-nine. I am the same age as my mother when I first saw her trying to die. I sat on a small stool in front of the wood stove and held on tight to the sides of it and I could not let Sher touch me. I could not cry for fear of letting my eyes close. I could not, would not look in the window. But I forced myself to see her. I forced myself to see how the light might play on her face and how it was only the light and my fear, my awful fear. She was not afraid. But she was not sucked in either, and I was stuck, far, far away.

We talked late into the night. He was still all around, had spread his evil stickiness on all the trees, dripping down from leaf to leaf like the rain. I finally fell asleep, rigid on the lbed, with my clothes on. The next morning, it was not better. In the morning, the rain dripped from the trees. Sher talked a little about how much she loved the land and I wanted it too and knew finally, I would have to see Tasha when I got home because I could not, would not be robbed of one more home.

Tasha is small and wiry-energied. She is not calm but she is generous and strong. She helps women with spirit things. I was raised in the Congregational Church in New England, but I refused their Christian communion and prayer and I would refuse them to this day. Since I came to California though, I found I could grow a tail into the center of the earth and once, as a present, Diane showed me how to put my small white-weak little roots down through the pavement into the earth, so I guess my washing in the blood of the lamb came in a yoga studio above an automobile showroom and the backyard of a women's bar in San Francisco.

Still, the spiritual makes me nervous and I don't like the words of it. But at some point in recovery you just have to start trusting somebody and use whatever you can. I think you have to breathe deep; you have to keep breathing and then, jump.

Tasha lives on the second floor of a Victorian in the Mission and her work room is scattered with things on the floor as if life on the material plane is not of interest to her, though what is scattered is often beautiful. There is no furniture in her room, just pillows and pallets on the floor and candles and an old record-player. Outside that day, the kids on the street shouted and shrieked in play. Tasha looked at me and held me steady and gentle and asked me did I have anyone to help us with this. I did, though who, I was reluctant to say.

When I was living with Marie and Cindy in Carolina, my angel came to me in a dream. I have never forgotten her, though for a very long time I didn't tell people because they thought it was too strange and I am not into being strange. It is hard enough as it is. But when I got back to town from that devil weekend, Sim called to fill me in on city news and I found myself forcing my mouth to make words against the air, trying to tell her about the devil. In her slow, careful way, Sim's love slipped over the line to me in a hush and she asked me did I have any one to help. And then I remembered my angel. After a long pause, I told her. She said she didn't think it was strange at all. So at Tasha's, it felt a little easier to talk about her aloud, but not much. Still, I told her.

My angel lives off-world and is about six feet tall and wears a long robe with a hood; under the robe are britches with hugh pouches. She has no hair and is quite beautiful. I can not now see what her face looks like but she smiles at me a lot and leans laconically against walls, waiting for me to ask for help. She won't help without being asked. She just waits. And she helps.

That day, when I went to Tasha and laid down on a pallet in her room, feeling raw and alone, I tried to let Tasha near me and tried to listen to her voice warm and steady in my ear. She began to breathe with me, giving me psychic directions, and I slipped behind my eyes, holding her hand and weeping. And then, shortly, the angel was with me and I asked her and she came back with me to that hunting lodge house back at the lake. There was so much sadness and fear stuck there, lingering in cold corners, that we burned the house to the ground. The angel firebombed it with a torch that sprang from her hand and the house exploded and the meadow and the lake all burned, flaming and wild in the night. After a while, we took the stones from the foundation and the porch and scattered them into the woods and replanted the meadow that had burned. And I could see the grass beginning to grow there, wild and green in the rainy Rhode Island winter.

I buried my face in the angel's breast and she wrapped her cloak around me. I breathed into her, felt her around me and then, when Tasha called us and I was ready, we flew to the winter city house. Someone else lived there now — but still my parent's things were in the house. The angel and I brought them out of the house and piled them in the front yard and burnt them, a big bonfire in between the house and the two maple trees at the edge of the street. In the back, the roses were still alive but they were different somehow; someone else was tending them and they looked like strangers to me. The angel held my hand as I stared.

And then I heard Tasha's voice again and she asked me what about my parents? Where were they? And as I looked around, I saw them standing in the street, bewildered and forlorn. Like a child who runs terrified to an adult in the face of fear, I turned to the angel and held my hand out. And the angel shook her head and I knew we could not help them and I buried my face into her again, so afraid I would run to them, so ashamed and devastated because at last I understood that the love I had for them burning like a hole in my chest would not make any difference, would not even be a soothing drop in the bonfire of their sadness. And the angel held me while I sobbed and then Tasha asked again what would I do with them.

I knew I couldn't leave them there alone, but I knew too I couldn't help, so I called Aunt Ida who has been dead for more than ten years to come with the car and drive them away; I didn't know to where. And she did and I sobbed and tried to wave good-by to them as they drove off, but they never looked out the window, never looked back into the night filled with flames.

Then I heard Tasha again, and she took us to the Albion farm. It was still night but the angel could see and she extended her fingers and wiped off each leaf in the forest and took the sticky-messy evil and wrapped it around the devil and burned them both in the small clearing in front of the cabin. He burnt like a flame of molten lead in the night and I watched as he turned into nothing but ash. I sat in the cabin and I watched and then sat still with the angel, holding her hand.

And then Tasha brought us back. The angel stayed with me, even walked home with me that day. The devil burnt and was gone then. Of course he was back the next week, but the angel kept him away from me until he changed one night at Misha's.

## I hear an old voice. Can you hear me?

My legs ache now. My legs ache as I wrap them around each other and try to keep my back straight as I type for eight to ten hours a day. The ache is in my knees and in my thighs and in my calves. I wake up in the night and find my legs clenched around each other. I am frightened by something in a dream from the day and the clenching pain of my legs wakes me. I find it hard to sleep. The next morning, I can barely walk. When it rains, my knees echo. I limp. First the right knee, then the left; at night it is both.

Misha says the wind of my body, the chi, moves from one leg to the next. We work with the needles. She says my liver is working overtime, that I have stored my fear and changed it to anger in my liver for years. She is not surprised to hear I am in recovery and she begins to rub the upper part of my ears. She says my chi is blocked. Tears are the sweat of the liver, she says. I scowl and tell her I don't cry much. She puts a needle in each of my palms and then one on the bottom of each foot, one on each wrist, one on each ankle, moving back and forth on my body like a mobius strip, opening the energy. She rubs my head. Just relax now, she says and she leaves the room.

As soon as she leaves, the devil comes in and makes the lamp over my head swing as though it would drop on me and finally I say, alright, goddamn it, you want to be in here so much, come in and sit in the chair and shut up. I have work to do. The angel, who has been watching all of this from the wall next to my right side, claps her hands and smiles at me. The devil sits down and rocks.

Next week, another opening. Misha inserts the needles, softly padding around the table and my body. The devil rocks in his chair and I begin to weep and the tears run off my face, out from under my eyes and the sadness fills the room. What sadness? I don't know from where, but the room is filled with it. I sob, quietly, like I've been taught. Never making a sound except when I try to breath. I try not to call attention to myself. The sadness in the room is as heavy as fog after rain all day, hugging the ground, filling the air. The devil rocks. Through my tears, I watch him. He becomes younger and younger in age until he is very small, just a baby. I get up and hold him and he becomes a real baby and after a while the baby jumps down and grows until he looks like he is about four or five years old and wanders off.

I find myself rocking myself as a baby. This baby is very sad. She is crying too, and quietly. The room is filled with sadness and it is too much. I can not bear it. I want to let it go, I want to just let go of all of it. I can not bear it anymore, I can not bear to have so much sadness near me in the world anymore and I sob. Then I remember the angel. I ask her and she nods and I hand the sadness to her. It takes a long time, but I gather it from the room and I hand it over to her. She fills the pouches in her britches with it and then covers it all with her robe and promises to take it off-world.

The next week it rains. And this week, my legs hurt less. This week at Misha's, she works on my elbows and my left knee and then my right knee heats up like it has a radiator in it. The evil chi is being released, she says. We know now how to get to it. When she leaves the room this time, I do not feel the sadness so much. I hear a very old voice, can you hear me? I am moving far away. The devil has not come back, and the angel is still here.

## Outside the rain begins

This afternoon Susan and I meet at the gym. I am late, of course. Susan asks about my knees. One of hers is covered with two long serpent scars. We do quat sets, her with weights, me without. We talk when our machines are next to each other. She is learning aikido. She is learning not to panic when someone grabs her, not to panic but to take the energy and turn it around, to throw, using the other person's energy. Her eyes open from their sleepiness. We talk. It's not about how to prevent panic, but about how to use it. Her incest survivor crystal dangles from her neck as she works her weights.

I look at her and watch her. Usually we meet three times a week at the crack of dawn before I have to go to the office and we talk and work out together, reporting on the survivor work from outside. Today, we meet in the afternoon, waiting on the rain. It's getting better, she says. Don't you think? I nod, wondering does she mean the rain or our work. Both are true, I think. It's getting better, I say. It's only when the old feelings come back and I recognize them again that I think I am stuck. It's like lifting weights. Inch by inch. She nods. She laughs, her long hair tossing in the shower.

We walk out into the rain. She won't cross Market Street like I do, in the middle of the road, so we walk to the intersection. She asks are you going to the country? If the roads hold out, I say. Sher will know. We need to take the roses. Susan nods. We kiss good-bye under her umbrella. She asks what we do up there in the country when it rains. We just watch and sit inside and be warm and dry, I say. It only rains in clumps, you know. We talk. We remember. We do our work. Susan smiles and kisses me. Have a good weekend, she says. See you Tuesday. She walks off in the other direction.

I walk towards my '63 Falcon. It is cold and gray. It is like Rhode Island in November. I get into the car and lean back on the seat, waiting before I push in the clutch, before I pull out the choke. I just sit there, my head tilted back on the top of the seat and I feel the sadness washing through me again, as though it were pressing out from the inside of all of my skin. The car is cold and damp. My tears slip down into my hair and then I remember to breathe. Breathe steady, feeling the sadness through me, then out through my feet. Breathe deeply, filling myself steady.

The air comes in through the old seams of the vent window and the car is silent with my tears. Then I realize I don't hear the rain on the roof. The rain has been stopped for a little while now. Well, maybe we will get there tonight. I keep my eyes closed and keep breathing my slow rhythm. Take in, let go, take in, let go. Well, if we can't, we'll figure something else out. We'll get the roses planted this weekend, even if we have to plant them in pots here in the city and take them up later.

Between me and Sher and the rest of us, we can probably figure this out. I begin to feel a little more soothed. I turn around and peek at the angel who is sitting in the back seat. She is smiling at me, softly, patiently. It will be okay. And soon, we'll be able to stay at the farm for good. Pretty soon. It's not so far away as it seems.

I look at the angel and she motions to me to dry my eyes off with my sleeve. This makes me smile and I turn back to the window and I wipe my eyes with my sleeve. The wind still comes cold and the sky is not clear, but the rain is holding off. Breathe. And then finally the sigh, which means my own rain is holding off. Just to be able to sit in the warm with Sher and be dry and talk seems like a home to me now. And this weekend, we will go to this home. When the rain stops, we will walk; Misha said I could walk if I use a strong stick. I know I can; it doesn't hurt so much as before, even in the rain.

*AUTHOR'S NOTE:* Women have asked me if this story is true; if it really happened. The answer is that this story is as true as I know how to make it; yes, everything I wrote here actually happened.

# The Day After Tomorrow Show

### by Patricia Piasecki

T: I'd like to introduce Priscilla Patience, who bills herself as a recovering lesbian alcoholic.

T: Tell me, Priscilla, what exactly is a recovering lesbian alcoholic?
P: Am I correct in assuming you know what a lesbian is?
T: I think so.
P: How about an alcoholic?
T: I guess I think of an alcoholic as someone whose inability to control their use of alcohol leads to major problems in their life.
P: That fits my definition closely enough.
T: I'm not sure what you mean by recovering — do you now have your drinking under control?
P: I believe the only way an alcoholic can have their drinking under control is to never have a drink.
T: You mean you abstain?
P: I haven't had a drink for three months now.
T: That doesn't seem like very long — I hope you're not offended by my saying that.
P: Not at all. From what I've read about alcohol treatment programs, most counselors don't consider their programs successful until the client has been off alcohol for a year. I'd be happy to come back in nine months if you feel the points I raise in my discussion would be more valid then.
T: No. We asked you here because our researchers tell us that alcoholism is currently a cause of great concern in the lesbian community and because our audience is interested in hearing what you have to say

about your own struggle with the problem. You were one of the few lesbians we contacted who was willing to appear.
P: Your researchers are correct. I'm glad you realize lesbians watch TV.
T: We try to do our best. Did you try controlling your drinking instead of completely giving it up?
P: I've been trying to control it ever since I started drinking ten years ago. It never seemed to work. For two months before I quit totally, I cut down to a couple of drinks a week with friends or for a special occasion. My last drink was for the Emmy Awards show.
T: A couple of drinks a week seems reasonable to me.
P: For someone who's not an alcoholic, it may be reasonable. But I was still having blackouts on just one drink and that's when I realized I had to get alcohol completely out of my life.
T: So you went to A.A.?
P: No, I decided to try quitting on my own with the hope that my friends would help out when I needed them.
T: Did they help?
P: They were wonderful. I wish they could be on this show with me. I had three people who I talked to or saw every day. When I was going through withdrawal, I sometimes talked to them several times a day.
T: I didn't realize you go through withdrawal when you quit drinking.
P: Let me tell you — I didn't realize it until I felt myself going through it! I know now that it's very common. I figured that if I didn't begin to see some progress in two weeks, I would seek professional help. Luckily, my friends seemed willing to continue their support for as long as it was needed and I've learned since then that it normally takes ten days to two weeks for the body to adjust. So setting a limit of two weeks turned out to be sound medical advice for myself.
T: So you don't think going to A.A. or some similar group is necessary.
P: So far, it hasn't been for me. But I have had the help of A.A. indirectly through a couple of generous people who attended meetings and shared lots of information that the three friends I mentioned earlier didn't have.
T: Does your family know about your alcoholism?
P: My family knows I quit drinking. The strange thing about all this is that being a lesbian, I've had many years of experience at keeping a secret. The word lesbian has never been mentioned to many of my close relatives and I suspect that the word alcoholic will never be mentioned to those same relatives. But just as my lovers have always been accepted at family gatherings without any explanations being necessary, I feel that my sobriety will be accepted without having to use the word alcoholic. But it's really too soon to tell.
T: You're comparing being a lesbian to being an alcoholic?!?

P: Only so far as the similarity in the fear, misunderstanding, and ignorance surrounding the two words. Admitting to myself that I was a lesbian wasn't *anywhere near* as hard as admitting to myself that I was an alcoholic. But both are, unfortunately, still socially unacceptable to mainstream America.

T: I never thought of it like that. So you feel like, as they say, you had to "come out of the closet" as an alcoholic like you had to as a lesbian.

P: Exactly. It was sort of funny when I first realized it. I thought "Oh no — coming out of another closet! I don't know if I can handle it." But then I told myself that since I had dealt with the fear of rejection from people who had known the "straight Priscilla", I would find some way to deal with the fear of rejection from people who had known the "drunk Priscilla".

T: We don't have much time left. I'd like to ask you a few questions about your life now. Other than no longer being an alcohol user, has it changed?

P: God, that's an entire show!

T: Well, how about telling us a little about the changes you notice on a daily basis.

P: That's easy. I have never felt better physically. I'm rarely tired and don't sleep half as much as I used to. I am happy and content most of the time. So many people forget that alcohol is a depressant. I don't have seemingly inexplicable mood swings. I can usually identify the problem when I'm feeling bad. When I was drinking, I was more often than not unable to understand why I was depressed all the time.

T: I assume you've remained close to the friends you've mentioned earlier. How about other people who may not know you as well and invite you to parties or out to bars? Do you turn those invitations down?

P: In the beginning, I felt I didn't have any other choice. I didn't feel strong enough to not have a drink in a situation where most people were drinking. But in the last month or so, I have begun going to parties again and being willing to meet people in bars. I can't expect my friends to stop drinking just because I have. Hopefully, none of them will ever let their drinking begin to destroy their lives like I let it begin to destroy mine.

T: You said you're happy and content most of the time. Can you pick one thing that makes you happiest now?

P: Sunlight. When it comes in my window in the morning, I welcome it instead of wanting to block it out by pulling the covers over my head. It doesn't hurt my eyes anymore.

T: I guess we can take a break for a commercial with that image. Priscilla has a message for someone who's getting to stay up late tonight. We'll do that when we return. Don't go away.

T: We're talking with Priscilla Patience, a recovering lesbian alcoholic. If you're just tuning in, you've missed a discussion of Priscilla's struggle with alcoholism. Before we move on to another guest, Priscilla wishes to read a short letter to a very special person in her life. Do you want to tell us a little about it, Priscilla?

P: Just that I was going to send this letter but when I found out I was going to be on the show, I knew that the person I wrote it to would be allowed to stay up and watch me so I asked if I could read it on the air. I really appreciate your letting me do this, Tad.

T: Hey, if it means we get an extra viewer, it's worth it. Go ahead.

P: Dear Georgia,

The last time I visited you in Texas, you asked me why I was drinking soda with dinner instead of my usual wine. I thought I would be ready for that question, but I wasn't. I've had some time to think about it and have come up with some answers:

So I will be in a good mood when you get me up at 7:00 a.m. to watch cartoons.

So I will be able to think quickly and answer your questions as best I can with the clarity and simplicity that a five-year-old girl requires.

So I will be able to understand the pictures you draw and give you the support and encouragement you need.

So I will always have enough money to buy you little presents that remind me of you.

So I can feel the joy that watching you do tricks for me on the swing set brings.

So I can feel the pain that is a natural part of saying good-bye to someone you love that you only get to see once or twice a year.

So I will remember all the sweet and funny things you say to me.

So I will have the courage to love you with all the power of that emotion.

So you will see that you can celebrate, have fun, and be uninhibited without having to use drugs.

There are probably many more reasons I could write to you about, but I think these are the most important.

The last time you visited me in Illinois, I gave you a glass of soda which you wanted to take with you in the car. Your mom was worried that you might spill it walking down the stairs and asked if you wanted her to carry it. You said "I can *han*-dle it." You did o.k. going down the stairs, but your mom told me later that you spilled it all over your nice outfit on the way to see your good friend.

I'm glad you have confidence in yourself — that's very important, especially for girls. But I hope you learned from that experience that sometimes you are wrong about what you can handle. It took me ten years (twice as many as you have been alive) to learn that I couldn't handle drinking alcohol. That's one more reason why I'm drinking cola now. Because I *can't* handle alcohol.

Love always,<br>PP

P.S. I haven't forgotten that too much sugar is bad for you — maybe next time we'll stick to five-alive like we always used to.

T: OK, Georgia, now it's time for bed. Thanks for sharing your experience with us, Priscilla.
P: Thanks for inviting me.
T: We'll be back after this commercial.

*(Thanks to Victoria, Joyce, Jeannie, Horace, Liz, to the kind-hearted woman whose vivid descriptions of the West Virginia hills finally convinced me I didn't need drugs to relax, and to Wally and Sue for making me Caroline's godmother.)*

**PATRICIA PIASECKI:** lives and works in Chicago. A practicing existentialist, she is one of Bruce Springsteen's biggest fans.

So many lesbians of all ages turn to drugs to numb the pain and frustration often associated with living in an imperfect society. Being clean and sober would not rid the society of its imperfections. However, it might result in more organized resources within the lesbian community since we would have additional energy and consistent clarity of thought to develop and maintain them. We would then be able to easily find and have each other for support and strength which is real and lasting instead of the superficial and temporary comfort being high or drunk brings. Also: we'd be the best dancers and marathon runners the world has ever seen, have the lowest car insurance rates since we'd be the safest drivers, all be employed since we'd have the best work records, and win all of our custody cases because we'd be the most stable parents on earth.

# Three Glasses Of Wine Have Been Removed From This Story
Excerpts from a Novel-In-Progress

### by Marian Michener

Streetlights flash in the round glasses on Flanner's round face. "So, you've never been to a women's bar before?"

Alison speeds her Birkenstock ramble to catch up to Flanner's stride. "When you call it a women's bar, does that mean straight women can go there, too? Or it is just for lesbians?"

"Both, I guess. Isn't a straight woman just a lesbian that hasn't figured it out yet?" Flanner is serious but Alison chortles a gleeful chortle that feeds on itself. And Olivia laughs, too, her heart filled with the summer night, her new friends Flanner and May, her lover Alison, and her vision of a place for women.

All there is to Alice B.'s is a storefront in a plain brown wrapper, a bar, a jukebox and a pool table. But when Olivia walks in and sees lesbians in Emma Goldman tee shirts, and lesbians in trousers with rainbow-colored suspenders, and lesbians with Panama hats and carnations in their lapels, and lesbians in overalls and lesbians with bow ties and lesbians with ink on their fingers and lesbians with chalk on their pants and lesbians in running shorts and tank tops showing off their biceps and breasts and thighs and sunburnt flesh, lesbians smoking pipes and lesbians wearing astrological symbols around their necks, lesbians with long hair, lesbians with beards, lesbians dancing, lesbians pouring from pitchers of beer, lesbians discussing politics and lesbians kissing and lesbians just sitting in chairs with their feet up being lesbians — the scene sways towards her and it feels like coming home.

"Don't stare," May whispers, blocked in the doorway behind Olivia. But Olivia has already noticed that most of the women in the room check out the newcomers at the creak of the door. Whether the look is a forward evaluation or a shy glance or a reflex so unconscious that it becomes a part of the gesture it interrupts, Olivia is certain that it is one of the foremost pleasures of being here.

Olivia and Alison snuggle in a booth and watch Flanner and May bumping on the dance floor like two long low slow-vibrating bass strings. Olivia touches Alison's elf silk hair with her cheek. Shy in their corner, in each other's arms, they look around a tavern much like all the taverns of life so far. But it's ours, Olivia thinks. On one wall, Janis Joplin wails in orange lights, southern comfort mouth turning inside out. On the other, Amelia Earhart is about to flip her propeller and fly. The night is street quiet outside, but Olivia and Alison huddle as if in protection from a storm.

In between the gangles and giggles of two games of pool, Flanner and Olivia plan a Sunday afternoon entertainment — watching Sappho's Sluggers play softball in the park. Olivia says, "Okay, we'll pick up a couple of six-packs and meet you there."

"You know, Olivia — " Alison's voice is cool and tired, coming in on a new tack. "We don't have to bring beer with us everywhere we go."

"Shesh. I know that." Olivia looks at her lover, soft as ever but far away. Alison's face grays under the pool table light. Her color-changing eyes flicker love and weary righteousness. Tenille is on the jukebox singing, "I never wanted to touch a man — the way I want to touch you," and Olivia thinks of Rick, Alison's alcoholic ex-husband; how Alison had been disgusted with his drinking and puking and sleeping and stinking. Alison never got drunk with Rick like Olivia did with the homebrew drinking man she lived with before. But none of this seems to Olivia to have anything to do with the glass of beer in front of her now, its fresh head fading.

"What are you getting at? Do I drink too much?"

Alison shrugs and shoots soggily into the cluster of poolballs. She is angry, Olivia knows, though it seems to her to have come out of nowhere. Angry in self-defense, Olivia raises her voice. "Flanner. Do I drink too much?"

Flanner blinks slowly at her. "I don't know. Do you?"

Flanner chalks her cue. Olivia challenges May, the weightlifter, the volleyball coach, who runs on carrot juice and doesn't care for the taste of booze herself. "May, tell me."

With the pained blankness of a sphinx who may only answer once, May nods.

"Hunh." Olivia pushes her glass away, spills beer, disproves her trusted friends. She will not take another drink. She will not say another word. She burns. She plays without pleasure, lines up her shot precisely and misses.

"Hey, come on." Alison rubs Olivia's shoulders.

Sympathetic, mournful May says, "Be a sport, Olivia."

And Flanner says, "Listen. If you're going to be such a drag when you don't drink, maybe you better just go ahead."

---

Olivia hops off the bus on Potrero and walks over to York. Champagne brunch at the Cliff House, the ocean roaring silently outside the large windows, still fills her head and she reminds herself to be a little uneasy on the street. In the three months that she has been in San Francisco, things have been ragged, as always, with the woman she moved here to live with. And neither of them has been well off. But they've celebrated anyway, champagne mornings and brandy evenings across the neighborhoods of the new city.

There is a long moment of stillness in these late winter afternoons as Olivia walks to her aikido class. The sun always hangs low, spilling gold over the row houses. The color of the hour breaks into Olivia's heart and she feels suspended in time. But, the fact is, she is late.

She hurries up the wooden warehouse stairs and bows her head at the entrance to the loft. She has an irreverent woman's reverence for the time and the place and the practice and the women she shares it with. But she can't help also feeling like a sound-of-music nun bustling into vespers late, disturbing her sisters.

She tiptoes to the dressing room. Penny and Joy and Verbana and Kitty and Sally and Linda and Estelle and Ruth and Marlene and Barbara and Margie Brown Belt and Margie Sensei, each gathering herself silently, kneel at the end of the red and yellow mat. Olivia tries to pull on her white gi quickly and quietly, but the drawstring on her pants sticks halfway up her hips until she bites out a curse and tugs at it. The ties inside her top fumble at her fingertips. And the belt ties clumsily as the swish of her footsteps follows her to the place that opens for her.

When she sits seiza everything sinks to a weighted place inside her. She feels the others through the mat and a common wave of breath. She opens her eyes to the window across the long white room. The sun rests behind the hill and the houses turn blue. She lets herself be with the breeze and the sky. The women bow and class begins.

They warm up wordlessly. Stretching arms, legs, fingers, toes, backbone, wrists, neck, Olivia hears her body, in a language of cracks, welcoming her wandering mind home.

Kneeling at the edge of the mat, she is embarrassed to have come to class woozy. Better woozy than not at all, she reasons, remembering how narrowly she escaped the seductions of staying home. But it *is* sloppy. It looks as if she cares less about aikido than she means to. It *is* hard to pay attention.

Margie is demonstrating. The long black skirts of her hakama follow the movements of her bare feet. Her pendulum braid accentuates her straight back.

"Wait until your uke is committed to her strike and then enter," she says. "It's hard because your natural reaction when you see her hand coming toward your head is this — " she puts her arms in front of her head and turns her face away, squeezing her eyes shut and shrinking into her shoulders. "That's like saying 'this can't be happening.' Don't do that. Watch the attack and see what it is. Try to stay conscious."

Olivia practices facing attacks. She blinks and blinks and even when she can force her eyes to stay open, her focus blurs. Her eyes refuse to see.

She takes some falls. She likes the solid thwack of her body on the mat. There is a clownishness that delights her in this ukemi — this art of falling away from harm. She can fall and she can roll and she can get up and do it again. But her eyes close also at the moment of the roll. She finds herself on her feet, confused at where she has landed.

She takes more attacks. She entreats her own attention. She determines she will relax now, smile, accept blows: gifts from her partner, something to play with, something she wants to see. She breathes. She stands her ground. Her ground stands her. She cries out when she sees the whole thing: the strike, the opening, the entry, the throw. Fascinated, she invites another attack and does it again. The third time, she is overconfident, forgets to watch, is caught by surprise and ducks. But now she knows she doesn't have to.

She wipes her face with her sleeve. Her mouth tastes clean. Margie is talking again.

"Take the attitude of practicing with a live blade. This is the attack. This is the sharp edge. If you don't pay attention, you are dead."

Olivia wonders what life would be like if every moment were a matter of life and death. And then she sees that, of course, it is. And this is a sobering thought. Every moment not paying attention is a moment dead. She is suddenly very tired of running from the blade without ever seeing its edge. Damn the time lost ducking blows. And not even just real blows, but imagined blows and anticipated blows, too: a whole life of ducking. She knows it's hard and it may take a long time, but damned if she isn't going to learn to keep her eyes open.

But there is another technique to practice. Attacks, blends, big circles, falls. Olivia is tired. She can't see the clock. This can't last forever, she advises herself. Hang in there. It will be over soon enough and looking back, you'll be glad you did.

In the Vietnamese restaurant near the hospital where Olivia and Kathleen work as clerks, the shades are drawn and there is nothing in the world but the two women, their cushioned corner, curried crab and tea. Kathleen is Olivia's ocelot-like high fidelity friend. It was Kathleen who took Olivia in when she had to move out from living with her lover. It is lunches with Kathleen that sustain Olivia when ranks and files of numbers besiege her. They are the ad-hoc leaflet writing committee for their union, the first editors of each other's literary efforts. Hungry mid-mornings, they bring each other bagels with lots of cream cheese. They argue over interpretations.

"It didn't bother me at first," Kathleen is saying. "But you did say you wanted to be aware of the pattern."

Olivia remembers saying this. It was at the end of their first sunny courtyard lunch together after discovering each other across a crowded discussion of loyalty oaths. She had found Kathleen intimidatingly cute and dry-cleaned and sure of herself. But she was an intelligent, politically-aware dyke writer; they were both new at the hospital; and Olivia needed a friend. After that lunch, when she suggested meeting after work for a beer, Kathleen sighed, squinted at the sky and said, "I guess now is the time to tell you — I'm a recovering alcoholic."

"A cup of tea then," Olivia said too quickly laughing reassuringly, embarrassed to have gaffed and uncovered something difficult. In her gut, she hung back, disoriented, nervous. She had never had a sober friend before. She had always had drinking buddies. Where could she even go with this woman? How could they get comfortable and talk? What would sit on the table between them? Feeling thirsty already, she began to formulate strategies for escaping the nascent relationship. It raised too many questions.

And yet she was curious about the questions and as her fingers pulled at blades of grass, she heard herself speaking calmly. "If you feel like talking about that sometime — I mean, I don't know much about it. I could probably learn a lot from your experience. I'm concerned about my own — I drink too much."

Three broken stone pillars stood beside them in the hospital courtyard, survivors from the original foundation. Olivia watched a red spider skitter up the shortest column.

"I'd like to try to understand the pattern," she had said then.

Now Kathleen is saying, "The pattern is you drink too much. You joke about getting hung up at the bar when there's work you want to do and I don't feel like laughing. It's not funny anymore. You have stories to tell. We need you to get out of the bar and do the work of writing them." Kathleen's pep talk and her stubborn cowlick make Olivia smile. But Kathleen pushes on beyond smiling.

"And I need you to be honest with me about something. You're full of support for me being sober. But then you make getting drunk sound like more fun than I think it really is."

Olivia sees the anger set in Kathleen's small but certain jaw. She hopes to get around it. She shrugs. "Maybe it isn't such a good time."

"Then why do it? And why, if it's so great that I'm sober, isn't it great for you?"

Olivia's own jaw quivers. She has no answer for this until the helplessness she feels reminds her of what she needs from the bar. "Listen," she says, "It's different for you. You have someone to go home to when I have the weekend to get through alone. The bar is my family, the place I can drop in and find someone to talk to. Or just watch the lesbian life go by."

"But that's what bothers me, Liv. You have this image of yourself as some sad, broken dyke sitting on a bar stool with the best of her life behind her — getting through the time that's left. That's bullshit. You have a lot to stay sober for."

Olivia's eyes fill. Their friendship is on the line. She wants to stop Kathleen before she demands something she can't do. There is no way to change the subject. Kathleen is not backing down.

"There are people who love you, Liv. Me for one. That lonely routine just won't get it."

Nothing ever makes Olivia's fundamental loneliness worse than someone breaking through it; the idea that it doesn't have to be that way; the awareness of how much she does it to herself; the implied questions: why don't you treat yourself better? Why don't you *like* yourself better? She wallows in red-faced sniffling.

Kathleen touches her arm. "I want you to know that you could quit drinking right now if you wanted to. I know it's hard. I could help."

Olivia shakes her head. She can't say she can't, but... Drinking seems such a small part of her general restless unhappiness. She pulls back to suspect Kathleen's biases, thinking: maybe she's projecting *her* problem onto *me*. Evangelic zeal. Alcoholic vampirism. Maybe she thinks I'm an alcoholic because she wants me to be like her. Kathleen's eyes are steady on her. Maybe, Olivia thinks, it takes one to know one.

She closes her eyes and tries to see the future with or without. Both are wide open passageways. She can't see anything yet in either. She imagines the chilled glass of white wine so dry it tastes like nothing is there. She imagines knowing she can't have it. She says, "I just can't see saying 'never again.'"

Her eyes still closed, she hears Kathleen's head shaking. "You don't have to."

Olivia opens her eyes. She does not want to be cornered into a decision she is not ready for. "Everything you say is true," she says. "I appreciate your honesty. I know you love me."

"But what are you going to do?"

"I'm going to cut down. Get off my ass."

Kathleen's gaze is not satisfied.

"I cut down on coffee, didn't I?"

"You don't have a problem with coffee, honey. And you do have a problem with alcohol."

Olivia grins at the doggedness she admires in Kathleen. She has always been glad to have her on her side. But just now she's not sure which side her side is on.

"Kathleen, I have to choose my own time. Believe me, I'll be thinking about it."

---

Olivia opens a bottle of mineral water for herself. She paces herself to take two bottles of water to one glass of wine. It's her last night in Portland and she's promised Jenny, her long-distance lover, they won't stay long at the party. Just catch up with some friends and then go home and make passionate love all night.

Jenny composes music that travels in circles, but she spoke quite directly when Olivia arrived for this visit. She said, "I'm glad you're here. And I want you to stay with me. But I don't want to be around you if you're going to be drunk." So Olivia instituted a three drink limit for the duration. She considers Jenny's ultimatum a gutsy kind of love. Of course, the risk is, if you tell a drunk not to be drunk around you, she may disappear. But this is the first time anyone has ever told Olivia that she's better to be with when she's sober. Did she somehow always think that the more she drank the better everyone would feel?

Maybe that's why she does sit down to a glass of wine with Beth, whose mother's death last spring is not far enough behind her. Beth's sentinel collarbones stand out letting a slow breath pass into her chest with every sad laugh or touch her friends bring. Olivia would love to surround her with the mournful foolishness she knows can keep you alive until you gain the distance from which you can stand to look back.

Olivia and Flanner compare the gray appearing in each other's hair. They call it silver and swear they would never trade back the years that brought it. Olivia pours another glass of wine to drink to change and old friends.

Flanner's guitar tunes and strums and Olivia joins it out on the porch between the glow of the house and the summer night. A bottle of wine goes with her because one more glass will soothe her fear of music.

And in short time she is pouring out her imitation Bobby Dylan nasal parlando and making commentary between the lines of ballads. She is making up new songs, mocking the burning torch of the old ones. And she is topping off her glass in case the night grows cold.

When Jenny tells her it is time to go home, it is not a tender suggestion.

"Why are you angry?" Olivia asks in the car. "Was I singing off key again?"

"You're drunk."

"I am not drunk. Am I drunk? What makes you think I'm drunk?" She feels a familiar turning under her and sees streetlights tilting in her direction. "I am drunk. How did I get drunk? Where were you while I was getting drunk? I didn't mean to get drunk."

Then she is on Jenny's couch. The bookcase is flickering like a Christmas-tree behind Jenny's head. Olivia would like to turn it down. It hurts her eyes.

"I can sleep out here," she says, sulkily. "I don't think you're very happy with me tonight."

Jenny holds her hand. Her focus steadies as something wavers across Jenny's face. Headlights from the street outside? Jenny says, "I want you to sleep with me. That's the point. It's our last night together and look what's happened to our precious time."

"I get it — you're angry because I'm leaving."

"I'm angry because I feel like you've already left. I wish you could see your eyes. It's scary the way they get. I don't feel like you see me."

Olivia understands that more presence is requested. She holds Jenny's hand tightly. "Okay. I'm going to get my shit together."

She closes her eyes and calls herself home. She lays her face in Jenny's lap. "I can't believe you still love me."

Jenny's face is hot and wet next to hers. Olivia sits up and commands the whirling electricity to settle. Satisfied, she takes a deep breath and then stands.

She laughs weakly as her balance trembles. "Okay, girl, you can lean on me if you like. We're going to bed and I bet I can still make love to you all night."

Jenny walks down the hall, arms around her. "I'll bet."

---

Olivia's pipes clang and she opens her eyes to sunshine on white walls, Sunday morning, her twenty-ninth birthday. She dresses and pulls her sheets into a duffel bag thinking, this is the laundry of my first sober day. She takes *Song of Solomon* with her to the laundromat but sits in the corner of the neighborhood bustle wondering that the old man who tends the machines doesn't notice what a different and rather special person she is becoming.

She makes her bed, the foam pad on the floor, smooths out the blue comforter thinking, I am making the bed of my first sober day. All the indications that it was time for her to quit drinking line up like the classic call to adventure and everything around her is subtly changed by her acceptance of the task. It's as if she has wakened in the poppy field and it's time to gather her tin, straw and animal forces and carry on towards Oz.

She meets Kathleen in a cafe on Haight for the first breakfast of her sober life. They toast each other with black coffee, as exciting a ceremony as any with champagne, as if the next step higher is the one that begins on the ground. The coffee sparkles in solid white mugs. A change begins in Olivia's gut like high tide turning to the long roll out to sea.

She walks, sober, to the other side of the city where the sky still has a distinct tint over the warehouses and her first aikido class as a sober woman. Her skills on the mat are not magically increased, but she does feel one less barrier to being there.

The exhilaration of the convert levels to a ride on the waves, on the new chemistry, or the old chemistry newly understood. It is a great experiment. Tacos without beer have a different flavor. She meets some people at Peg's Place for her first sober evening of dancing.

Will it feel odd, she wonders, to be in a bar without drinking? She has to change the physical habit of stepping immediately up to the tap for the security of holding a glass in her hand. She sees how buying beer after beer after beer was a way of paying dues to the regular club, visibly supporting the bars, drinking to their health. And how a woman with a shot of whiskey in front of her always had an inalienable right to her place at the bar. Did you come here to drink or what?

Olivia dances. This is what *she* came here for. She is not afraid. But she is shyer than before. Loosening up comes slower, but she knows it is coming. They have made the music she grew up to a disco medley of oldie tunes. She laughs. Friends bring her Calistoga and lime.

Before, when she got tired, she would drink more and that would keep her going until it dropped her flat. Tonight, when she is tired, she goes home.

She waits at the bus stop with a friend of a friend, Diana, the rock-and-roll teddy bear with the interested eyes.

"It's impressive what you're doing," Diana says, intent on the streetlight. "But what, exactly is the point?"

Olivia looks at the short, soft, dark furry head of hair, dark eyes set in a face that insists that it has overgrown its own innocence. Diana's mouth is drawn expectantly as if it already knows the answers, while the arch of one eyebrow demands that the answers be recited out loud. Olivia slips her hands in her pockets and leans against the lamppost.

"Well, it's that old bottle-meets-girl, bottle-gets-girl, bottle-loses-girl story. It's like I've been in a bad but seductive, obsessive relationship for ten years. It leads me on and it makes me cry and it never really gives me what I want. It *seems* to take care of me when I'm afraid or tired. But I always wind up with a pain in my head. I've been crazy and rude around booze to where I'd walk over my grandmother for a drink. And I'm tired of walking over my sweet old grandmother. The damned thing saps my energy and I need that back so I can be a good friend to my friends and write the Great American Lesbian novel and enjoy my life as it passes."

Olivia looks down the funneling gutter drain at her feet. Diana says, "There's something else?"

"I was thinking today about how you go into an airport to meet a plane and it's late so you go into the bar to kill some time. And I was thinking, I'm not sure a person has all that much time that she can afford to be hanging out in bars killing it."

"I know," Diana says. She nods Olivia on.

Olivia follows the thought towards its center. "I'm twenty-nine years old and I'm more than a little afraid of dying. My mother has this disease — and I may have it too in time — it takes away your nervous system's control of your muscles. That's what death looks like to me. And when you have this thing, in its advanced stages, people sometimes think you're drunk because you lurch when you walk and you slur your words. I'll face that when I have to. But I *don't* have to meet it half-way."

She opens her fist and looks at the change. "You know what I mean?"

---

Reptilian, she feels like a reptile, Olivia reflects as she stretches out on the grass at Dolores Park. Or is it amphibian? Some kind of creature whose blood runs cold and still as the stone it hibernates under, who warms to activity only after bathing in the morning sun. She follows Diana's story, mostly listening to the melodic tones it is told in. Given the long eight years between their ages, her hardest image of them is the dinosaur and the teddy bear. But there's more than stuffing in the girl's head (even though she *doesn't* laugh at some of Olivia's jokes) and Olivia is feeling a few million years this side of extinct today.

They are watching children bounce on the wood and metal and sand constructions. Two small boys push the merry-go-round and jump on for a half turn before it cranks to a stop and they push again. The sun has almost heated through to Olivia's heart when Diana stands and runs knock-kneed across the grass to the grinding wheel. She pushes it by the hoops that quarter it. Olivia is behind her and pushing as well, soon as she grasps the project. The two boys squeal, riding free at last. Another half dozen playground kids join them.

"Get on," Olivia says to Diana. And she puts her shoulder to the steel and runs with it until she thinks the thing should fly.

Lizardlike no longer, she sweats and huffs and collaspes on the nubby surface of the disc. It screams and stops. She stretches out with her head in the center and her feet against an arch.

"Okay, you guys give us a ride," Diana challenges. The kids laugh. The wheel turns. Diana's head touches Olivia's. Clouds and blue sky turn sassily. Under the creaking of the spindle, Olivia can hear the music that sounds in the ears of a strange young girl who looks up into the sky too long.

The merry-go-round slows. Children's shouting fades back in. "Push us again."

"Another day," Diana tells them. And by the time Olivia realizes she's gone, she's halfway across the park, diving into the ship/train/treehouse jungle gym complex. The ground under Olivia's feet feels old or new or differently present as she follows.

Three and four-year-olds track over the planks above Diana's hiding place. Grains of sand trickle down on the hair of both women there. Shafts of sunlight fall over their faces. Olivia kisses Diana's soft, not at all childish mouth.

Diana laughs, "So. Sober doesn't mean you don't play."

---

Olivia walks off the elevator on the twelfth floor and into the half-lab half-office where Kathleen works. She paces, looking out the window at the ocean and a few thousand houses while Kathleen types footnotes to the day's work.

"Well," Olivia asks when the clatter stops. They never pretend to have anything else on their minds at a time like this.

Kathleen looks up and lets only a few seconds pass because she knows it's too important and vulnerable to tease.

"Well," she says, grinning proud. "Well, it's great that's what."

She always says something like this, but it is still a relief to Olivia to hear it. Kathleen packs things up from her desk drawers into her canvas briefcase — promising manila envelopes, books, an empty yoghurt cup. She hands Olivia the almost finished draft of Olivia's short story. Across the top she has written, "It's a dance."

Olivia's arm is around Kathleen as they walk to the elevator. "God, I'm glad we like each other's stuff."

"Well, you really pulled this one out. It seemed so hung up for a long time. You had me holding my breath."

As they walk up and down the hills home, Olivia watches the Cole Valley women in the hardware store, the laundromat, the doorway of the bar. Kathleen watches the sidewalk. "There's just one thing that bothers me at the end of your story."

"What's that?"

"The wine."

Olivia breathes thinly, thinking about the wine. "Well, that's the way it was."

She has cleaned up her act about drinking and she's glad, but she's not about to censor the life this story comes out of. "I mean, that's what this character would do — at that time."

"Does she have to?"

"*Yeah,* she does. Those glasses of wine mark a progression toward the insight the whole thing winds up on. It's *in vino veritas* - the truth in the wine."

"Don't you think that's romaticizing drinking?"

"Don't *you* think there's some truth to it? Aren't there things that only come clear when you're a little ways out there after a few glasses of wine?"

They stop at the corner where Olivia's way continues down Cole and Kathleen's turns up Haight. Kathleen shifts the briefcase under her arm and looks steadily up at Olivia. "What really happened to that character that night?"

Olivia frowns at the corner of a brick wall. She likes to see what's real. "She went out to the bar and got drunk and went home."

"And what did she think?"

"She didn't *think* anything. She *felt* sorry for herself. Well, shit. Maybe there is something dishonest about putting a sober insight into a drunk's mouth."

Olivia rubs her head and pulls the hair at the back of her neck. "If I have to cut out either the insight or the wine, the wine will have to go."

"Of course." Kathleen waits.

Olivia sighs. "I don't know, Kathleen. I just don't know if I can get the feeling I want without those glasses of wine."

"I know." Kathleen hugs her. "That's the question, isn't it."

---

Because there are about five hundred thousand gay people marching down Market Street in the sunshine this morning, Olivia's spirit is on the rise. She laughs at the bearded fellow in the Glinda-the-good-witch get-up: crinoline skirts, glittering crown and wand and a sign around his neck that says, "It takes balls to be a fairy." Dykes on Bikes roar by at the front of the parade. Women on Wheels pump their bicycles, singing "Daisy" and smiling broadly. Gay caucuses from a spectrum of religions and political parties, and floats from Castro and South of Market bars pass. The Parents of Gays draw the most enthusiastic applause, a shiver passing along the sidelines as onlookers fantasize the distant dream of support from their families.

The division between the parade and the crowd lining the sidewalk is ambiguous with constant movement of people in and out of the surging dragon. A large group approaches, gay men and lesbians, striking in the everydayness of their appearance among the costumes and decorations. They carry a banner reading "Clean and Sober." Olivia joins the cheers and recognizes that something has changed. Last year she applauded when the Clean and Sober contingent passed and she thought their statement terribly courageous in a community where booze is so highly regarded an instrument of seduction and communion. But she had felt hypocritical applauding last year because the possibility of being sober and proud seemed as remote to her as the possibility of visits from another planet. And the fear of alienating herself from the sisterhood of her drinking sisters — missing the party in some basic way — kept her from even contemplating that incredible reach. And right now — any time now — she could march behind that banner without a thought. And even seeing it here makes the city look a little more like home.

She follows Diana's gaze up the street where a wave of excitement precedes the women's percussion band — sixty women dressed in white and playing drums and tambourines: a salsa march. Diana squeezes Olivia's hand. "This is it."

They find their place in front of the band and in back of the Women's Health Collective — red tee shirts and plastic speculums held high. Olivia and Diana let rhythm run through them and they dance. The asphalt heats up. Towers tower.

Olivia's silk shirt, orchid to overstate the lavender occasion, is half open for air. Diana teases her to take it off. Olivia is tempted, hesitates, then dances on, thinking, if I see one more bare-chested boy, I will.

Of course, she does. And dancing half-naked down Market Street feels pretty good to her. She dances harder, smiles down in her gut. Get it now, she thinks. This moment will never come again. Two other women nearby follow her example, one handing her baby to a friend while she pulls off her shirt.

This is something Olivia used to do drunk. Then she would be embarrassed, as if it had been a mistake. But this is intentional. The mistake would be to have to get drunk to do it.

By the end of the thirty block march, turning in to Civic Center square, Olivia is very high and very dry. She would pawn her shoes for a drink.

Large placards on the nearest wall proclaim, "Cold Beer."

"Jesus," Olivia points to the signs. "This is what's at the end of the long march for freedom and pride?"

She plans to scream if there isn't a glass of water to be had. It's funny because last night she'd been feeling edgy about going to a house party with Diana. She was afraid she would be bored. She didn't know anyone there. Before, when she was bored, she would drink to the intellectual level of the situation. Now she has to either change it or leave. When she's bored or nervous, now, especially when she's nervous about being tempted to drink, she dances. She had said, "I have this terrible fantasy that I dance half the night and then I'm dying of thirst and there's nothing in the house but cold beer and chilled wine."

Diana had laughed at her. "This house — it has running water."

In the coolers at the Civic Center, arranged to invite parade participants, the only alternative to beer is chilly red cans of Coke. Olivia compromises on two of these in spite of her reformed caffeine and sugar habits. It's a special day. You've got to rot your gut with something if it's a special day.

As they sit on the curb watching the great gay parade come in, Olivia says, "You know, when I used to drink, I was always thirsty."

"I know," Diana says. "It dehydrates you."

"The old man used to make fun of me when I'd wake up hungover, tongue-curling thirsty. He'd say 'Why? You were drinking all night.' And it's taken me ten years to get the joke. Half the reason I drank all those years was because I was always so thirsty."

---

Olivia slips her beige clerk smock over her street clothes and strides down the hall to the nurses' station with an Ellington tune in her head. There was blue sky over Rainier as she walked up from downtown Seattle and her lungs woke to the cold October air.

The assignment board on the wall is half empty and she almosts laughs, disoriented after only a day off. "What's happening?"

Ilsa, the day secretary looks up. "Marna Thayer expired at 9:30 this morning." Olivia hears, now, the quiet on the ward she just threaded her cheerful, almost whistling, way through. Ilsa is explaining the other transfers and discharges but Olivia is stopped on how sharp the colors of the leaves outside become when the girl down the hall can't see them anymore.

And this is it. She has worked for two months on the leukemia floor and before she took the job she agonized over whether she was ready to work with dying patients, with the realization that we are all dying. The week before she started here, she dreamed the death of her mother, explicit drowned body and a silent funeral circle beside the lake. Her mother *had* been a swimmer as a young woman and there was something wonderful in the dream, finally, about her swimming without being afraid, without having to try not to die at the end.

Until today there had been improvements, declines, delicate moments, remissions, relapses, discharges, but no deaths on the floor. The routine of death turns out to be fairly simple. Olivia organizes Marna's chart to go to Medical Records. There is a problem about the autopsy and a mortician to entertain. Olivia types Marna's address on the Death Certificate, though in what sense it could be said to be her address now escapes her. She tracks down Dr. Deems, who is on call for the weekend, but was not present at Marna's death, to sign the certificate.

Deems is a tall young woman busy with another patient on another floor when Olivia finds her. She resents having to sign the certificate for another doctor's patient, but she is the only one available, so she sits down to it at the desk while Olivia waits.

"Was there an autopsy?" she asks.

"No."

Deems fills in a few words and then stops, tapping her pen on the blotter. "Immediate cause of death?"

"I don't know," Olivia says, realizing how little she understands of the causes of death, the causes of life.

"Did she stop breathing?" Deems asks.

"I don't know," Olivia says. "I wasn't there." This strikes her as absurd. Is it a trick question? Of course she stopped breathing. We wouldn't be writing a Death Certificate if she were still breathing.

Deems writes "respiratory arrest" in a tiny, precise hand in the immediate cause of death rectangle.

As Olivia walks back to her own floor, the whole hospital seems silly, unequal to the most basic questions. So much technology, research, care; and in the end, people die because they stop breathing.

Marna's primary nurse sits at the front desk, comtemplative, angry.

"I'm trying to understand why this one got to me. I've lost patients before."

"It's worth figuring out," Olivia says. "You wouldn't feel you've lost something if you hadn't felt you'd had something special."

Other patients and their families are quiet, picking at their dinner trays, looking out the windows at the sunset glowing over the city.

The pharmacist has been listening to a football game, and when it is over, he lets Olivia set the radio on her desk. She can't find a classical station but settles for jazz turned low by her ear while she works through lab requests and reports. One patient's wife walks by and says, "That's pretty upbeat." Olivia is not sure whether she means that the music is inappropriate on the night of Marna's death. But life is too short, in her view tonight, to do without a little piano, a little saxophone.

At the bus stop, at midnight, Olivia leans against the wood and glass shelter. On the half-inch ledge, beside her hand, she finds a green marble.

Cat's eye, she remembers the name as she picks up the scratched, oddly abandoned globe. She slips it in her pocket.

City blocks flicker cooly past the bus window. Kathleen had told her that the second year of sobriety was the hard part, where the excitement of cleaning up and taking control has passed and the issues drinking had obscured emerge to be dealt with. She wonders if it is this or turning thirty that has her thinking so much of her own mortality lately. Sometimes she feels like a bundle of sticks and tubes and knows it can't last.

Even though it is late when she gets home, she reaches back in her closet and finds the canvas-covered case by touch. She pulls the tarnished pieces of her mother's flute out of the bald red velvet lining. And she sits on the floor for what must be a long time and yet is no time at all. There is something equitable here that settles her face. Her mother sang off-key lullabies to her when she was a babe in arms. Olivia knows she'll never really sing. But her mother did give her the flute. And the flute does have a perfectly lovely voice. Olivia feels the weight and fit of possibilities in the silver segments. She thinks, as she has before, it's a long sight finer instrument than I'll ever be musician.

The lip of the mouthpiece is cold against her own as her fingers find the keys and some notes that please her. Part of a song of Jenny's. A ballad that reminds her of Flanner. A phrase that's just a piece of music. It's only warm air and metal after all. But tonight it seems to Olivia that life is nothing more than a stream of breath and whatever you can make of that.

**MARIAN MICHENER:** was born in Boston in 1952. She left town six months later and even today receives pieces of mail plastered with forwarding addresses. Her mother wanted her to be the first woman president. Her father would have settled for a doctor or lawyer. But she has her eye on the Great American Lesbian novel and only wishes she could explain her work to her grandmother.

If my community were clean and sober, it would look like: For starts, just think of the money our community spends on booze (or, if you prefer, the time we spend to earn the money we spend on booze). Then think of the time and energy spent thinking about drinking, being drunk, being hungover. Then the strength and awareness drained. Reclaim all of this — this is exciting enough a process as individuals, but as a community — there is nothing humanly possible we could not accomplish: cure cancer, create a literature, climb mountains, make incredible love to each other, foment revolution. Then there's the honesty, because alcohol is not the truth drug it has been reputed to be. And getting sober, on the other hand, presupposes and demands increasing honesty. And that means increasing trust between us. Sure we'd still have those wonderful terrible intense differences. Sure we'd still fool ourselves sometimes. And it would still take our whole lives to know and accept our ecstasies and sorrows. But along the way, we'd be that much closer to being the unfailing army of lovers Sappho told us about.

# The Sober Dyke

## by Sherry Thomas

"I like sober dykes" the button read. I pinned it on my jacket collar as I walked down the street to her apartment, smiling as I anticipated her slow grin when she saw it. Though "like" isn't the word for it: am crazy in love with one sober dyke would be more like it.

This began as a story about her, my wonderful sober dyke lover. I fell in love with her (among other reasons) when she was still an almost total stranger and she stood up to introduce herself at a women's community meeting, saying that she was a recovering alcoholic. I had grown up with an alcoholic father, had known lesbians who drank alcoholically, was ending a relationship with another child of an alcoholic, but I had never heard the word "recovery" spoken. A great leap of hope flooded through me, a name for the painful, blind changes I had been groping with. She stood small and sturdy, illuminated for a moment by her own power. I was intensely attracted, wanted to walk out the door and go home with her.

Months later, when I walked to her apartment pinning on my "sober dykes" button, she opened the door to me and I was struck again, as I am so often, by her beauty: the sensual pleasure in her being that delights me. My so un-sober dyke! She was standing in the doorway, a white shirt open to show the full curve of her breasts, her nakedness beneath, a navy vest chastely offering an essential ambiguity; her pants thin cotton touching all the curves of her. Only later, running my hand over her ass, savoring the perfect fit of hand and buttock, cupped desire, only then did I realize that there was nothing on under the pants either.

But coming through the door, I was watching her face, those eyes that can (and have) knocked me across a room, her butchy crew cut at its perfect baby-soft length.

"Girl," she said, seeing the roses I held out. And then she saw the button, threw back her head and laughed. "Girl, come over here," she said, still laughing, enfolding me.

She is an alcoholic, this lover of mine, who had been sober almost a year to the day when we met. And there has never been a moment when we were together that would have been richer, more fun, less inhibited, with alcohol between us. This is a relationship about joy, about coming alive: with all the demons of the past, so long repressed, out among us, but also all the vitality of the present here to slay them. Belief, acceptance, choosing to live: these are effective weapons. She has steadily invited me to grow, applauded every leap of daring that I took. She has taken her own leaps, remembering, recovering the past, recreating the present.

That night, she sat me down and listened to my demons from a hard confrontation with my recently ex-lover. My ex-lover, also the child of an alcoholic, had accosted me at work, angry and accusing, freely mixing fact with fantasy until I doubted the ground I stood on. At the sober dyke's house, I ended up on the floor, a wild-eyed child, afraid of being hit again. For the first time ever, it seemed, I was feeling the fear and remembering clearly the then and the now. I was not masking the fear with anger, not shutting down with coldness. Two years before, when my former lover had tried to strangle me, I said to myself, "People do things like that." I thought I had no feelings. Rocking on the floor in my sober dyke's arms, I dared to go all the way back, not coldly, but feeling what it was like for the little girl I'd been, who was never safe. And something cracked in me, wild grief and wild possibility: that I could start trying to be fully alive.

"I don't want to just dump all this garbage in here," I said (not saying what I meant: "Will you love me anyway?").

She reminded me that we can only have our space by going through, by being all that we are. So I told of the anger and the fear, the fear that seems so present and goes so far back: that I will get hit, hurt, killed. That I don't know what will happen next, am ducking blows and don't know where the next is coming from, then will be told that it didn't happen. We sat there with the terror, quietly.

It is a great gift to me, this bearing witness. She does not try to fix it, fix me, stop me. She is not repulsed by my vulnerability or my wildness. We sat with it and I grew more relaxed, came back to the present and asked what was for dinner.

"Scampi," she told me. And I was afraid to ask what it was, having always been afraid to ask in restaurants. But she always feeds me well, this woman, and this time it was prawns: an abundance of prawns, more prawns than I could eat. When was the last time I had too many prawns?

A lot of our connection is about feeding and about abundance. I'm coming out of the closet as a food lover and a good cook, no longer embarrassed to produce candlelight and flowers. She brings me fresh baked whole grain bread from the Zen center, crumpets from the English tea shop, introduces me to the delights of fresh pasta. We feed each other, and food is only the beginning. With the physical food has come spiritual food: rocking in the nights as one or the other of us reclaimed our past, listening to our stories, believing when we stopped denying.

"Outrageousness should be a virtue in love affairs," she told me, when she sent me a dozen lavender roses for Valentine's Day. I was enchanted, after a lifetime of control and denial; outrageousness seeps into my bloodstream, my bones loosen up, my face cracks open.

"I want you," she said to me after dinner, sitting on the couch, talking more casually.

"Take me," I said, looking her in the eye. Do I have the right to this much physical desire, to be so compellingly attracted? I ask myself often, as though there is something wrong with having so much.

She was kneeling on the floor; I was sprawled on the couch. She unbuttoned my shirt, removed it. I was lying in a lace undershirt, another new piece of daring, hidden-longing assuaged. My shoulders strong, arms lean and muscular, breasts outlined in soft lace, being all of myself. And she teased me through the shirt, licking my nipples, holding them in her teeth, oh so gently, persistently arousing me. Claiming what was still half-hidden from myself: how the shirt, the convergence of powerful arms and soft lace is about reclaiming my sexuality, the strength of my passion, the fullness of my invitation for her to take me.

And take me she did, fearlessly crossing boundary after boundary. I gave myself over, knowing she would bring me back, and I her. Lying naked before her on the couch, she caressed me, all of me, both gently and insistently: fingertips arousing underarms to hips, fingernails on inner thighs, tongue in the hollows of my neck. She laid me out and invited me to feel all of myself, to go all the way through with taking. And when her hand at last came to my vagina, I was open, wet, soaking wet, begging for her there. Her finger on my clitoris, her tongue. "I love the taste of you," she said to me there.

"Take your clothes off," I said to her.

"What?" she asked startled.

"Take your clothes off," I repeated, sliding her hand out of me, still throbbing, still wanting.

And I stretched her out on the floor, lying down beside her, stroked her, until she moaned and felt she could not wait. And then I was inside her, four fingers; she opened for me, sucked me in, held me tight. I was in her and she in me and we were flying, electrified. "Synergy," she calls it. More than the sum of its parts.

And so we moved instinctively, turning intensity and attention first to one and then to the other, wordlessly; no score kept in an internal rhythm of desire: desire to give and to take. I *will* have her as lover and beloved.

When at last I came, some momentarily final explosion, my back-arched body flying up off the floor; at first I saw only empty space, feeling taken to such fullness there was no consciousness, and then light, blazing light. And she was stroking my belly, gentling me back into life.

Later, moving my hand strong and sure in her vagina, spiraling deeper and harder to wave after wave of contraction. "Enough!" she screamed.

"Enough?" I asked provocatively.

She propped herself up on her elbows, looking down at my face by her vulva. She was laughing and crying at the same time, tears streaming down a radiant face, her chest heaving. "All my life, I've been told I wanted too much," she cried.

Soberness is about having it all, staying with and going through. Having the passion, the nakedness, the often painful vulnerability. Feeling desire rekindle after being so long absent. Discovering, repeatedly, in a momentary pause that it is indeed safe to want again. Not dancing away from the desire, risking instead, to choose it. Sometimes just asking, and not turning to take her: pulsing with the fullness of being with myself; the explosive revolution that is loving myself, accepting love.

Soberness is letting the memories of the past surface, whenever they come through. Often, for us, they come in the still openness after we make love. For the sober dyke, the memories have been hidden, deadened, transformed by ten years of drinking. A year into sobriety, they were coming back to her, a daily confrontation.

"But you don't laugh," she said, lying naked beside me in bed. She had just finished a wry, self-mocking story of being labeled incorrigible at fourteen by the Christian Youth leader whose sexual advances she had rejected. Pain turned inside out into irony, made "funny", the unspeakable spoken when drunk, then denied. Now it came through different: sobered. I didn't laugh. She looked again at the familiar puzzle piece of her past, cried instead, and began to re-know that part of herself.

Still, I thought recovery was about her. And how lucky I was to be in a relationship with someone who was in recovery. Recovery by osmosis. She would do her work, and I would learn from it. Not that it looked unequal: there was the exhilaration of our companionship, our laughter, our passion, bunches of flowers delivered by the local dyke florist, romance grounded in hard work and deep sharing.

But I had brought demons too, though I had no name for the process. My own remembering had also been so long buried, not by drink but by not-feeling, another kind of slow death. Terror strikes me often now. Fear so long present and "not felt", cumulative, striking now with the force of years.

I sat huddled on the couch, knees bundled protectively against my chest. The sober dyke sat beside me, lightly touching me.

"What can you see?" she asked me gently.

I went backwards, deep. As always, the fear is a gray fog. I am a child again faced with my mother's bottled rage, afraid that she will leave altogether; a child believing that pain is better than being abandoned. I go down into it, sit with feelings that were cut off young in the effort to survive. My earliest memory is screaming and screaming in a crib and no one coming. Last year, my mother told me that she used to leave me alone all night while she hunted for my father who stayed away, drunk. Timeless now, I am alone, screaming, and no one comes. I don't believe they will ever come. It feels like it must be my fault that they don't come; it must be something wrong with me.

I sat and breathed deeply. I slowly breathed myself back into life, breathed myself large again, breathed myself strong.

And the sober dyke sat with me all the way through, not afraid (or not too afraid): saw me through. I could not go so deep alone, not yet anyway. We do not rescue each other, cannot do it for the other, yet how profound the comfort is. I am not alone anymore. I'm slow to know this, but it's sinking in.

Having our feelings keeps being the key for us. We had each learned not to feel, had found effective ways to deaden feelings. Each of us now had to break that instinctive reaction, to find a new way. When I had started therapy two years before, I wanted a list of feelings. I didn't know what was a feeling and what wasn't.

"How do you feel about that?" my therapist would ask.

"I think it's a big problem," I would answer.

One day, nearly two years into therapy, the therapist gave me a book she had just discovered, Sharon Wegscheider's *Another Chance: Hope and Health for the Alcoholic Family*. At the end of the book, Wegscheider gives a list of some feelings. She says that adult children of alcoholics frequently know only the grossest feelings: fear, rage, abandonment. Adult children commonly can't distinguish between feelings either: between hurt and hate or anger; between excitement and tension or anxiety; between shame and guilt or embarrassment. I copied her list and pinned it up on my bedroom wall:

| | | |
|---|---|---|
| love | hate | confidence |
| cockiness | disgust | resentment |
| irritation | tension | anxiety |
| excitement | discomfort | fulfillment |
| concern | curiosity | discouragement |
| uneasiness | shame | sadness |

| | | |
|---|---|---|
| anger | comfort | courage |
| humility | embarrassment | relief |
| hurt | need | guilt |
| fear | happiness | amusement |
| affection | hopelessness | |

"What are you feeling?" the sober dyke would ask me. I would feel very confused. Before I could even name the feeling, the censors began: is what I'm feeling appropriate, can I justify it, what good will it do me to feel that, what will she (they) do to me if I feel that?

Often, with my back to the wall, I would answer her, "I don't know." It seemed easier than saying "betrayed."

And sometimes, I *didn't* know. The questions, the lifelong hiding was overwhelming. Sometimes it took me a "long" time to know, though I got there in the end: five minutes or the next morning. Sometimes, now, I know what I feel immediately and can say it; it has taken a lot of practice.

Early on, the sober dyke got the idea that feelings didn't have any reason at all (weren't good or bad, useful or not useful). And that one can't choose to not have them: they just are. This idea made me furious.

Sometimes, it still does. If I was going to be rocked from one end to another, if I was going to be overwhelmed, flooded, immobilized, galvanized... I would, by god, still have choices about when and where. And if I wasn't going to feel something, I wasn't. I'd suppressed feelings for thirty-three years and I wasn't about to be at their mercy now.

My therapist said any feeling feels overwhelming after long disuse, that one probably feels out of control all the time. I agreed wholeheartedly. And didn't budge. The problem was, feelings began to come unbidden. It became steadily harder to not-know; it took active denial instead of general amnesia. And denial was what I was trying to rid myself of. I began to see the sober dyke's point.

My coping mechanisms began to break down when the feelings started coming back. "Leave me alone! I can do it myself!" I would still scream, only this time flooded with the aching panic of my unnurtured self, the terror of being so alone. Pushing away turned to fury. Couldn't she see (intuit, read my mind) that I needed to be held?

In one spectacular fight, I said the ugliest things I could think of for two hours, pulling everything out of the ragbag. I wanted to keep her away from me, having decided she wouldn't be there anyway. I ended up pitching a temper tantrum and sobbing uncontrollably that she wasn't there for me, that no one was ever there for me.

"Come and hold me," I demanded. "Please."

By some mercy, she let go and came.

"I would have held you two hours ago if you'd asked me," she said. "But you have to stop pushing me away so much. And you have to ask."

Gradually, we learned I don't have defenses against touch, having been touched so infrequently. The sober dyke would step around and hold me from behind when I started screaming — until, surrounded by warmth, I had nothing but my own demons to confront. And more often than not, I could see that it was not the sober dyke I was yelling at.

The sober dyke will not hurt me when my guard is down, will not tell me that I'm crazy, will not forget the next day everything that happened the day before. The voices inside me that once made sense, the child who believed that such erratic care must be her fault, who sought to control the universe by acute observation of others; the radar queen, eyes to the ground, head tilted forward, huge antennae sweeping the area for signals, nuances of voice or movement: these are not what I need now. Staying with myself, listening to my feelings, asking for what I need, checking out my fears: there is another way to be.

Just before our first anniversary, I went away for a week on a business trip. On the plane flight east, came my first, unexpected, confrontation with alcohol for my own sake, not the sober dyke's. Nominally, I was still drinking, though I didn't when I was with the sober dyke.

Alone, on my way to New York, nothing sounded better than a drink: calming, relaxing. Didn't I have the right to relax? I hadn't had a drink in over a month, having been spending almost every night with the sober dyke. Then, suddenly, I needed to know what it was like to say "no" to alcohol, for me, not to protect her. I looked at the flight attendant and asked for milk.

The next night, staying with acquaintances, I faced my first alarm: could I sleep without alcohol? Where was the sober dyke's warm body when I needed her? I had no trouble sleeping when I was with her. I cursed myself for toughing this trip out, not asking her to come. Equally, I cursed myself for not packing hot chocolate as routinely as I pack Twinings tea. Hadn't I been serving hot chocolate to the sober dyke for months? I got through that week one night at a time, deep breathing, counting to five hundred, reading mysteries late into the night — and sleeping, to my surprise, I did sleep!

On the plane coming home, I decided to choose to stay sober for three months. It sounded like an eternity. If three months was an eternity and I didn't think I was addicted to alcohol, what was going on? I sat remembering all the holes in my life that alcohol had filled up: relaxing, letting go from the high-pitched intensity of my workaholic self; numbing panic, when I've gone to the edge of rage or self-destruction; a drink to "calm me down"; solace in those times of desperation and despair, when the pain came through too sharply, when I "couldn't cope".

Sitting on the plane in broad daylight, tears streaming down my face, I tried to imagine what other ways I knew to relax. Hot baths, novels, maybe I could relearn to knit. I felt empty, hollow, my imagination stunted. About comfort, solace, sitting with the panic — at that moment there was an enormous void. It was hard to even remember the sober dyke's arms. As far back as I could remember, alcohol was the solution to pain, the only solution. Even if I hadn't had a drink very often, in extremity, it was the only solution I could think of.

I decided not to drink again until alcohol had shrunk down in size; until I had a whole world of options about relaxation and comfort, until ways I hadn't even explored yet were as familiar to me as alcohol was now. I began to choose my own sobriety.

And the world started to look different. I was no longer protecting the sober dyke; I had my own deeper stake in recovery. I began banging up against billboards, novels, friends' assumptions, restaurant menus. . . alcohol suddenly seemed to be everywhere. Two months after I returned, the sober dyke and I went to the annual women's crafts fair at the Women's Building. As we came through the door, two dykes I knew hoisted a large sign across one end of the room: "Beer! Wines! Other Goodies!" I tried to ignore it, knew I couldn't, wondered how I could stay, wondered when I would ever enter a space not devoted to promoting alcohol. The sober dyke was tired and didn't want to fight this once. And this time, it was my issue. *I* didn't want to be in that room with that sign.

The dykes putting up the sign weren't interested; the craftswoman I knew thought I should mellow out; the fair co-ordinator was openly hostile — "Beer and wine make money for us. Don't you support the Women's Building?" Fourth try, deep breaths to explain myself clearly, the food coordinator listened, thought, asked a few questions. "It'll take an hour or so," she said. The new sign read: "Hot Cider! Calistoga! Cake! Sandwiches! Other Goodies!"

I began to look like a fanatic to almost everyone I knew. My favorite sister stopped speaking to me. I stopped seeing my parents. My co-workers (a lesbian feminist collective with three out of four children of alcoholics) thought I was an extremist. Many of my old friends seemed suddenly to be on the other side of a steadily widening gulf.

Almost every woman I told that I was sober, turned around and called me an alcoholic. I felt crazy — I was not my father! I sounded like an alcoholic, what was I? How to explain that abusing alcohol wasn't the issue, but that the place that alcohol always held in my life was the issue. Did it matter?

The sober dyke and I tried for a language to describe what we were doing: getting healthy, being in recovery — it sounded self-righteous and crude. We were talking short-hand for something that had no language in our histories, something we were inventing moment by moment. And even in a lesbian feminist collective there was punishment for not-rescuing, not-fixing, not being super-responsible, not participating in the constant dramas. Whenever I went outside my relationship with the sober dyke, changing how I was created new conflicts. I wanted my whole community in recovery.

The sober dyke and I went to the country for a weekend and took along *Another Chance* and Claudia Black's new book *It Will Never Happen To Me*. Somehow, I had skipped some key chapters the first time through. The sober dyke and I were beginning to identify as ACA's (Adult Children of Alcoholics).

We sat in the late fall sunshine, in the enormous silence of the woods, and shared our family histories — everything we could remember or thought we had imagined. We told the family secrets, and waited for the ground to start shaking. Each of us felt as though Wegscheider had been peering through the windows of our childhood homes. The roles she described: dependent, enabler, hero, scapegoat, lost child, mascot; they showed up in our families in a spiraling web. Sometimes we played one role, sometimes another. But the descriptions in the book were so uncannily accurate as to lay to rest forever the question of our "craziness" for naming what went on. And then Claudia Black came along and did for emotions what Wegscheider did for family dynamics — until I saw my and my sisters' stories spread before me. Remembering how heros tend to become enablers (co's) and how scapegoats tend to become dependents (alcoholics) — I looked at the sober dyke and me now, and our journeys into adulthood. And I looked at my work collective: saw me enabling like mad in a feminist institution; took another look at a recent political confrontation and found a dependent, a hero and a scapegoat without much difficulty.

"Ain't it a bitch," the sober dyke said, when we could finally laugh a little, "to be both the scapegoat and the alcoholic?"

One night, the sober dyke came home and announced, "Guess what? There is a group starting at my recovery center for lesbian adult children of alcoholics!" She was excited for me.

I resisted. I didn't need a group; I was doing fine with my therapist. My life with the sober dyke was wonderful. My schedule suddenly seemed very full. It was my loneliness that finally got me there; I didn't want to feel so different any more.

"Aren't you lucky," the facilitator said at my initial interview, "that you quit drinking before it was more of a problem?"

Later, she told me that she had quit when no one around her saw any signs of a problem. "Sixty percent of all children of alcoholics become alcoholics themselves. One day I said to myself, 'Why play Russian roulette?'" she said. "Then what I found is that there's a process of emotional dependency that's parallel to the physical dependency for alcoholics, and that what I had to learn was emotional sobriety."

I decided I had come to the right place, though my heart was thumping so badly at the first meeting of the group that I thought I'd never be able to speak. At that stage, I was still going on teeth-gritted determination anyway. To my surprise, the redhead across the circle from me said out loud, "I get sick to my stomach every time I come here." The facilitator told us that ACA's have more than the usual resistance to sitting in a group.

In the following weeks, we did all sorts of exercises. Week by week, we took each part of the victim/rescuer/persecutor triangle and listed all the feelings we could remember for each role. The feelings about rescuing covered a whole chalkboard: self-righteous, powerful, manipulative, pissed-off, overburdened, important, helpful, strong, vindictive. Being either victim or rescuer was never quite the same again after seeing those lists on the board.

We did deep breathing exercises and guided meditations, something I was sure you'd never catch me dead doing. By the end of three months, we were starting every meeting that way, sprawled on the floor. I was learning to stay, very literally, with myself.

We each told our family histories, bringing photographs and charting the family roles on the chalkboard. In every family, the alcoholism went back three, four, maybe more generations. If it skipped one, it showed up just behind it. Each story was particular and specific, its own web of pain and denial, but such common threads wove between them that we all drew closer.

The redhead talked of being coerced by an older sister into searching the house for murderers when they were left alone at night. I had made my younger sister do the same for me. The Texan showed photos of herself bloated and dying at fifteen from heavy drug use with her family standing around her smiling in desperate oblivion. The twin in the group looked at that picture and cried, seeing her own twin sister's destruction mirrored back. The blame for who got picked to be lost child, scapegoat or hero lessened; we began to know each other whole.

And we each did our own work, with the nitty-gitty practical problems of our individual lives being a source of inspiration or acknowledgment for each other. For me, a breakthrough came when I got into my first head-on conflict, saying to myself "Oh my god, am I really going to do this?" Then I challenged the Texan's chip-on-the-shoulder response to me, and kept going until she was finally able to ask, "Is it true you really don't like me and think I'm stupid?" Surprised, I answered, "I learn more from you than anyone else here right now, because you take such risks." Weeks later, another woman would say to me, "You keep showing me that conflict doesn't have to be devastating, and that's meant a lot to me."

I found I was falling in love with my group. I couldn't wait for Tuesday nights and kept arriving most uncoolly early, so I could hang out with anyone else who was early. That very rosy period ended, finally, with a big conflict about including new women in the group, and it became clear to me that it was time to take new risks, to test limits, grow some more. We each emerged a little more human, rough edges showing, but the love grew and the foundations felt more solid.

The group members would call me up at mid-week to see how I was doing. For a while I dismissed the caring. "Oh, it's just the redhead in my group," I'd tell the sober dyke. After a while, I realized I could call them too; I'd spent my whole life waiting for people to approach me. I had to make a list at first, of who I could call — I was back in grade school with my list of emergency numbers pinned inside my coat. I was learning how to ask. At nine, I hadn't been able to; at thirty-four, I was starting.

I made other new friends, began exploring how to play. Going to movies, swimming, picnics at the ocean. Having deep, deep talks, risking intimacy that had been reserved only for the sober dyke. And we met other couples in recovery — a new experience, this not-closeting our intimacy (or our fights), not denying our commitment. We went away for the weekend with another couple, a photographer who is also an incest survivor and a bookkeeper who is also a recovering addict. Sharing stories of recovery, we found deep similarities in any family that practices secrecy and denial. That weekend, the four of us let all of our complexities be present, took long walks, ate wonderful food, fought and loved around each other; when we talked about sex, all four of us cried. It scared me to death, but I came home bigger, profoundly hopeful. Two weeks later, the photographer and I started swimming together every Tuesday at noon. I pick her up at work and bring a picnic lunch.

The sober dyke is better at making friends than I am. She doesn't wait for them to call. But I have a few friends now, who speak the same faltering language, who are learning new laughter that's not turned in on ourselves, who are risking being fully alive. There is joy in these friendships as well as fear.

It is beginning to be spring now, my second spring with the sober dyke, my second spring in recovery. It was a hard winter. "Why isn't recovery easy?" an old friend writes. It hasn't been easy; if anything, the second year has been harder, being deeper. But I have known times of real unadulterated happiness, too; something I never had before.

The sober dyke and I are planting a garden this year. We started with artichokes and raspberries. It's been five years since I last turned soil, worked it deep with my hands, felt my heart leap at the sight of the first new shoots. I look at the sober dyke working over by the fence and am flooded with delight in her being, wonder at all her daring. She has only to turn and smile at me and passion rushes through me. Her body and her mind never cease to excite me. I stand here in the feeble spring sunshine, muck up to my elbows, feet firmly on the ground, my face cracked open in a wide grin. And I know I am going to live, really live: no part cut off, dying or denied. I stand here smiling, at peace.

This started as a story about her, that first step into a world I could not yet imagine. But to embrace her, I had to also love me, and that's when the journey really started. Now in this second spring, it is a story about her, about me, and finally about us. About each of us separately growing more whole and about both of us together risking having, risking being happy.

**SHERRY THOMAS:** I have done a number of exciting and fulfilling things in my life — sheep ranching, editing a magazine, writing two books, running a bookstore, and publishing — but the greatest joy has come the last two years, understanding what it is to be the adult child of an alcoholic and building a partnership with another sober dyke.

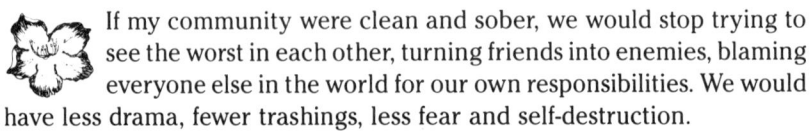

If my community were clean and sober, we would stop trying to see the worst in each other, turning friends into enemies, blaming everyone else in the world for our own responsibilities. We would have less drama, fewer trashings, less fear and self-destruction.

If my community were clean and sober, we'd celebrate each other's victories, encourage each other's growth. We'd be in touch with our feelings and claim them as our own; we'd shine with the power and joy of women who are fully alive, who love themselves and each other.

# Selected Bibliography

The following references were gathered during a year's worth of unguided, informal and unscientific reading. They are the result of my own curiosity, recommendations from friends, contributors and professional associates, and the general underground of photocopied/hand-held/friends-passed/unattributed literature which flourishes in the recovery communities. I say this so that you will understand this bibliography is incomplete and limited. If you want more information, I urge you to write the National Association of Gay Alcoholism Professionals (204 West 20th Street, New York City, NY 10011), which publishes an extensive bibliography of the literature pertaining to lesbians and gay men as well as a separate listing of services available to us, or write the National Clearinghouse for Alcohol Information (P.O. Box 2345, Rockville, MD 20852), for more general information. Good luck. — *JS*

## Specific Recovery References

"Flare-Up: Stress Time in Recovery from Alcoholism." Scott, Fitz, Simpson and Walker (1969) *Osteopathic Physician* (Feb. issue)

"Checklist of Symptoms Leading to Relapse." Alcoholism Treatment Unit. (Sequoia Hospital District, Whipple and Alameda, Redwood City, CA 94062)

"Is There Sex After Sobriety?" G. Rosellini (1982) *Alcoholism* Sept.-Oct. pp. 31-33.

"Alcoholism: Acute and Delayed Withdrawal." T. M. Smith (1978) (This is an extremely helpful article. I have not been able to find where this was originally published, but Dr. Smith is currently employed at the Alcoholism Evaluation and Treatment Center, San Francisco, CA.)

*Living Sober* (1975) (A.A. World Services, Inc., Box 459, Grand Central Station, New York City, NY 10163.) (A.A. has a great many pamphlets addressing a wide range of issues from the A.A. perspective. Order forms are available at the above address.)

## Literature Reviews

"Alcoholism and Homosexuality: A Theoretical Perspective." P.M. Nardi (1982) *Journal of Homosexuality* 7(4): 9-25. (This is an excellent review, and includes an extensive bibliography.)

"Alcoholism and Women." S. Johnson, S. R. Garzon (1978) *American Journal of Drug Abuse* 5(1) pp. 107-122.

"Alcoholism Among Women." J. D. Homiller (1980) *Chemical Dependencies: Behavioral and Biomedical Issues* 4(1): 1-31.

"The Female Alcoholic." E. S. Gomberg (1976) in *Alcoholism: Interdisciplinary Approaches to an Enduring Problem* (Addison-Wesley) p. 603-636.

"Women Alcoholics: A Review of Social and Psychological Studies." L. Beckman (1975) *Journal of Studies on Alcohol,* 36(7):797-824.

Bibilography on Alcoholism in 13 lesbian periodicals. Bibliography source: Lesbian Periodicals Index, (West Coast Lesbian Collections, 66 Hamilton, Oakland, CA)

"Women and Drug Concerns Bibliography." R. Hargraves and M. Nellis, eds. (1974) in *Developments in the Field of Drug Abuse: Proceedings of the National Drug Abuse Council* E. Senay, V. Shorty and A. Atksne, eds. (Shenkman Publishing Co., Cambridge, MA) p. 524.

## Lesbian/Gay References

"Lesbian Alcoholics: Climbing Up From Nowhere." K. Hendrix (1975) *L.A. Times* July 16.

"Alcoholism and Co-Alcoholism: There is a Solution." M. O'Donnell (1978) in *Lesbian Health Matters!* (Santa Cruz Women's Health Collective, 250 Locust Street, Santa Cruz, CA 95060)

"The Ties That Bind: Strategies for Counseling the Gay Male Alcoholic." Scott Whitney (1982) *Journal of Homosexuality* 7(4):37-41). (This is a very interesting article which concerns gay alcoholic relationships with co-alcoholism and gay non-traditional family structures.)

*The Way Back: The Stories of Gay and Lesbian Alcoholics.* Gay Council on Drinking Behavior (Whitman-Walker Clinic, 2335 18th Street, NW, Washington, D.C. 20009)

*Alcoholism and the Lesbian Community* B. Weathers (1976, 1980) Gay Council on Drinking Behavior (Whitman-Walker Clinic, 2335 18th Street, NW, Washington, D.C. 20009)

"Alcoholics Anonymous and The Gay Alcoholic." W.E. Bittle (1982) *Journal of Homosexuality* 7(4): 81-88.

"Preventing Alcohol Abuse in the Gay Community: Towards a Theory and Model." J.E. Mongeon, T.O. Ziebold (1982) *Journal of Homosexuality* 7(4): 89-99. (This was extremely interesting.)

*Alcoholism in the Lesbian/Gay Community: Coming to Terms with an Epidemic* L. Schwartz. (1980) (Do It Now Foundation, P.O. Box 5115, Phoenix, AZ 85010) (They have a variety of publications on alcoholism.)

"On My Way to Nowhere: An Analysis of Gay Alcohol Abuse and an Evaluation of Alcoholism Rehabilitation Sources of the Los Angeles Gay Community." L. Fifield (1975) (Contract #25125. County of Los Angeles.)

"Substance Abuse in the Lesbian Community." *Rag Times* July 1982 (Portland, Oregon.)

"Homosexuality: IV. Psychiatric Disorders and Disability in the Female Homosexual." M.T. Saghir, G. Robins, B. Walbran, K.A. Gentry (1970) *American Journal of Psychiatry* 127:2, 147-154.

"Drinking Patterns in Homosexual and Heterosexual Women." C.E. Lewis, M.T. Saghir and E. Robins (1982) *Journal of Clinical Psychiatry* 43(7): 277-279.

"Stresses on Lesbians and Gay Men Leading to Alcohol Abuse." T. Smith, S. Balcer (1982) (Alcoholism Evaluation and Treatment Center, San Francisco, CA.) (This provides a clear view of the similarities between psychological states from oppression and alcohol abuse and is very interesting.)

"Alcohol Treatment and the Non-Traditional 'Family' Structure of Gays and Lesbians." P.M. Nardi (1982) *Journal of Alcohol and Drug Education* V. 27(2):83-89.

*The gay drinking problem: There is a solution.* J. Michael (1976) (Compcare Publications, Minneapolis, MN)

*Sober, clean and gay!* J. Michael (1977) (Compcare Publications, Minneapolis, MN) (These people do a whole list of readings on alcoholism and recovery and will send a free catalogue. Address: Compcare Publications, 2415 Annapolis Lane, Suite 140, Minneapolis, MN 55441.)

"Alcohol abuse among lesbians: A descriptive study." D. Diamond and S. Wilsnack (1978) *Journal of Homosexuality* 4(2): 123-142.

"Lesbianism and alcoholism." J. Hawkins (1976) in *Alcoholism Problems in Women and Children* (Grune and Stratton, NY).

## Adult Children of Alcoholics References

"What Can You Do For The Child Of An Alcoholic?" flyer from Women's Alcohol Coalition (3380 26th Street, San Francisco, CA 94110)

"Group Therapy with the Adult Children of Alcoholics." S. Brown and T. Cermak (1982) *California Society for the Treatment of Alcoholism and Other Drug Dependencies Newsletter* 7(1): 1-6. (This is a very interesting article for ACA's. One of the authors, S. Brown can be contacted at the Stanford Alcoholic Clinic, Stanford University Medical Center, Stanford, CA 94305. For $2.00, her helpful assistant will provide you with a packet of reprints and a bibliography for ACA literature.)

*Another Chance: Hope and Health for the Alcoholic Family* S. Wegscheider (1981) (Science and Behavior Books, Inc., P.O. Box 11457, Palo Alto, CA 94306)

*It Will Never Happen To Me: Children of Alcoholics as Youngsters, Adolescents and Adults* C. Black (1981) (MAC Printing and Publication Division, 1850 High Street, Denver, CO 80218)

*My Dad Loves Me, My Dad Has a Disease: A Workbook for Children of Alcoholics* C. Black (1979) (distributed by MAC Printing and Publication Division, 1850 High Street, Denver, CO 80218)

# References About Women in General

"Radical Feminism: A Treatment Modality for Addicted Women." A.M. Schultz (1974) in *Developments in the Field of Drug Abuse: Proceedings of the National Drug Abuse Council* E. Senay, V. Shorty and A. Alksne, eds. (Shenkman Publishing Co., Cambridge, MA) pp. 484-502.

"The Impact of Feminist Psychotherapy on the Treatment of Alcoholics." B. Connor and M.L. Babcock (1980) *Journal of Addictions and Health, Vol. 1, #2, "Focus on Women"* Summer 1980 (G.F. Stickley Co.) (This whole issue was devoted to women's issues, and this article in particular was excellent.)

"A Comparison of Male and Female Patients at an Alcoholism Treatment Center." J. Curlee (1970) *Journal of Psychology,* 74:239-247.

*Turnabout: Help For a New Life* J. Kirkpatrick (1977) (Doubleday, NY) (This is the autobiography of the woman who started Women for Sobriety, a 12-step program which was developed for women. Though Women for Sobriety is not well represented in this anthology, a great many women find it works for them. For more information, write Women for Sobriety, P.O. Box 68, Quakertown, PA 18951)

*Empowering Female Alcoholics to Help Themselves and Their Sisters in the Workplace* Robin J. Milstead (1981) (Kendall/Hunt Publishing Co., Dubuque, IA) (This book deals with structures to help women at work. It has a great bibliography.)

"Addiction." (Spring, 1982) *The Speculum Speaks* (Leichardt Women's Community Health Centre, 164 Flood Street, Leichardt, N.S.W., 2040, Australia.)

"Addiction—A Woman's Issue." (March/April 1982) *Girls' Own* (P.O. Box 188, Wentworth Building, Sydney University 2006, Sydney, Australia.) (This is a great double issue from Sydney's feminist newpaper, filled with all kinds of material for women, straight and lesbian. Well worth getting.)

*High and Outside* L. A. Due (1980) (Harper and Row, NY)

*Women and Alcohol* (1980) Comberwell Council on Alcoholism (Tavistock Publications, London, England)

*The Invisible Alcoholics: Women and Alcohol Abuse in America* M. Sandmaier (1980) (McGraw-Hill, NY)

*Alcoholism in Women* C. C. Eddy and J. L. Ford, eds. (1980) (Kendall/Hunt Publishing Co., Dubuque, IA)

*Women: Their Use of Alcohol and Other Legal Drugs* A. MacLennan, ed. (1976) (Addiction Research Foundation of Ontario, Toronto, Ontario, Canada)

*I'm Dancing As Fast As I Can* B. Gordon (1979) (Bantam, NY)

*The Late Great Me* S. Scoppettone (1976) (Bantam, NY)

# General Alcoholism/Substance Abuse References

*Alcoholism: Development, consequences and interventions.* N. Estes and E. Heinermann, eds. (1977) (C.V. Mosby, St. Louis, MO)

*Understanding Alcohol* J. Kinney and G. Leaton (1982) (Plume/New American Library)

*Young Alcoholics.* T. Alibrandi (1978) (CompCare Publications, Minneapolis, MN)

*Beyond Alcoholism* D. Beauchamp (1980) Alcohol and Public Health Policy. (Temple University Press, Philadelphia)

"Alcohol: Servant or Master?" S. Brown (1982) *Stanford Magazine* (Stanford University, Stanford, CA) (This is interesting in the information it gives for upper-middle class straight alcoholics.)

*Early Recognition of Alcoholism and Other Drug Dependence* (1980) (Hazelden, Center City, MN) (These folks also publish or distribute a variety of publications about substance abuse and they have a catalogue available: write Hazelden Educational Services, Box 176, Center City, MN 55012.)

*Love and Addiction* S. Peele (1975) (New American Library, New York, NY)

*Healing Alcoholism* C. Steiner (1979) (Grove Press, San Francisco)

*Games Alcoholics Play* C. Steiner. (1974) (Grove Press, San Francisco)

*Alcoholics Anonymous Big Book* (1939) (A.A. World Services, Inc., Box 459, Grand Central Station, New York City, NY 10163)

Spinsters, Ink is a women's independent publishing company that survives despite financial and cultural obstacles. Our commitment is to publishing works of literature and non-fiction that are beyond the scope of mainstream commercial publishers. We emphasize work by feminists and lesbians.

Your support through buying our books or making donations will enable us to continue to bring out new books — to publish between the cracks of what can be imagined and what will be accepted.

For a complete list of our titles, please write to us.

Spinsters, Ink<br>
803 DeHaro Street<br>
San Francisco, CA 94107